INEQUALITY

INEQUALITY

CLASSIC READINGS IN RACE, CLASS, AND GENDER

edited by David B. Grusky
and Szonja Szelényi

A Member of the Perseus Books Group

Westview Press books are available at special discounts for bulk purchases in the United
States by corporations, institutions, and other organizations. For more information, please
contact the Special Markets Department at the Perseus Books Group, 11 Cambridge Center,
Cambridge MA 02142, or call (617) 252-5298 or (800) 255-1514, or e-mail
special.markets@perseusbooks.com.

Library of Congress Cataloging-in-Publication Data
Classic readings in race, class, and gender / edited by David B. Grusky and Szonja Szelényi.
    p. cm.
Includes bibliographical references and index.
ISBN-13: 978-0-8133-4330-3 (pbk. : alk. paper)
ISBN-10: 0-8133-4330-5
1. Equality. 2. Social stratification. 3. Social classes. 4. Race. 5. Sex role. I. Grusky,
David B. II. Szelényi, Szonja, 1960-
  HM821.C584 2006
  305.01—dc22
                                    2005028911

06 07 08 / 10 9 8 7 6 5 4 3 2 1

For Bob Hauser

CONTENTS

INEQUALITY AT THE EXTREMES

RACIAL, ETHNIC, AND GENDER INEQUALITY

GENERATING INEQUALITY

THE CONSEQUENCES OF INEQUALITY

LIST OF TABLES AND FIGURES

PREFACE AND ACKNOWLEDGMENTS

◆◆◆

The main rationale for publishing an anthology of classic readings is that doing so frees instructors and other scholars from the time-consuming and routine task of assembling the readings themselves. It is unlikely, we think, that such a task is regarded by many as an attractive one, especially because there is rather little room for creativity or discretion in making the selections. To the contrary, our recent analysis of graduate and undergraduate syllabi in inequality courses revealed that instructors across the country are assigning much the same classics, almost as if some invisible hand guided them. That is, just as high school teachers of U.S. literature find themselves obliged to assign Hemingway, Faulkner, Steinbeck, and Fitzgerald, so too instructors of graduate and undergraduate inequality courses evidently find themselves obliged to assign Marx, Weber, Wilson, and Bourdieu (among others). Whatever our personal tastes or preferences might be, these classics have become part of the intellectual world in which we live, and any student who is to be inducted into that world simply must know of them. There are accordingly real economies to be had in owning up to the standardization of our syllabi and centralizing the task of assembling the classics.

If there is much consensus on the classics, it is coupled, however, with an equally striking dissensus on how one might best cull from the massive contemporary literature on inequality. In our analysis of inequality syllabi, we found that the various contemporary pieces that are chosen to supplement the common core are quite idiosyncratic and betray a host of differing viewpoints about the areas or approaches that are most important, most likely to yield a payoff in the future, or most appropriate given the interests or needs of the students being taught.

It was precisely this combination of consensus and dissensus in inequality syllabi that motivated Steve Catalano, our Westview Press editor, to approach us about editing a new anthology that represents exclusively the common core and foregoes the temptation to cull from the contemporary research literature. We were instantly attracted to the idea. The present reader is intended, then, to represent the classical core alone, a core that may then be supplemented with contemporary selections of the instructor's choosing that presumably reflect the approach that is most appropriate for her or his students.

We of course hope that many scholars will continue to appreciate the convenience of a more comprehensive reader that combines the classics with contemporary pieces. For those scholars, we unsurprisingly recommend our own comprehensive reader, *Social Stratification: Class, Race, and Gender in Sociological Perspective* (2001, Boulder, CO: Westview Press). This reader will continue to be updated at regular intervals to reflect current developments in the field. Although we stand by the contemporary readings in that anthology as a defensible, if not necessarily consensual, representation of the state of the field, we appreciate that some scholars will inevitably wish to chart a different course through the contemporary literature. We offer our new anthology for precisely those renegade scholars.

We don't mean to suggest that our selection of classics in the present anthology was a completely mechanical process lacking altogether in discretion or judgment on our end. As suggested by the Table P. 1, the concept of a classic is itself something of an amalgam, as it pertains at once to (a) pieces that are widely regarded as examples of excellent scholarship (i.e., a reputational criterion), and (b) pieces that, whatever their reputational ranking may be, have decisively affected either the course of scholarship or, more spectacularly, the course of human history (e.g., Marx). Although some classics are regarded as such by virtue of a reputational criterion, others are regarded as classics not because scholars find them intellectually persuasive but because they appreciate that the world of inequality scholarship has, for whatever reason, been irrevocably influenced by them.

	Influence	
Reputation	Low	High
Disparaged	Type I (i.e., nonclassics)	Type II (e.g., Parsons)
Well-liked	Type III (e.g., Tumin)	Type IV (e.g., Marx)

Table P.1 Typology of Classics

The vast majority of inequality scholarship fails to satisfy either of these tests and thus falls outside the space of classics (see [1,1] cell). The remaining cells in our 2×2 table represent, however, three quite distinct types of classics, all of which are represented in our anthology. First, the Type II classic is one which has profoundly affected the course of research and theorizing in the field, even though a sizable contingent of sociologists no longer embrace the ideas, theories, or approaches it represents. By way of example, consider the influential work of Parsons on the structure of modern stratification systems, a line of work that spawned an industry of scholarship on prestige scales and other gradational representations of inequality. Influential though it was, Parsons is hardly worshipped by contemporary inequality scholars in the way that, say, Weber still is, although no one would question the influence of Parsons. Likewise, there are very few Davis-Moore functionalists among the ranks of contemporary inequality scholars, yet presumably no one would question the influence of functionalism or the role of Davis and Moore in popularizing it.

Obversely, the Type III classic is one that most everyone still appreciates as unusually insightful or creative, yet for any number of reasons it never engendered a school of research or had substantial impact on the development of inequality research. For a classic of this sort, there is much in the way of deferential and decorative citing, but it nonetheless remains largely on the sidelines because it was introduced at an impropitious time or because it wasn't readily convertible into a research program. This category includes, perhaps, the pieces by Tumin, Turner, Veblen, and Hartmann.

Finally, the remaining pieces in our anthology arguably fall into the (2,2) cell, a category reserved for classics that deeply influenced the course of the field and are still well-received among a very broad constituency. For example, few scholars indeed would dispute the creativity and continuing relevance of the Blau-Duncan status attainment model, nor would they dispute the impact of this model on the field. We would of course like to believe that many of our selections fall into the (2,2) cell representing such doubly blessed classics.

To be sure, the foregoing characterizations are merely our own inferences about disciplinary sentiments, inferences that are not only colored by our own tastes and biases but are also necessarily judgments about the average sociologist and hence subject to some variability around that average. The Blau-Duncan model is an especially instructive case in point. Clearly, some scholars regard that model as a spectacular wrong turn for the field, however widely embraced the wrong turn was. Although these skeptics might therefore categorize the Blau-Duncan piece as a Type II classic rather than a Type IV (on the assumption that their skepticism about the Blau-Duncan model is widely shared), they aren't likely to dispute its place within the anthology as a legitimate classic. More generally, we suspect that there is often some disagreement about the type of classic that a piece represents, but not typically much disagreement about whether it is a classic at all. The latter interpretation is consistent with our finding that inequality syllabi quite predictably share a common core of classic readings.

We sought, then, to include classics of one of the three types represented in the table. In making our selections, we decided explicitly against the strategy of ensuring adequate representation of certain core areas in the discipline, preferring instead to reflect the consensual core in whatever form it takes. The implication of this decision is that subfields that came into prominence later in the history of the field, such as those of gender and race, are perforce under-represented relative to what our current sensibilities would dictate. This outcome is altogether consistent with the rationale underlying the volume. That is, whenever a field is (relatively) new and a large body of classics have not yet emerged within it, we prefer to avoid imposing our particularistic tastes and instead will leave it to the individual instructor to tailor selections that reflect her or his tastes and needs. By implication, the selections represented here will reflect disproportionately the subfields of the past, not the present.

There is nonetheless a very important sense in which this volume must be understood as a presentist artifact that is deeply affected by contemporary sensibilities. It is not merely that the defining feature of some classics is that they were influential enough to spawn much contemporary scholarship. Additionally, our excerpting decisions will serve in the main to exaggerate this connection between the classical and contemporary worlds, as the natural (and largely desirable) tendency of the editor is to retain those sections of the classics that seem most relevant and to excise those sections that seem least relevant. The novice reader may be left, then, with the misleading impression that all past sociological work leads directly and inevitably to current disciplinary interests. Although the resulting pieces provide, by virtue of our careful excerpting, much payoff for those engaging with the contemporary literature, we would never discourage a rereading of the classics in their entirety nor of course an effort to poach from less-known scholars who are not considered part of our classical legacy. Indeed, when students have had enough of mastering the field and wish to turn to producing creative scholarly works of their own, there is much to be said for abandoning well-traveled roads.

The editing rules adopted throughout this anthology were in most cases conventional. For example, brackets were used to mark off a passage that was inserted for the purpose of clarifying meaning, whereas ellipses were used whenever a passage appearing in the original contribution was excised altogether. The latter convention was violated, however, if the excised text was merely a footnote or a minor reference to a table or passage (e.g., "see Table 1") that was itself excerpted out. When necessary, tables and endnotes were renumbered without so indicating in the text, and all articles that were cited in excised passages were likewise omitted, without indication, from the list of references appearing at the end of the chapters. The spelling, grammar, and stylistic conventions of the original contributions were otherwise preserved. In this respect, the reader should be forewarned that some of the terms appearing in the original contributions would now be regarded as inappropriate (e.g., *Negro*), whereas others have passed out of common usage and will possibly be unfamiliar. While a strong argument could clearly be made for eliminating all language that is no longer acceptable, this type of sanitizing would not only exceed usual editorial license but would also generate a final text that contained inconsistent, and possibly confusing, temporal cues. In the lead footnotes for each article, we detail any of the potentially controversial editing decisions, such as omitting tables, resequencing paragraphs, and smoothing out transitional prose between adjacent sections.

The selections reproduced here have all been pretested in graduate and undergraduate inequality classes at the University of Chicago, Stanford University, and Cornell University. We are indebted to the many students in these classes who shared their reactions to the selections and thereby shaped the final product more than they may realize. The anonymous reviewers of an earlier proposal for this book also provided unusually constructive criticisms that were helpful in assembling the final book. As we all know, those who consent to write such reviews are only barely compensated, and no amount of gratitude on our part will ever correct for that. We are thankful that top scholars can still be found who will temporarily suspend the laws of rational action and altruistically provide us with their reactions.

We are also grateful for the expert market research carried out by Karl Yambert. From the start, we sought to develop a book that was carefully tailored to meet the needs of graduate and undergraduate students, and much of course rides on having done our market research right and properly identified what those needs are. If we have at all succeeded in that task, it is in large part because of the unstinting labor of Karl.

Finally, it is fitting to close by again thanking Steve Catalano, not just for conceiving of the project but also and more importantly for his sage advice throughout the gestation period. Like all good editors, Steve showed consummate skill in coaxing out the sometimes recalcitrant product, expertly administering painkillers as necessary (e.g., advances on royalties) and thereby making the process as tolerable as possible.

David B. Grusky and Szonja Szelényi
Palo Alto, California, 2005

I

SOME PRINCIPLES OF STRATIFICATION

Kingsley Davis and Wilbert E. Moore

♦♦♦

In a previous paper some concepts for handling the phenomena of social inequality were presented.[1] In the present paper a further step in stratification theory is undertaken—an attempt to show the relationship between stratification and the rest of the social order.[2] Starting from the proposition that no society is "classless," or unstratified, an effort is made to explain, in functional terms, the universal necessity which calls forth stratification in any social system.

Throughout, it will be necessary to keep in mind one thing—namely, that the discussion relates to the system of positions, not to the individuals occupying those positions. It is one thing to ask why different positions carry different degrees of prestige, and quite another to ask how certain individuals get into those positions. Although, as the argument will try to show, both questions are related, it is essential to keep them separate in our thinking.

Kingsley Davis and Wilbert E. Moore, "Some Principles of Stratification," *American Sociological Review* 10 (April 1945), pp. 242–249.

Most of the literature on stratification has tried to answer the second question (particularly with regard to the ease or difficulty of mobility between strata) without tackling the first. The first question, however, is logically prior and, in the case of any particular individual or group, factually prior.

THE FUNCTIONAL NECESSITY OF STRATIFICATION

Curiously the main functional necessity explaining the universal presence of stratification is precisely the requirement faced by any society of placing and motivating individuals in the social structure. As a functioning mechanism a society must somehow distribute its members in social positions and induce them to perform the duties of these positions. It must thus concern itself with motivation at two different levels: to instill in the proper individuals the desire to fill certain positions, and, once in these positions, the desire to perform the duties attached to them. Even though the social order may be relatively static in form, there is a continuous process of metabolism as new individuals are born into it, shift with age, and die off. Their absorption into the positional system must somehow be arranged and motivated. This is true whether the system is competitive or non-competitive. A competitive system gives greater importance to the motivation to achieve positions, whereas a non-competitive system gives perhaps greater importance to the motivation to perform the duties of the positions; but in any system both types of motivation are required.

If the duties associated with the various positions were all equally pleasant to the human organism, all equally important to societal survival, and all equally in need of the same ability or talent, it would make no difference who got into which positions, and the problem of social placement would be greatly reduced. But actually it does make a great deal of difference who gets into which positions, not only because some positions are inherently more agreeable than others, but also because some require special talents or training and some are functionally more important than others. Also, it is essential that the duties of the positions be performed with the diligence that their importance requires. Inevitably, then, a society must have, first, some kind of rewards that it can use as inducements, and, second, some way of distributing these rewards differentially according to positions. The rewards and their distribution become a part of the social order, and thus give rise to stratification.

One may ask what kind of rewards a society has at its disposal in distributing its personnel and securing essential services. It has, first of all, the things that contribute to sustenance and comfort. It has, second, the things that contribute to humor and diversion. And it has, finally, the things that contribute to self-respect and ego expansion. The last, because of the peculiarly social character of the self, is largely a function of the opinion of others, but it nonetheless ranks in importance with the first two. In any social system all three kinds of rewards must be dispensed differentially according to positions.

In a sense the rewards are "built into" the position. They consist in the "rights" associated with the position, plus what may be called its accompaniments or perquisites. Often the rights, and sometimes the accompaniments, are functionally related to the duties of the position. (Rights as viewed by the incumbent are usually duties as viewed by other members of the community.) However, there may be a host of subsidiary rights and perquisites that are not essential to the function of the position and have only an indirect and symbolic connection with its duties, but which still may be of considerable importance in inducing people to seek the positions and fulfil the essential duties.

If the rights and perquisites of different positions in a society must be unequal, then the society must be stratified, because that is precisely what stratification means. Social inequality is thus an unconsciously evolved device by which societies insure that the most important positions are conscientiously filled by the most qualified persons. Hence every society, no matter how simple or complex, must differentiate persons in terms of both prestige and esteem, and must therefore possess a certain amount of institutionalized inequality.

It does not follow that the amount or type of inequality need be the same in all societies. This is largely a function of factors that will be discussed presently.

THE TWO DETERMINANTS OF POSITIONAL RANK

Granting the general function that inequality subserves, one can specify the two factors that determine the relative rank of different positions. In general those positions convey the best reward, and hence have the highest rank, which (a) have the greatest importance for the society and (b) require the greatest training or talent. The first factor concerns function and is a matter of relative significance; the second concerns means and is a matter of scarcity.

Differential Functional Importance.   Actually a society does not need to reward positions in proportion to their functional importance. It merely needs to give sufficient reward to them to insure that they will be filled competently. In other words, it must see that less essential positions do not compete successfully with more essential ones. If a position is easily filled, it need not be heavily rewarded, even though important. On the other hand, if it is important but hard to fill, the reward must be high enough to get it filled anyway. Functional importance is therefore a necessary but not a sufficient cause of high rank being assigned to a position.[3]

Differential Scarcity of Personnel.   Practically all positions, no matter how acquired, require some form of skill or capacity for performance. This is implicit in the very notion of position, which implies that the incumbent must, by virtue of his incumbency, accomplish certain things.

There are, ultimately, only two ways in which a person's qualifications come about: through inherent capacity or through training. Obviously, in concrete activities both are always necessary, but from a practical standpoint the scarcity may lie primarily in one or the other, as well as in both. Some positions require innate talents of such high degree that the persons who fill them are bound to be rare. In many cases, however, talent is fairly abundant in the population but the training process is so long, costly, and elaborate that relatively few can qualify. Modern medicine, for example, is within the mental capacity of most individuals, but a medical education is so burdensome and expensive that virtually none would undertake it if the position of the M.D. did not carry a reward commensurate with the sacrifice.

If the talents required for a position are abundant and the training easy, the method of acquiring the position may have little to do with its duties. There may be, in fact, a virtually accidental relationship. But if the skills required are scarce by reason of the rarity of talent or the costliness of training, the position, if functionally important, must have an attractive power that will draw the necessary skills in competition with other positions. This means, in effect, that the position must be high in the social scale—must command great prestige, high salary, ample leisure, and the like.

How Variations Are to Be Understood.   In so far as there is a difference between one system of stratification and another, it is attributable to whatever factors affect the two determinants of differential reward—namely, functional importance and scarcity of personnel. Positions important in one society may not be important in another, because the conditions faced by the societies, or their degree of internal development, may be different. The same conditions, in turn, may affect the question of scarcity; for in some societies the stage of development, or the external situation, may wholly obviate the necessity of certain kinds of skill or talent. Any particular system of stratification, then, can be understood as a product of the special conditions affecting the two aforementioned grounds of differential reward.

NOTES

[1] Kingsley Davis, "A Conceptual Analysis of Stratification," *American Sociological Review.* 7:309–321, June, 1942.

[2] The writers regret (and beg indulgence) that the present essay, a condensation of a longer study, covers so much in such short space that adequate evidence and qualification cannot be given and that as a result what is actually very tentative is presented in an unfortunately dogmatic manner.

[3] Unfortunately, functional importance is difficult to establish. To use the position's prestige to establish it, as is often unconsciously done, constitutes circular reasoning from our point of view. There are, however, two independent clues: (a) the degree to which a position is functionally unique, there being no other positions that can perform the same function satisfactorily; (b) the degree to which other positions are dependent on the one in question. Both clues are best exemplified in organized systems of positions built around one major function. Thus, in most complex societies the religious, political, economic, and educational functions are handled by distinct structures not easily interchangeable. In addition, each structure possesses many different positions, some clearly dependent on, if not subordinate to, others. In sum, when an institutional nucleus becomes differentiated around one main function, and at the same time organizes a large portion of the population into its relationships, the *key* positions in it are of the highest functional importance. The absence of such specialization does not prove functional unimportance, for the whole society may be relatively unspecialized; but it is safe to assume that the more important functions receive the first and clearest structural differentiation.

2

SOME PRINCIPLES OF
STRATIFICATION

A CRITICAL ANALYSIS

Melvin M. Tumin

◆◆◆

The fact of social inequality in human society is marked by its ubiquity
and its antiquity. Every known society, past and present, distributes its
scarce and demanded goods and services unequally. And there are attached to
the positions which command unequal amounts of such goods and services
certain highly morally toned evaluations of their importance for the society.

The ubiquity and the antiquity of such inequality has given rise to the assumption that there must be something both inevitable and positively
functional about such social arrangements.

Clearly, the truth or falsity of such an assumption is a strategic question
for any general theory of social organization. It is therefore most curious that
the basic premises and implications of the assumption have only been most
casually explored by American sociologists.

Melvin M. Tumin, "Some Principles of Stratification: A Critical Analysis," American Sociological Review
18 (August 1953), pp. 387–394.

The most systematic treatment is to be found in the well-known article by Kingsley Davis and Wilbert Moore, entitled "Some Principles of Stratification."[1] More than twelve years have passed since its publication, and though it is one of the very few treatments of stratification on a high level of generalization, it is difficult to locate a single systematic analysis of its reasoning. It will be the principal concern of this paper to present the beginnings of such an analysis.

The central argument advanced by Davis and Moore can be stated in a number of sequential propositions, as follows:

1. Certain positions in any society are functionally more important than others, and require special skills for their performance.

2. Only a limited number of individuals in any society have the talents which can be trained into the skills appropriate to these positions.

3. The conversion of talents into skills involves a training period during which sacrifices of one kind or another are made by those undergoing the training.

4. In order to induce the talented persons to undergo these sacrifices and acquire the training, their future positions must carry an inducement value in the form of differential, i.e., privileged and disproportionate access to the scarce and desired rewards which the society has to offer.[2]

5. These scarce and desired goods consist of the rights and perquisites attached to, or built into, the positions, and can be classified into those things which contribute to (a) sustenance and comfort, (b) humor and diversion, (c) self-respect and ego expansion.

6. This differential access to the basic rewards of the society has as a consequence the differentiation of the prestige and esteem which various strata acquire. This may be said, along with the rights and perquisites, to constitute institutionalized social inequality, i.e., stratification.

7. Therefore, social inequality among different strata in the
   amounts of scarce and desired goods, and the amounts
   of prestige and esteem which they receive, is both positively functional and inevitable in any society.

Let us take these propositions and examine them *seriatim.*[3]

*(1) Certain positions in any society are more functionally important than oth-
ers, and require special skills for their performance.*
   The key term here is "functionally important." The functionalist theory
of social organization is by no means clear and explicit about this term. The
minimum common referent is to something known as the "survival value" of
a social structure.[4] This concept immediately involves a number of perplex-
ing questions. Among these are: (a) the issue of minimum vs. maximum
survival, and the possible empirical referents which can be given to those
terms; (b) whether such a proposition is a useless tautology since any *status
quo* at any given moment is nothing more and nothing less than everything
present in the *status quo.* In these terms, all acts and structures must be
judged positively functional in that they constitute essential portions of the
status quo; (c) what kind of calculus of functionality exists which will enable
us, at this point in our development, to add and subtract long and short
range consequences, with their mixed qualities, and arrive at some summa-
tive judgment regarding the rating an act or structure should receive on a
scale of greater or lesser functionality? At best, we tend to make primarily in-
tuitive judgments. Often enough, these judgments involve the use of
value-laden criteria, or, at least, criteria which are chosen in preference to
others not for any sociologically systematic reasons but by reason of certain
implicit value preferences.
   Thus, to judge that the engineers in a factory are functionally more important to the factory than the unskilled workmen involves a notion
regarding the dispensability of the unskilled workmen, or their replace-
ability, relative to that of the engineers. But this is not a process of choice
with infinite time dimensions. For at some point along the line one must
face the problem of adequate motivation for *all* workers at all levels of skill
in the factory. In the long run, *some* labor force of unskilled workmen is as
important and as indispensable to the factory as *some* labor force of engineers. Often enough, the labor force situation is such that this fact is
brought home sharply to the entrepreneur in the short run rather than in
the long run.

Moreover, the judgment as to the relative indispensability and replace-ability of a particular segment of skills in the population involves a prior judgment about the bargaining-power of that segment. But this power is itself a culturally shaped *consequence* of the existing system of rating, rather than something inevitable in the nature of social organization. At least the contrary of this has never been demonstrated, but only assumed.

A generalized theory of social stratification must recognize that the pre-vailing system of inducements and rewards is only one of many variants in the whole range of possible systems of motivation which, at least theoreti-cally, are capable of working in human society. It is quite conceivable, of course, that a system of norms could be institutionalized in which the idea of threatened withdrawal of services, except under the most extreme circum-stances, would be considered as absolute moral anathema. In such a case, the whole notion of relative functionality, as advanced by Davis and Moore, would have to be radically revised.

(2) Only a limited number of individuals in any society have the talents which can be trained into the skills appropriate to these positions (i.e., the more functionally important positions).

The truth of this proposition depends at least in part on the truth of proposition 1 above. It is, therefore, subject to all the limitations indicated above. But for the moment, let us assume the validity of the first proposition and concentrate on the question of the rarity of appropriate talent.

If all that is meant is that in every society there is a *range* of talent, and that some members of any society are by nature more talented than others, no sensible contradiction can be offered, but a question must be raised here regarding the amount of sound knowledge present in any society concerning the presence of talent in the population.

For in every society there is some demonstrable ignorance regarding the amount of talent present in the population. *And the more rigidly stratified a society is, the less chance does that society have of discovering any new facts about the talents of its members.* Smoothly working and stable systems of stratifica-tion, wherever found, tend to build-in obstacles to the further exploration of the range of available talent. This is especially true in those societies where the opportunity to discover talent in any one generation varies with the dif-ferential resources of the parent generation. Where, for instance, access to education depends upon the wealth of one's parents, and where wealth is differentially distributed, large segments of the population are likely to be deprived of the chance even to *discover* what are their talents.

Whether or not differential rewards and opportunities are functional in any one generation, it is clear that if those differentials are allowed to be socially inherited by the next generation, then, the stratification system is specifically dysfunctional for the discovery of talents in the next generation. In this fashion, systems of social stratification tend to limit the chances available to maximize the efficiency of discovery, recruitment and training of "functionally important talent."[5]

Additionally, the unequal distribution of rewards in one generation tends to result in the unequal distribution of motivation in the succeeding generation. Since motivation to succeed is clearly an important element in the entire process of education, the unequal distribution of motivation tends to set limits on the possible extensions of the educational system, and hence, upon the efficient recruitment and training of the widest body of skills available in the population.[6]

Lastly, in this context, it may be asserted that there is some noticeable tendency for elites to restrict further access to their privileged positions, once they have sufficient power to enforce such restrictions. This is especially true in a culture where it is possible for an elite to contrive a high demand and a proportionately higher reward for its work by restricting the numbers of the elite available to do the work. The recruitment and training of doctors in modern United States is at least partly a case in point.

Here, then, are three ways, among others which could be cited, in which stratification systems, once operative, tend to reduce the survival value of a society by limiting the search, recruitment and training of functionally important personnel far more sharply than the facts of available talent would appear to justify. It is only when there is genuinely equal access to recruitment and training for all potentially talented persons that differential rewards can conceivably be justified as functional. And stratification systems are apparently *inherently antagonistic* to the development of such full equality of opportunity.

(3) The conversion of talents into skills involves a training period during which sacrifices of one kind or another are made by those undergoing the training.

Davis and Moore introduce here a concept, "sacrifice" which comes closer than any of the rest of their vocabulary of analysis to being a direct reflection of the rationalizations, offered by the more fortunate members of a society, of the rightness of their occupancy of privileged positions. It is the least critically thought-out concept in the repertoire, and can also be shown to be least supported by the actual facts.

In our present society, for example, what are the sacrifices which talented persons undergo in the training period? The possibly serious losses involve the surrender of earning power and the cost of the training. The latter is generally borne by the parents of the talented youth undergoing training, and not by the trainees themselves. But this cost tends to be paid out of income which the parents were able to earn generally by virtue of *their* privileged positions in the hierarchy of stratification. That is to say, the parents' ability to pay for the training of their children is part of the differential *reward* they, the parents, received for their privileged positions in the society. And to charge this sum up against sacrifices made by the youth is falsely to perpetrate a bill or a debt already paid by the society to the parents.

So far as the sacrifice of earning power by the trainees themselves is concerned, the loss may be measured relative to what they might have earned had they gone into the labor market instead of into advanced training for the "important" skills. There are several ways to judge this. One way is to take all the average earnings of age peers who did go into the labor market for a period equal to the average length of the training period. The total income, so calculated, roughly equals an amount which the elite can, on the average, earn back in the first decade of professional work, over and above the earnings of his age peers who are not trained. Ten years is probably the maximum amount needed to equalize the differential.[7] There remains, on the average, twenty years of work during each of which the skilled person then goes on to earn far more than his unskilled age peers. And, what is often forgotten, there is then still another ten or fifteen year period during which the skilled person continues to work and earn when his unskilled age peer is either totally or partially out of the labor market by virtue of the attrition of his strength and capabilities.

One might say that the first ten years of differential pay is perhaps justified, in order to regain for the trained person what he lost during his training period. But it is difficult to imagine what would justify continuing such differential rewards beyond that period.

Another and probably sounder way to measure how much is lost during the training period is to compare the per capita income available to the trainee with the per capita income of the age peer on the untrained labor market during the so-called sacrificial period. If one takes into account the earlier marriage of untrained persons, and the earlier acquisition of family dependents, it is highly dubious that the per capita income of the wage worker is significantly larger than that of the trainee. Even assuming, for the moment, that there is a difference, the amount is by no means sufficient to justify a lifetime of continuing differentials.

What tends to be completely overlooked, in addition, are the psychic and spiritual rewards which are available to the elite trainees by comparison with their age peers in the labor force. There is, first, the much higher prestige enjoyed by the college student and the professional-school student as compared with persons in shops and offices. There is, second, the extremely highly valued privilege of having greater opportunity for self-development. There is, third, all the psychic gain involved in being allowed to delay the assumption of adult responsibilities such as earning a living and supporting a family. There is, fourth, the access to leisure and freedom of a kind not likely to be experienced by the persons already at work.

If these are never taken into account as rewards of the training period it is not because they are not concretely present, but because the emphasis in American concepts of reward is almost exclusively placed on the material returns of positions. The emphases on enjoyment, entertainment, ego enhancement, prestige and esteem are introduced only when the differentials in these which accrue to the skilled positions need to be justified. If these other rewards were taken into account, it would be much more difficult to demonstrate that the training period, as presently operative, is really sacrificial. Indeed, it might turn out to be the case that even at this point in their careers, the elite trainees were being differentially rewarded relative to their age peers in the labor force.

All of the foregoing concerns the quality of the training period under our present system of motivation and rewards. Whatever may turn out to be the factual case about the present system—and the factual case is moot—the more important theoretical question concerns the assumption that the training period under *any* system must be sacrificial.

There seem to be no good theoretical grounds for insisting on this assumption. For while under any system certain costs will be involved in training persons for skilled positions, these costs could easily be assumed by the society-at-large. Under these circumstances, there would be no need to compensate anyone in terms of differential rewards once the skilled positions were staffed. In short, there would be no need or justification for stratifying social positions on *these* grounds.

(4) In order to induce the talented persons to undergo these sacrifices and acquire the training, their future positions must carry an inducement value in the

form of differential, i.e., privileged and disproportionate access to the scarce and desired rewards which the society has to offer.

Let us assume, for the purposes of the discussion, that the training period is sacrificial and the talent is rare in every conceivable human society. There is still the basic problem as to whether the allocation of differential rewards in scarce and desired goods and services is the only or the most efficient way of recruiting the appropriate talent to these positions.

For there are a number of alternative motivational schemes whose efficiency and adequacy ought at least to be considered in this context. What can be said, for instance, on behalf of the motivation which De Man called "joy in work," Veblen termed "instinct for workmanship" and which we latterly have come to identify as "intrinsic work satisfaction"? Or, to what extent could the motivation of "social duty" be institutionalized in such a fashion that self interest and social interest come closely to coincide? Or, how much prospective confidence can be placed in the possibilities of institutionalizing "social service" as a widespread motivation for seeking one's appropriate position and fulfilling it conscientiously?

Are not these types of motivations, we may ask, likely to prove most appropriate for precisely the "most functionally important positions"? Especially in a mass industrial society, where the vast majority of positions become standardized and routinized, it is the skilled jobs which are likely to retain most of the quality of "intrinsic job satisfaction" and be most readily identifiable as socially serviceable. Is it indeed impossible then to build these motivations into the socialization pattern to which we expose our talented youth?

To deny that such motivations could be institutionalized would be to overclaim our present knowledge. In part, also, such a claim would seem to derive from an assumption that what has not been institutionalized yet in human affairs is incapable of institutionalization. Admittedly, historical experience affords us evidence we cannot afford to ignore. But such evidence cannot legitimately be used to deny absolutely the possibility of heretofore untried alternatives. Social innovation is as important a feature of human societies as social stability.

On the basis of these observations, it seems that Davis and Moore have stated the case much too strongly when they insist that a "functionally important position" which requires skills that are scarce, "must command great prestige, high salary, ample leisure, and the like," if the appropriate talents are to be attracted to the position. Here, clearly, the authors are postulating the unavoidability of very specific types of rewards and, by implication, denying the possibility of others.

(5) These scarce and desired goods consist of the rights and perquisites attached to, or built into, the positions, and can be classified into those things which contribute to (a) sustenance and comfort, (b) humor and diversion, (c) self-respect and ego expansion.

(6) This differential access to the basic rewards of the society has as a consequence the differentiation of the prestige and esteem which various strata acquire. This may be said, along with the rights and perquisites, to constitute institutionalized social inequality, i.e., stratification.

With the classification of the rewards offered by Davis and Moore there need be little argument. Some question must be raised, however, as to whether any reward system, built into a general stratification system, must allocate equal amounts of all three types of reward in order to function effectively, or whether one type of reward may be emphasized to the virtual neglect of others. This raises the further question regarding which type of emphasis is likely to prove most effective as a differential inducer. Nothing in the known facts about human motivation impels us to favor one type of reward over the other, or to insist that all three types of reward must be built into the positions in comparable amounts if the position is to have an inducement value.

It is well known, of course, that societies differ considerably in the kinds of rewards they emphasize in their efforts to maintain a reasonable balance between responsibility and reward. There are, for instance, numerous societies in which the conspicuous display of differential economic advantage is considered extremely bad taste. In short, our present knowledge commends to us the possibility of considerable plasticity in the way in which different types of rewards can be structured into a functioning society. This is to say, it cannot yet be demonstrated that it is *unavoidable* that differential prestige and esteem shall accrue to positions which command differential rewards in power and property.

What does seem to be unavoidable is that differential prestige shall be given to those in any society who conform to the normative order as against those who deviate from that order in a way judged immoral and detrimental. On the assumption that the continuity of a society depends on the continuity and stability of its normative order, some such distinction between conformists and deviants seems inescapable.

It also seems to be unavoidable that in any society, no matter how literate its tradition, the older, wiser and more experienced individuals who are charged with the enculturation and socialization of the young must have more power than the young, on the assumption that the task of effective socialization demands such differential power.

But this differentiation in prestige between the conformist and the deviant is by no means the same distinction as that between strata of individuals each of which operates *within* the normative order, and is composed of adults. The *latter* distinction, in the form of differentiated rewards and prestige between social strata is what Davis and Moore, and most sociologists, consider the structure of a stratification system. The *former* distinctions have nothing necessarily to do with the workings of such a system nor with the efficiency of motivation and recruitment of functionally important personnel.

Nor does the differentiation of power between young and old necessarily create differentially valued strata. For no society rates its young as less morally worthy than its older persons, no matter how much differential power the older ones may temporarily enjoy.

(7) Therefore, social inequality among different strata in the amounts of scarce and desired goods, and the amounts of prestige and esteem which they receive, is both positively functional and inevitable in any society.

If the objections which have heretofore been raised are taken as reasonable, then it may be stated that the only items which any society *must* distribute unequally are the power and property necessary for the performance of different tasks. If such differential power and property are viewed by all as commensurate with the differential responsibilities, and if they are culturally defined as *resources* and not as rewards, then, no differentials in prestige and esteem need follow.

Historically, the evidence seems to be that every time power and property are distributed unequally, no matter what the cultural definition, prestige and esteem differentiations have tended to result as well. Historically, however, no systematic effort has ever been made, under propitious circumstances, to develop the tradition that each man is as socially worthy as all other men so long as he performs his appropriate tasks conscientiously. While such a tradition seems utterly utopian, no known facts in psychological or social science have yet demonstrated its impossibility or its dysfunctionality for the continuity of a society. The achievement of a full institutionalization of such a tradition seems far too remote to contemplate. Some successive approximations at such a tradition, however, are not out of the range of prospective social innovation.

What, then, of the "positive functionality" of social stratification? Are there other, negative, functions of institutionalized social inequality which can be identified, if only tentatively? Some such dysfunctions of stratification have already been suggested in the body of this paper. Along with others they may now be stated, in the form of provisional assertions, as follows:

1. Social stratification systems function to limit the possibility of discovery of the full range of talent available in a society. This results from the fact of unequal access to appropriate motivation, channels of recruitment and centers of training.

2. In foreshortening the range of available talent, social stratification systems function to set limits upon the possibility of expanding the productive resources of the society, at least relative to what might be the case under conditions of greater equality of opportunity.

3. Social stratification systems function to provide the elite with the political power necessary to procure acceptance and dominance of an ideology which rationalizes the *status quo,* whatever it may be, as "logical," "natural" and "morally right." In this manner, social stratification systems function as essentially conservative influences in the societies in which they are found.

4. Social stratification systems function to distribute favorable self-images unequally throughout a population. To the extent that such favorable self-images are requisite to the development of the creative potential inherent in men, to that extent stratification systems function to limit the development of this creative potential.

5. To the extent that inequalities in social rewards cannot be made fully acceptable to the less privileged in a society, social stratification systems function to encourage hostility, suspicion and distrust among the various segments of

a society and thus to limit the possibilities of extensive social integration.

6. To the extent that the sense of significant membership in a society depends on one's place on the prestige ladder of the society, social stratification systems function to distribute unequally the sense of significant membership in the population.

7. To the extent that loyalty to a society depends on a sense of significant membership in the society, social stratification systems function to distribute loyalty unequally in the population.

8. To the extent that participation and apathy depend upon the sense of significant membership in the society, social stratification systems function to distribute the motivation to participate unequally in a population.

Each of the eight foregoing propositions contains implicit hypotheses regarding the consequences of unequal distribution of rewards in a society in accordance with some notion of the functional importance of various positions. These are empirical hypotheses, subject to test. They are offered here only as exemplary of the kinds of consequences of social stratification which are not often taken into account in dealing with the problem. They should also serve to reinforce the doubt that social inequality is a device which is uniformly functional for the role of guaranteeing that the most important tasks in a society will be performed conscientiously by the most competent persons.

The obviously mixed character of the functions of social inequality should come as no surprise to anyone. If sociology is sophisticated in any sense, it is certainly with regard to its awareness of the mixed nature of any social arrangement, when the observer takes into account long as well as short range consequences and latent as well as manifest dimensions.

SUMMARY

In this paper, an effort has been made to raise questions regarding the inevitability and positive functionality of stratification, or institutionalized social inequality in rewards, allocated in accordance with some notion of the greater and lesser functional importance of various positions. The possible alternative meanings of the concept "functional importance" has been shown to be one difficulty. The question of the scarcity or abundance of available talent has been indicated as a principal source of possible variation. The extent to which the period of training for skilled positions may reasonably be viewed as sacrificial has been called into question. The possibility has been suggested that very different types of motivational schemes might conceivably be made to function. The separability of differentials in power and property considered as resources appropriate to a task from such differentials considered as rewards for the performance of a task has also been suggested. It has also been maintained that differentials in prestige and esteem do not necessarily follow upon differentials in power and property when the latter are considered as appropriate resources rather than rewards. Finally, some negative functions, or dysfunctions, of institutionalized social inequality have been tentatively identified, revealing the mixed character of the outcome of social stratification, and casting doubt on the contention that

> Social inequality is thus an unconsciously evolved device by which societies insure that the most important positions are conscientiously filled by the most qualified persons.[8]

Notes

The writer has had the benefit of a most helpful criticism of the main portions of this paper by Professor W. J. Goode of Columbia University. In addition, he has had the opportunity to expose this paper to criticism by the Staff Seminar of the Sociology Section at Princeton. In deference to a possible rejoinder by Professors Moore and Davis, the writer has not revised the paper to meet the criticisms which Moore has already offered personally.

[1] *American Sociological Review,* 10 (April, 1945), pp. 242–249. An earlier article by Kingsley Davis, entitled, "A Conceptual Analysis of Stratification," *American Sociological Review,* VII (June, 1942), pp. 309–321, is devoted primarily to setting forth a vocabulary for stratification analysis. A still earlier article by Talcott Parsons, "An Analytical Approach to the Theory of Social Stratification," *American Journal of Sociology,* XLV (November, 1940), pp. 849–862, approaches the problem in terms of why "differential ranking is considered a really fundamental phenomenon of social systems and what are the respects in which such ranking is important." The principal line of integration asserted by Parsons is with the fact of the normative orientation of any society. Certain crucial lines of connection are left unexplained, however, in this article, and in the Davis and Moore article of 1945 only some of these lines are made explicit.

[2] The "scarcity and demand" qualities of goods and services are never explicitly mentioned by Davis and Moore. But it seems to the writer that the argument makes no sense unless the goods and services are so characterized. For if rewards are to function as differential inducements they must not only be differentially distributed but they must be both scarce and demanded as well. Neither the scarcity of an item by itself nor the fact of its being in demand is sufficient to allow it to function as a differential inducement in a system of unequal rewards. Leprosy is scarce and oxygen is highly demanded.

[3] The arguments to be advanced here are condensed versions of a much longer analysis entitled, *An Essay on Social Stratification*. Perforce, all the reasoning necessary to support some of the contentions cannot be offered within the space limits of this article.

[4] Davis and Moore are explicitly aware of the difficulties involved here and suggest two "independent clues" other than survival value. See footnote 3 on p. 244 of their article.

[5] Davis and Moore state this point briefly on p. 248 but do not elaborate it.

[6] In the United States, for instance, we are only now becoming aware of the amount of productivity we, as a society, lose by allocating inferior opportunities and rewards, and hence, inferior motivation, to our Negro population. The actual amount of loss is difficult to specify precisely. Some rough estimate can be made, however, on the assumption that there is present in the Negro population about the same range of talent that is found in the White population.

[7] These are only very rough estimates, of course, and it is certain that there is considerable income variation within the so-called elite group, so that the proposition holds only relatively more or less.

[8] Davis and Moore, *op. cit.,* p. 243.

3

CLASSES IN CAPITALISM
AND PRE-CAPITALISM

Karl Marx

♦♦♦

The history of all hitherto existing society[1] is the history of class struggles.

Freeman and slave, patrician and plebeian, lord and serf, guild-master[2] and
journeyman, in a word, oppressor and oppressed, stood in constant opposition to one another, carried on an uninterrupted, now hidden, now open
fight, a fight that each time ended, either in a revolutionary re-constitution
of society at large, or in the common ruin of the contending classes.

In the earlier epochs of history, we find almost everywhere a complicated
arrangement of society into various orders, a manifold gradation of social

Karl Marx, "The Communist Manifesto," in *Selected Works*, vol. 1 (Moscow: Progress Publishers, 1964),
pp. 108–119. Reprinted by permission of Progress Publishers. *The Poverty of Philosophy* (New York: International Publishers, 1963), pp. 172–175. Reprinted by permission of International Publishers. "The
Eighteenth Brumaire of Louis Bonaparte," in *Selected Works*, vol. 1 (Moscow: Progress Publishers, 1963),
pp. 478–479. Reprinted by permission of Progress Publishers. *Capital*, vol. 3 (Moscow: Progress Publishers, 1967), pp. 885–886. Reprinted by permission of Progress Publishers.

rank. In ancient Rome we have patricians, knights, plebeians, slaves; in the Middle Ages, feudal lords, vassals, guild-masters, journeymen, apprentices, serfs; in almost all of these classes, again, subordinate gradations.

The modern bourgeois society that has sprouted from the ruins of feudal society has not done away with class antagonisms. It has but established new classes, new conditions of oppression, new forms of struggle in place of the old ones.

Our epoch, the epoch of the bourgeoisie, possesses, however, this distinctive feature: it has simplified the class antagonisms. Society as a whole is more and more splitting up into two great hostile camps, into two great classes directly facing each other: Bourgeoisie and Proletariat.

From the serfs of the Middle Ages sprang the chartered burghers of the earliest towns. From these burgesses the first elements of the bourgeoisie were developed.

The discovery of America, the rounding of the Cape, opened up fresh ground for the rising bourgeoisie. The East-Indian and Chinese markets, the colonisation of America, trade with the colonies, the increase in the means of exchange and in commodities generally, gave to commerce, to navigation, to industry, an impulse never before known, and thereby, to the revolutionary element in the tottering feudal society, a rapid development.

The feudal system of industry, under which industrial production was monopolised by closed guilds, now no longer sufficed for the growing wants of the new markets. The manufacturing system took its place. The guild-masters were pushed on one side by the manufacturing middle class; division of labour between the different corporate guilds vanished in the face of division of labour in each single workshop.

Meantime the markets kept ever growing, the demand ever rising. Even manufacture no longer sufficed. Thereupon, steam and machinery revolutionised industrial production. The place of manufacture was taken by the giant, Modern Industry, the place of the industrial middle class, by industrial millionaires, the leaders of whole industrial armies, the modern bourgeois.

Modern industry has established the world-market, for which the discovery of America paved the way. This market has given an immense development to commerce, to navigation, to communication by land. This development has, in its turn, reacted on the extension of industry; and in proportion as industry, commerce, navigation, railways extended, in the same proportion the bourgeoisie developed, increased its capital, and pushed into the background every class handed down from the Middle-Ages.

We see, therefore, how the modern bourgeoisie is itself the product of a long course of development, of a series of revolutions in the modes of production and of exchange.

Each step in the development of the bourgeoisie was accompanied by a corresponding political advance of that class. An oppressed class under the sway of the feudal nobility, an armed and self-governing association in the mediaeval commune;[3] here independent urban republic (as in Italy and Germany), there taxable "third estate" of the monarchy (as in France), afterwards, in the period of manufacture proper, serving either the semi-feudal or the absolute monarchy as a counterpoise against the nobility, and, in fact, cornerstone of the great monarchies in general, the bourgeoisie has at last, since the establishment of Modern Industry and of the world-market, conquered for itself, in the modern representative State, exclusive political sway. The executive of the modern State is but a committee for managing the common affairs of the whole bourgeoisie.

The bourgeoisie, historically, has played a most revolutionary part. The bourgeoisie, wherever it has got the upper hand, has put an end to all feudal, patriarchal, idyllic relations. It has pitilessly torn asunder the motley feudal ties that bound man to his "natural superiors," and has left remaining no other nexus between man and man than naked self-interest, than callous "cash payment." It has drowned the most heavenly ecstasies of religious fervour, of chivalrous enthusiasm, of philistine sentimentalism, in the icy water of egotistical calculation. It has resolved personal worth into exchange value, and in place of the numberless indefeasible chartered freedoms, has set up that single, unconscionable freedom—Free Trade. In one word, for exploitation, veiled by religious and political illusions, it has substituted naked, shameless, direct, brutal exploitation.

The bourgeoisie has stripped of its halo every occupation hitherto honoured and looked up to with reverent awe. It has converted the physician, the lawyer, the priest, the poet, the man of science, into its paid wage-labourers.

The bourgeoisie has torn away from the family its sentimental veil, and has reduced the family relation to a mere money relation.

The bourgeoisie has disclosed how it came to pass that the brutal display of vigour in the Middle Ages, which Reactionists so much admire, found its fitting complement in the most slothful indolence. It has been the first to show what man's activity can bring about. It has accomplished wonders far surpassing Egyptian pyramids, Roman aqueducts, and Gothic cathedrals; it has conducted expeditions that put in the shade all former Exoduses of nations and crusades.

The bourgeoisie cannot exist without constantly revolutionising the instruments of production, and thereby the relations of production, and with them the whole relations of society. Conservation of the old modes of production in unaltered form, was, on the contrary, the first condition of existence for all earlier industrial classes. Constant revolutionising of production, uninterrupted disturbance of all social conditions, everlasting uncertainty and agitation distinguish the bourgeois epoch from all earlier ones. All fixed, fast-frozen relations, with their train of ancient and venerable prejudices and opinions, are swept away, all new-formed ones become antiquated before they can ossify. All that is solid melts into air, all that is holy is profaned, and man is at last compelled to face with sober senses, his real conditions of life, and his relations with his kind.

The need of a constantly expanding market for its products chases the bourgeoisie over the whole surface of the globe. It must nestle everywhere, settle everywhere, establish connexions everywhere.

The bourgeoisie has through its exploitation of the world-market given a cosmopolitan character to production and consumption in every country. To the great chagrin of Reactionists, it has drawn from under the feet of industry the national ground on which it stood. All old-established national industries have been destroyed or are daily being destroyed. They are dislodged by new industries, whose introduction becomes a life and death question for all civilised nations, by industries that no longer work up indigenous raw material, but raw material drawn from the remotest zones; industries whose products are consumed, not only at home, but in every quarter of the globe. In place of the old wants, satisfied by the productions of the country, we find new wants, requiring for their satisfaction the products of distant lands and climes. In place of the old local and national seclusion and self-sufficiency, we have intercourse in every direction, universal inter-dependence of nations. And as in material, so also in intellectual production. The intellectual creations of individual nations become common property. National one-sidedness and narrow-mindedness become more and more impossible, and from the numerous national and local literatures, there arises a world literature.

The bourgeoisie, by the rapid improvement of all instruments of production, by the immensely facilitated means of communication, draws all, even the most barbarian, nations into civilisation. The cheap prices of its commodities are the heavy artillery with which it batters down all Chinese walls, with which it forces the barbarians' intensely obstinate hatred of foreigners to capitulate. It compels all nations, on pain of extinction, to adopt the bourgeois mode of production; it compels them to introduce what it calls civilisation into their midst, *i.e.,* to become bourgeois themselves. In one word, it creates a world after its own image.

The bourgeoisie has subjected the country to the rule of the towns. It has created enormous cities, has greatly increased the urban population as compared with the rural, and has thus rescued a considerable part of the population from the idiocy of rural life. Just as it has made the country dependent on the towns, so it has made barbarian and semi-barbarian countries dependent on the civilised ones, nations of peasants on nations of bourgeois, the East on the West.

The bourgeoisie keeps more and more doing away with the scattered state of the population, of the means of production, and of property. It has agglomerated population, centralised means of production, and has concentrated property in a few hands. The necessary consequence of this was political centralisation. Independent, or but loosely connected provinces, with separate interests, laws, governments and systems of taxation, became lumped together into one nation, with one government, one code of laws, one national class-interest, one frontier and one customs-tariff.

The bourgeoisie, during its rule of scarce one hundred years, has created more massive and more colossal productive forces than have all preceding generations together. Subjection of Nature's forces to man, machinery, application of chemistry to industry and agriculture, steam-navigation, railways, electric telegraphs, clearing of whole continents for cultivation, canalisation of rivers, whole populations conjured out of the ground—what earlier century had even a presentiment that such productive forces slumbered in the lap of social labour?

We see then: the means of production and of exchange, on whose foundation the bourgeoisie built itself up, were generated in feudal society. At a certain stage in the development of these means of production and of exchange, the conditions under which feudal society produced and exchanged, the feudal organisation of agriculture and manufacturing industry, in one word, the feudal relations of property became no longer compatible with the already developed productive forces; they became so many fetters. They had to be burst asunder; they were burst asunder.

Into their place stepped free competition, accompanied by a social and political constitution adapted to it, and by the economical and political sway of the bourgeois class.

A similar movement is going on before our own eyes. Modern bourgeois society with its relations of production, of exchange and of property, a society that has conjured up such gigantic means of production and of exchange, is like the sorcerer, who is no longer able to control the powers of the nether world whom he has called up by his spells. For many a decade past the history of industry and commerce is but the history of the revolt of modern productive forces against modern conditions of production, against the property relations that are the conditions for the existence of the bourgeoisie and of its rule. It is enough to mention the commercial crises that by their periodical return put on its trial, each time more threateningly, the existence of the entire bourgeois society. In these crises a great part not only of the existing products, but also of the previously created productive forces, are periodically destroyed. In these crises there breaks out an epidemic that, in all earlier epochs, would have seemed an absurdity—the epidemic of over-production. Society suddenly finds itself put back into a state of momentary barbarism; it appears as if a famine, a universal war of devastation had cut off the supply of every means of subsistence; industry and commerce seem to be destroyed; and why? Because there is too much civilisation, too much means of subsistence, too much industry, too much commerce. The productive forces at the disposal of society no longer tend to further the development of the conditions of bourgeois property; on the contrary, they have become too powerful for these conditions, by which they are fettered, and so soon as they overcome these fetters, they bring disorder into the whole of bourgeois society, endanger the existence of bourgeois property. The conditions of bourgeois society are too narrow to comprise the wealth created by them. And how does the bourgeoisie get over these crises? On the one hand by enforced destruction of a mass of productive forces; on the other, by the conquest of new markets, and by the more thorough exploitation of the old ones. That is to say, by paving the way for more extensive and more destructive crises, and by diminishing the means whereby crises are prevented.

The weapons with which the bourgeoisie felled feudalism to the ground are now turned against the bourgeoisie itself.

But not only has the bourgeoisie forged the weapons that bring death to itself; it has also called into existence the men who are to wield those weapons—the modern working class—the proletarians.

In proportion as the bourgeoisie, i.e., capital, is developed, in the same proportion is the proletariat, the modern working class, developed—a class of labourers, who live only so long as they find work, and who find work only so long as their labour increases capital. These labourers, who must sell themselves piecemeal, are a commodity, like every other article of commerce, and are consequently exposed to all the vicissitudes of competition, to all the fluctuations of the market.

Owing to the extensive use of machinery and to division of labour, the work of the proletarians has lost all individual character, and, consequently, all charm for the workman. He becomes an appendage of the machine, and it is only the most simple, most monotonous, and most easily acquired knack, that is required of him. Hence, the cost of production of a workman is restricted, almost entirely, to the means of subsistence that he requires for his maintenance, and for the propagation of his race. But the price of a commodity, and therefore also of labour, is equal to its cost of production. In proportion, therefore, as the repulsiveness of the work increases, the wage decreases. Nay more, in proportion as the use of machinery and division of labour increases, in the same proportion the burden of toil also increases, whether by prolongation of the working hours, by increase of the work exacted in a given time or by increased speed of the machinery, etc.

Modern industry has converted the little workshop of the patriarchal master into the great factory of the industrial capitalist. Masses of labourers, crowded into the factory, are organised like soldiers. As privates of the industrial army they are placed under the command of a perfect hierarchy of officers and sergeants. Not only are they slaves of the bourgeois class, and of the bourgeois State; they are daily and hourly enslaved by the machine, by the overlooker, and, above all, by the individual bourgeois manufacturer himself. The more openly this despotism proclaims gain to be its end and aim, the more petty, the more hateful and the more embittering it is.

The less the skill and exertion of strength implied in manual labour, in other words, the more modern industry becomes developed, the more is the labour of men superseded by that of women. Differences of age and sex have no longer any distinctive social validity for the working class. All are instruments of labour, more or less expensive to use, according to their age and sex.

No sooner is the exploitation of the labourer by the manufacturer, so far, at an end, and he receives his wages in cash, than he is set upon by the other portions of the bourgeoisie, the landlord, the shopkeeper, the pawnbroker, etc.

The lower strata of the middle class—the small tradespeople, shopkeepers, and retired tradesmen generally, the handicraftsmen and peasants—all these sink gradually into the proletariat, partly because their diminutive capital does not suffice for the scale on which Modern Industry is carried on, and is swamped in the competition with the large capitalists, partly because their specialised skill is rendered worthless by new methods of production. Thus the proletariat is recruited from all classes of the population.

The proletariat goes through various stages of development. With its birth begins its struggle with the bourgeoisie. At first the contest is carried on by individual labourers, then by the workpeople of a factory, then by the operatives of one trade, in one locality, against the individual bourgeois who directly exploits them. They direct their attacks not against the bourgeois conditions of production, but against the instruments of production themselves: they destroy imported wares that compete with their labour, they smash to pieces machinery, they set factories ablaze, they seek to restore by force the vanished status of the workman of the Middle Ages.

At this stage the labourers still form an incoherent mass scattered over the whole country, and broken up by their mutual competition. If anywhere they unite to form more compact bodies, this is not yet the consequence of their own active union, but of the union of the bourgeoisie, which class, in order to attain its own political ends, is compelled to set the whole proletariat in motion, and is moreover yet, for a time, able to do so. At this stage, therefore, the proletarians do not fight their enemies, but the enemies of their enemies, the remnants of absolute monarchy, the landowners, the non-industrial bourgeois, the petty bourgeoisie. Thus the whole historical movement is concentrated in the hands of the bourgeoisie; every victory so obtained is a victory for the bourgeoisie.

But with the development of industry the proletariat not only increases in number; it becomes concentrated in greater masses, its strength grows, and it feels that strength more. The various interests and conditions of life within the ranks of the proletariat are more and more equalised, in proportion as machinery obliterates all distinctions of labour, and nearly everywhere reduces wages to the same low level. The growing competition among the bourgeois, and the resulting commercial crises, make the wages of the workers ever more fluctuating. The unceasing improvement of machinery, ever more rapidly developing, makes their livelihood more and more precarious; the collisions between individual workmen and individual bourgeois take more and more the character of collisions between two classes. Thereupon the workers begin to form combinations (Trades' Unions) against the bourgeois; they club together in order to keep up the rate of wages; they found permanent associations in order to make provision beforehand for these occasional revolts. Here and there the contest breaks out into riots.

Now and then the workers are victorious, but only for a time. The real fruit of their battles lies, not in the immediate result, but in the ever-expanding union of the workers. This union is helped on by the improved means of communication that are created by modern industry and that place the workers of different localities in contact with one another. It was just this contact that was needed to centralise the numerous local struggles, all of the same character, into one national struggle between classes. But every class struggle is a political struggle. And that union, to attain which the burghers of the Middle Ages, with their miserable highways, required centuries, the modern proletarians, thanks to railways, achieve in a few years.

This organisation of the proletarians into a class, and consequently into a political party, is continually being upset again by the competition between the workers themselves. But it ever rises up again, stronger, firmer, mightier. It compels legislative recognition of particular interests of the workers, by taking advantage of the divisions among the bourgeoisie itself. Thus the ten-hours' bill in England was carried.

Altogether collisions between the classes of the old society further, in many ways, the course of development of the proletariat. The bourgeoisie finds itself involved in a constant battle. At first with the aristocracy; later on, with those portions of the bourgeoisie itself, whose interests have become antagonistic to the progress of industry; at all times, with the bourgeoisie of foreign countries. In all these battles it sees itself compelled to appeal to the proletariat, to ask for its help, and thus, to drag it into the political arena. The bourgeoisie itself, therefore, supplies the proletariat with its own elements of political and general education, in other words, it furnishes the proletariat with weapons for fighting the bourgeoisie.

Further, as we have already seen, entire sections of the ruling classes are, by the advance of industry, precipitated into the proletariat, or are at least threatened in their conditions of existence. These also supply the proletariat with fresh elements of enlightenment and progress.

Finally, in times when the class struggle nears the decisive hour, the process of dissolution going on within the ruling class, in fact within the whole range of old society, assumes such a violent, glaring character, that a small section of the ruling class cuts itself adrift, and joins the revolutionary class, the class that holds the future in its hands. Just as, therefore, at an earlier period, a section of the nobility went over to the bourgeoisie, so now a portion of the bourgeoisie goes over to the proletariat, and in particular, a portion of the bourgeois ideologists, who have raised themselves to the level of comprehending theoretically the historical movement as a whole.

Of all the classes that stand face to face with the bourgeoisie today, the proletariat alone is a really revolutionary class. The other classes decay and finally disappear in the face of Modern Industry; the proletariat is its special and essential product.

The lower middle class, the small manufacturer, the shopkeeper, the artisan, the peasant, all these fight against the bourgeoisie, to save from extinction their existence as fractions of the middle class. They are therefore not revolutionary, but conservative. Nay more, they are reactionary, for they try to roll back the wheel of history. If by chance they are revolutionary, they are so only in view of their impending transfer into the proletariat, they thus defend not their present, but their future interests, they desert their own standpoint to place themselves at that of the proletariat.

The "dangerous class," the social scum, that passively rotting mass thrown off by the lowest layers of old society, may, here and there, be swept into the movement by a proletarian revolution, its conditions of life, however, prepare it far more for the part of a bribed tool of reactionary intrigue.

In the conditions of the proletariat, those of old society at large are already virtually swamped. The proletarian is without property; his relation to his wife and children has no longer anything in common with the bourgeois family-relations; modern, industrial labour, modern subjection to capital, the same in England as in France, in America as in Germany, has stripped him of every trace of national character. Law, morality, religion, are to him so many bourgeois prejudices, behind which lurk in ambush just as many bourgeois interests.

All the preceding classes that got the upper hand, sought to fortify their already acquired status by subjecting society at large to their conditions of appropriation. The proletarians cannot become masters of the productive forces of society, except by abolishing their own previous mode of appropriation, and thereby also every other previous mode of appropriation. They have nothing of their own to secure and to fortify; their mission is to destroy all previous securities for, and insurances of, individual property.

All previous historical movements were movements of minorities, or in the interests of minorities. The proletarian movement is the self-conscious, independent movement of the immense majority, in the interests of the immense majority. The proletariat, the lowest stratum of our present society, cannot stir, cannot raise itself up, without the whole superincumbent strata of official society being sprung into the air.

Though not in substance, yet in form, the struggle of the proletariat with the bourgeoisie is at first a national struggle. The proletariat of each country must, of course, first of all settle matters with its own bourgeoisie.

In depicting the most general phases of the development of the proletariat, we traced the more or less veiled civil war, raging within existing society, up to the point where that war breaks out into open revolution, and where the violent overthrow of the bourgeoisie lays the foundation for the sway of the proletariat.

Hitherto, every form of society has been based, as we have already seen, on the antagonism of oppressing and oppressed classes. But in order to oppress a class, certain conditions must be assured to it under which it can, at least, continue its slavish existence. The serf, in the period of serfdom, raised himself to membership in the commune, just as the petty bourgeois, under the yoke of feudal absolutism, managed to develop into a bourgeois. The modern labourer, on the contrary, instead of rising with the progress of industry, sinks deeper and deeper below the conditions of existence of his own class. He becomes a pauper, and pauperism develops more rapidly than population and wealth. And here it becomes evident, that the bourgeoisie is unfit any longer to be the ruling class in society, and to impose its conditions of existence upon society as an overriding law. It is unfit to rule because it is incompetent to assure an existence to its slave within his slavery, because it cannot help letting him sink into such a state, that it has to feed him, instead of being fed by him. Society can no longer live under this bourgeoisie, in other words, its existence is no longer compatible with society.

The essential condition for the existence, and for the sway of the bourgeois class, is the formation and augmentation of capital; the condition for capital is wage-labour. Wage-labour rests exclusively on competition between the labourers. The advance of industry, whose involuntary promoter is the bourgeoisie, replaces the isolation of the labourers, due to competition, by their revolutionary combination, due to association. The development of Modern Industry, therefore, cuts from under its feet the very foundation on which the bourgeoisie produces and appropriates products. What the bourgeoisie, therefore, produces, above all, is its own grave-diggers. Its fall and the victory of the proletariat are equally inevitable.

NOTES

[1] That is, all *written* history. In 1847, the pre-history of society, the social organisation existing previous to recorded history, was all but unknown. [*Note by Engels to the English edition of 1888.*]

[2] Guild-master, that is, a full member of a guild, a master within, not a head of a guild. [*Note by Engels to the English edition of 1888.*]

^{3} "Commune" was the name taken, in France, by the nascent towns even before they had conquered from their feudal lords and masters local self-government and political rights as the "Third Estate." Generally speaking, for the economical development of the bourgeoisie, England is here taken as the typical country; for its political development, France. [*Note by Engels to the English edition of 1888.*]

   This was the name given their urban communities by the townsmen of Italy and France, after they had purchased or wrested their initial rights of self-government from their feudal lords. [*Note by Engels to the German edition of 1890.*]

The Communist Manifesto, pp. 108–119

The first attempts of workers to *associate* among themselves always take place in the form of combinations.

   Large-scale industry concentrates in one place a crowd of people unknown to one another. Competition divides their interests. But the maintenance of wages, this common interest which they have against their boss, unites them in a common thought of resistance—*combination*. Thus combination always has a double aim, that of stopping competition among the workers, so that they can carry on general competition with the capitalist. If the first aim of resistance was merely the maintenance of wages, combinations, at first isolated, constitute themselves into groups as the capitalists in their turn unite for the purpose of repression, and in face of always united capital, the maintenance of the association becomes more necessary to them than that of wages. This is so true that English economists are amazed to see the workers sacrifice a good part of their wages in favour of associations, which, in the eyes of these economists, are established solely in favour of wages. In this struggle—a veritable civil war—all the elements necessary for a coming battle unite and develop. Once it has reached this point, association takes on a political character.

   Economic conditions had first transformed the mass of the people of the country into workers. The combination of capital has created for this mass a common situation, common interests. This mass is thus already a class as against capital, but not yet for itself. In the struggle, of which we have noted only a few phases, this mass becomes united, and constitutes itself as a class for itself. The interests it defends become class interests. But the struggle of class against class is a political struggle.

   In the bourgeoisie we have two phases to distinguish: that in which it constituted itself as a class under the regime of feudalism and absolute monarchy, and that in which, already constituted as a class, it overthrew feudalism and monarchy to make society into a bourgeois society. The first of these phases was the longer and necessitated the greater efforts. This too began by partial combinations against the feudal lords.

Much research has been carried out to trace the different historical phases that the bourgeoisie has passed through, from the commune up to its constitution as a class.

But when it is a question of making a precise study of strikes, combinations and other forms in which the proletarians carry out before our eyes their organization as a class, some are seized with real fear and others display a *transcendental* disdain.

An oppressed class is the vital condition for every society founded on the antagonism of classes. The emancipation of the oppressed class thus implies necessarily the creation of a new society. For the oppressed class to be able to emancipate itself it is necessary that the productive powers already acquired and the existing social relations should no longer be capable of existing side by side. Of all the instruments of production, the greatest productive power is the revolutionary class itself. The organization of revolutionary elements as a class supposes the existence of all the productive forces which could be engendered in the bosom of the old society.

Does this mean that after the fall of the old society there will be a new class domination culminating in a new political power? No.

The condition for the emancipation of the working class is the abolition of every class, just as the condition for the liberation of the third estate, of the bourgeois order, was the abolition of all estates[1] and all orders.

The working class, in the course of its development, will substitute for the old civil society an association which will exclude classes and their antagonism, and there will be no more political power properly so-called, since political power is precisely the official expression of antagonism in civil society.

Meanwhile the antagonism between the proletariat and the bourgeoisie is a struggle of class against class, a struggle which carried to its highest expression is a total revolution. Indeed, is it at all surprising that a society founded on the opposition of classes should culminate in brutal *contradiction*, the shock of body against body, as its final *dénouement*?

Do not say that social movement excludes political movement. There is never a political movement which is not at the same time social.

It is only in an order of things in which there are no more classes and class antagonisms that *social evolutions* will cease to be *political revolutions*. Till then, on the eve of every general reshuffling of society, the last word of social science will always be:

"Le combat ou la mort; la lutte sanguinaire ou le néant. C'est ainsi que la question est invinciblement posée." [2]

NOTES

[1] Estates here in the historical sense of the estates of feudalism, estates with definite and limited privileges. The revolution of the bourgeoisie abolished the estates and their privileges. Bourgeois society knows only *classes*. It was, therefore, absolutely in contradiction with history to describe the proletariat as the "fourth estate." [*Note by F. Engels to the German edition*, 1885.]

[2] "Combat or death; bloody struggle or extinction. It is thus that the question is inexorably put." George Sand, *Jean Ziska*.

The Poverty of Philosophy, pp. 172–175

The small-holding peasants form a vast mass, the members of which live in similar conditions but without entering into manifold relations with one another. Their mode of production isolates them from one another instead of bringing them into mutual intercourse. The isolation is increased by France's bad means of communication and by the poverty of the peasants. Their field of production, the small holding, admits of no division of labour in its cultivation, no application of science and, therefore, no diversity of development, no variety of talent, no wealth of social relationships. Each individual peasant family is almost self-sufficient; it itself directly produces the major part of its consumption and thus acquires its means of life more through exchange with nature than in intercourse with society. A small holding, a peasant and his family; alongside them another small holding, another peasant and another family. A few score of these make up a village, and a few score of villages make up a Department. In this way, the great mass of the French nation is formed by simple addition of homologous magnitudes, much as potatoes in a sack form a sack of potatoes. In so far as millions of families live under economic conditions of existence that separate their mode of life, their interests and their culture from those of the other classes, and put them in hostile opposition to the latter, they form a class. In so far as there is merely a local interconnection among these small-holding peasants, and the identity of their interests begets no community, no national bond and no political organisation among them, they do not form a class. They are consequently incapable of enforcing their class interests in their own name, whether through a parliament or through a convention. They cannot represent themselves, they must be represented. Their representative must at the same time appear as their master, as an authority over them, as an unlimited governmental power that protects them against the other classes and sends them rain and sunshine from above. The political influence of the small-holding peasants, therefore, finds its final expression in the executive power subordinating society to itself.

The Eighteenth Brumaire of Louis Bonaparte, pp. 478–479

The owners merely of labour-power, owners of capital, and landowners, whose respective sources of income are wages, profit and ground-rent, in other words, wage-labourers, capitalists and landowners, constitute then three big classes of modern society based upon the capitalist mode of production.

In England, modern society is indisputably most highly and classically developed in economic structure. Nevertheless, even here the stratification of classes does not appear in its pure form. Middle and intermediate strata even here obliterate lines of demarcation everywhere (although incomparably less in rural districts than in the cities). However, this is immaterial for our analysis. We have seen that the continual tendency and law of development of the capitalist mode of production is more and more to divorce the means of production from labour, and more and more to concentrate the scattered means of production into large groups, thereby transforming labour into wage-labour and the means of production into capital. And to this tendency, on the other hand, corresponds the independent separation of landed property from capital and labour, or the transformation of all landed property into the form of landed property corresponding to the capitalist mode of production.

The first question to be answered is this: What constitutes a class?—and the reply to this follows naturally from the reply to another question, namely: What makes wage-labourers, capitalists and landlords constitute the three great social classes?

At first glance—the identity of revenues and sources of revenue. There are three great social groups whose members, the individuals forming them, live on wages, profit and ground-rent respectively, on the realisation of their labour-power, their capital, and their landed property.

However, from this standpoint, physicians and officials, e.g., would also constitute two classes, for they belong to two distinct social groups, the members of each of these groups receiving their revenue from one and the same source. The same would also be true of the infinite fragmentation of interest and rank into which the division of social labour splits labourers as well as capitalists and landlords—the latter, e.g., into owners of vineyards, farm owners, owners of forests, mine owners and owners of fisheries.

[Here the manuscript breaks off.]

Capital, Vol. III, pp. 885–886

4

CLASS, STATUS, PARTY

Max Weber

♦♦♦

ECONOMICALLY DETERMINED POWER
AND THE SOCIAL ORDER

Law exists when there is a probability that an order will be upheld by a specific staff of men who will use physical or psychical compulsion with the intention of obtaining conformity with the order, or of inflicting sanctions for infringement of it.[1] The structure of every legal order directly influences the distribution of power, economic or otherwise, within its respective community. This is true of all legal orders and not only that of the state. In general, we understand by 'power' the chance of a man or of a number of men to realize their own will in a communal action even against the resistance of others who are participating in the action.

'Economically conditioned' power is not, of course, identical with 'power' as such. On the contrary, the emergence of economic power may be the

Max Weber, "Class, Status, Party," in *From Max Weber: Essays in Sociology*, edited and translated by H. H. Gerth and C. Wright Mills, pp. 180–195. Translation copyright 1946, 1958 by H. H. Gerth and C. Wright Mills.

consequence of power existing on other grounds. Man does not strive for power only in order to enrich himself economically. Power, including economic power, may be valued 'for its own sake.' Very frequently the striving for power is also conditioned by the social 'honor' it entails. Not all power, however, entails social honor: The typical American Boss, as well as the typical big speculator, deliberately relinquishes social honor. Quite generally, 'mere economic' power, and especially 'naked' money power, is by no means a recognized basis of social honor. Nor is power the only basis of social honor. Indeed, social honor, or prestige, may even be the basis of political or economic power, and very frequently has been. Power, as well as honor, may be guaranteed by the legal order, but, at least normally, it is not their primary source. The legal order is rather an additional factor that enhances the chance to hold power or honor; but it cannot always secure them.

The way in which social honor is distributed in a community between typical groups participating in this distribution we may call the 'social order.' The social order and the economic order are, of course, similarly related to the 'legal order.' However, the social and the economic order are not identical. The economic order is for us merely the way in which economic goods and services are distributed and used. The social order is of course conditioned by the economic order to a high degree, and in its turn reacts upon it.

Now: 'classes,' 'status groups,' and 'parties' are phenomena of the distribution of power within a community.

Determination of Class-Situation by Market-Situation

In our terminology, 'classes' are not communities; they merely represent possible, and frequent, bases for communal action. We may speak of a 'class' when (1) a number of people have in common a specific causal component of their life chances, in so far as (2) this component is represented exclusively by economic interests in the possession of goods and opportunities for income, and (3) is represented under the conditions of the commodity or labor markets. [These points refer to 'class situation,' which we may express more briefly as the typical chance for a supply of goods, external living conditions, and personal life experiences, in so far as this chance is determined by the amount and kind of power, or lack of such, to dispose of goods or skills for the sake of income in a given economic order. The term 'class' refers to any group of people that is found in the same class situation.]

It is the most elemental economic fact that the way in which the disposition over material property is distributed among a plurality of people, meeting competitively in the market for the purpose of exchange, in itself creates specific life chances. According to the law of marginal utility this mode of distribution excludes the non-owners from competing for highly valued goods; it favors the owners and, in fact, gives to them a monopoly to acquire such goods. Other things being equal, this mode of distribution monopolizes the opportunities for profitable deals for all those who, provided with goods, do not necessarily have to exchange them. It increases, at least generally, their power in price wars with those who, being propertyless, have nothing to offer but their services in native form or goods in a form constituted through their own labor, and who above all are compelled to get rid of these products in order barely to subsist. This mode of distribution gives to the propertied a monopoly on the possibility of transferring property from the sphere of use as a 'fortune,' to the sphere of 'capital goods'; that is, it gives them the entrepreneurial function and all chances to share directly or indirectly in returns on capital. All this holds true within the area in which pure market conditions prevail. 'Property' and 'lack of property' are, therefore, the basic categories of all class situations. It does not matter whether these two categories become effective in price wars or in competitive struggles.

Within these categories, however, class situations are further differentiated: on the one hand, according to the kind of property that is usable for returns; and, on the other hand, according to the kind of services that can be offered in the market. Ownership of domestic buildings; productive establishments; warehouses; stores; agriculturally usable land, large and small holdings—quantitative differences with possibly qualitative consequences— ownership of mines; cattle; men (slaves); disposition over mobile instruments of production, or capital goods of all sorts, especially money or objects that can be exchanged for money easily and at any time; disposition over products of one's own labor or of others' labor differing according to their various distances from consumability; disposition over transferable monopolies of any kind—all these distinctions differentiate the class situations of the propertied just as does the 'meaning' which they can and do give to the utilization of property, especially to property which has money equivalence. Accordingly, the propertied, for instance, may belong to the class of rentiers or to the class of entrepreneurs.

Those who have no property but who offer services are differentiated just as much according to their kinds of services as according to the way in which they make use of these services, in a continuous or discontinuous relation to a recipient. But always this is the generic connotation of the concept of class: that the kind of chance in the *market* is the decisive moment which presents a common condition for the individual's fate. 'Class situation' is, in this sense, ultimately 'market situation.' The effect of naked possession *per se*, which among cattle breeders gives the nonowning slave or serf into the power of the cattle owner, is only a forerunner of real 'class' formation. However, in the cattle loan and in the naked severity of the law of debts in such communities, for the first time mere 'possession' as such emerges as decisive for the fate of the individual. This is very much in contrast to the agricultural communities based on labor. The creditor-debtor relation becomes the basis of 'class situations' only in those cities where a 'credit market,' however primitive, with rates of interest increasing according to the extent of dearth and a factual monopolization of credits, is developed by a plutocracy. Therewith 'class struggles' begin.

Those men whose fate is not determined by the chance of using goods or services for themselves on the market, e.g. slaves, are not, however, a 'class' in the technical sense of the term. They are, rather, a 'status group.'

COMMUNAL ACTION FLOWING FROM CLASS INTEREST

According to our terminology, the factor that creates 'class' is unambiguously economic interest, and indeed, only those interests involved in the existence of the 'market.' Nevertheless, the concept of 'class-interest' is an ambiguous one: even as an empirical concept it is ambiguous as soon as one understands by it something other than the factual direction of interests following with a certain probability from the class situation for a certain 'average' of those people subjected to the class situation. The class situation and other circumstances remaining the same, the direction in which the individual worker, for instance, is likely to pursue his interests may vary widely, according to whether he is constitutionally qualified for the task at hand to a high, to an average, or to a low degree. In the same way, the direction of interests may vary according to whether or not a *communal* action of a larger or smaller portion of those commonly affected by the 'class situation,' or even an association among them, e.g. a 'trade union,' has grown out of the class situation from which the individual may or may not expect promising results. [Communal action refers to that action which is oriented to the feeling of the actors that they belong together. Societal action, on the other hand, is oriented to a rationally motivated adjustment of interests.] The rise of societal or even of communal action from a common class situation is by no means a universal phenomenon.

The class situation may be restricted in its effects to the generation of essentially *similar* reactions, that is to say, within our terminology, of 'mass actions.' However, it may not have even this result. Furthermore, often merely an amorphous communal action emerges. For example, the 'murmuring' of the workers known in ancient oriental ethics: the moral disapproval of the work-master's conduct, which in its practical significance was probably equivalent to an increasingly typical phenomenon of precisely the latest industrial development, namely, the 'slow down' (the deliberate limiting of work effort) of laborers by virtue of tacit agreement. The degree in which 'communal action' and possibly 'societal action,' emerges from the 'mass actions' of the members of a class is linked to general cultural conditions, especially to those of an intellectual sort. It is also linked to the extent of the contrasts that have already evolved, and is especially linked to the *transparency* of the connections between the causes and the consequences of the 'class situation.' For however different life chances may be, this fact in itself, according to all experience, by no means gives birth to 'class action' (communal action by the members of a class). The fact of being conditioned and the results of the class situation must be distinctly recognizable. For only then the contrast of life chances can be felt not as an absolutely given fact to be accepted, but as a resultant from either (1) the given distribution of property, or (2) the structure of the concrete economic order. It is only then that people may react against the class structure not only through acts of an intermittent and irrational protest, but in the form of rational association. There have been 'class situations' of the first category (1), of a specifically naked and transparent sort, in the urban centers of Antiquity and during the Middle Ages; especially then, when great fortunes were accumulated by factually monopolized trading in industrial products of these localities or in foodstuffs. Furthermore, under certain circumstances, in the rural economy of the most diverse periods, when agriculture was increasingly exploited in a profit-making manner. The most important historical example of the second category (2) is the class situation of the modern 'proletariat.'

Types of 'Class Struggle'

Thus every class may be the carrier of any one of the possibly innumerable forms of 'class action,' but this is not necessarily so: In any case, a class does not in itself constitute a community. To treat 'class' conceptually as having the same value as 'community' leads to distortion. That men in the same class situation regularly react in mass actions to such tangible situations as economic ones in the direction of those interests that are most adequate to their average number is an important and after all simple fact for the understanding of historical events. Above all, this fact must not lead to that kind of pseudo-scientific operation with the concepts of 'class' and 'class interests' so frequently found these days, and which has found its most classic expression in the statement of a talented author, that the individual may be in error concerning his interests but that the 'class' is 'infallible' about its interests. Yet, if classes as such are not communities, nevertheless class situations emerge only on the basis of communalization. The communal action that brings forth class situations, however, is not basically action between members of the identical class; it is an action between members of different classes. Communal actions that directly determine the class situation of the worker and the entrepreneur are: the labor market, the commodities market, and the capitalistic enterprise. But, in its turn, the existence of a capitalistic enterprise presupposes that a very specific communal action exists and that it is specifically structured to protect the possession of goods *per se,* and especially the power of individuals to dispose, in principle freely, over the means of production. The existence of a capitalistic enterprise is preconditioned by a specific kind of 'legal order.' Each kind of class situation, and above all when it rests upon the power of property *per se,* will become most clearly efficacious when all other determinants of reciprocal relations are, as far as possible, eliminated in their significance. It is in this way that the utilization of the power of property in the market obtains its most sovereign importance.

Now 'status groups' hinder the strict carrying through of the sheer market principle. In the present context they are of interest to us only from this one point of view. Before we briefly consider them, note that not much of a general nature can be said about the more specific kinds of antagonism between 'classes' (in our meaning of the term). The great shift, which has been going on continuously in the past, and up to our times, may be summarized, although at the cost of some precision: the struggle in which class situations are effective has progressively shifted from consumption credit toward, first, competitive struggles in the commodity market and, then, toward price wars on the labor market. The 'class struggles' of antiquity—to the extent that they were genuine class struggles and not struggles between status groups—were initially carried on by indebted peasants, and perhaps also by artisans threatened by debt bondage and struggling against urban creditors. For debt bondage is the normal result of the differentiation of wealth in commercial cities, especially in seaport cities. A similar situation has existed among cattle breeders. Debt relationships as such produced class action up to the time of Cataline. Along with this, and with an increase in provision of grain for the city by transporting it from the outside, the struggle over the means of sustenance emerged. It centered in the first place around the provision of bread and the determination of the price of bread. It lasted throughout antiquity and the entire Middle Ages. The propertyless as such flocked together against those who actually and supposedly were interested in the dearth of bread. This fight spread until it involved all those commodities essential to the way of life and to handicraft production. There were only incipient discussions of wage disputes in antiquity and in the Middle Ages. But they have been slowly increasing up into modern times. In the earlier periods they were completely secondary to slave rebellions as well as to fights in the commodity market.

The propertyless of antiquity and of the Middle Ages protested against monopolies, pre-emption, forestalling, and the withholding of goods from the market in order to raise prices. Today the central issue is the determination of the price of labor.

This transition is represented by the fight for access to the market and for the determination of the price of products. Such fights went on between merchants and workers in the putting-out system of domestic handicraft during the transition to modern times. Since it is quite a general phenomenon we must mention here that the class antagonisms that are conditioned through the market situation are usually most bitter between those who actually and directly participate as opponents in price wars. It is not the rentier, the share-holder, and the banker who suffer the ill will of the worker, but almost exclusively the manufacturer and the business executives who are the direct opponents of workers in price wars. This is so in spite of the fact that it is precisely the cash boxes of the rentier, the share-holder, and the banker into which the more or less 'unearned' gains flow, rather than into the pockets of the manufacturers or of the business executives. This simple state of affairs has very frequently been decisive for the role the class situation has played in the formation of political parties. For example, it has made possible the varieties of patriarchal socialism and the frequent attempts—formerly, at least—of threatened status groups to form alliances with the proletariat against the 'bourgeoisie.'

STATUS HONOR

In contrast to classes, *status groups* are normally communities. They are, however, often of an amorphous kind. In contrast to the purely economically determined 'class situation' we wish to designate as 'status situation' every typical component of the life fate of men that is determined by a specific, positive or negative, social estimation of *honor*. This honor may be connected with any quality shared by a plurality, and, of course, it can be knit to a class situation: class distinctions are linked in the most varied ways with status distinctions. Property as such is not always recognized as a status qualification, but in the long run it is, and with extraordinary regularity. In the subsistence economy of the organized neighborhood, very often the richest man is simply the chieftain. However, this often means only an honorific preference. For example, in the so-called pure modern 'democracy,' that is, one devoid of any expressly ordered status privileges for individuals, it may be that only the families coming under approximately the same tax class dance with one another. This example is reported of certain smaller Swiss cities. But status honor need not necessarily be linked with a 'class situation.' On the contrary, it normally stands in sharp opposition to the pretensions of sheer property.

Both propertied and propertyless people can belong to the same status group, and frequently they do with very tangible consequences. This 'equality' of social esteem may, however, in the long run become quite precarious. The 'equality' of status among the American 'gentlemen,' for instance, is expressed by the fact that outside the subordination determined by the different functions of 'business,' it would be considered strictly repugnant—wherever the old tradition still prevails—if even the richest 'chief,' while playing billiards or cards in his club in the evening, would not treat his 'clerk' as in every sense fully his equal in birthright. It would be repugnant if the American 'chief' would bestow upon his 'clerk' the condescending 'benevolence' marking a distinction of 'position,' which the German chief can never dissever from his attitude. This is one of the most important reasons why in

America the German 'clubby-ness' has never been able to attain the attraction that the American clubs have.

GUARANTEES OF STATUS STRATIFICATION

In content, status honor is normally expressed by the fact that above all else a specific *style of life* can be expected from all those who wish to belong to the circle. Linked with this expectation are restrictions on 'social' intercourse (that is, intercourse which is not subservient to economic or any other of business's 'functional' purposes). These restrictions may confine normal marriages to within the status circle and may lead to complete endogamous closure. As soon as there is not a mere individual and socially irrelevant imitation of another style of life, but an agreed-upon communal action of this closing character, the 'status' development is under way.

In its characteristic form, stratification by 'status groups' on the basis of conventional styles of life evolves at the present time in the United States out of the traditional democracy. For example, only the resident of a certain street ('the street') is considered as belonging to 'society,' is qualified for social intercourse, and is visited and invited. Above all, this differentiation evolves in such a way as to make for strict submission to the fashion that is dominant at a given time in society. This submission to fashion also exists among men in America to a degree unknown in Germany. Such submission is considered to be an indication of the fact that a given man *pretends* to qualify as a gentleman. This submission decides, at least *prima facie,* that he will be treated as such. And this recognition becomes just as important for his employment chances in 'swank' establishments, and above all, for social intercourse and marriage with 'esteemed' families, as the qualification for dueling among Germans in the Kaiser's day. As for the rest: certain families resident for a long time, and, of course, correspondingly wealthy, e.g. 'F. F. V., i.e. First Families of Virginia,' or the actual or alleged descendants of the 'Indian Princess' Pocahontas, of the Pilgrim fathers, or of the Knickerbockers, the members of almost inaccessible sects and all sorts of circles setting themselves apart by means of any other characteristics and badges . . . all these elements usurp 'status' honor. The development of status is essentially a question of stratification resting upon usurpation. Such usurpation is the normal origin of almost all status honor. But the road from this purely conventional situation to legal privilege, positive or negative, is easily traveled as

soon as a certain stratification of the social order has in fact been 'lived in'
and has achieved stability by virtue of a stable distribution of economic
power.

'ETHNIC' SEGREGATION AND 'CASTE'

Where the consequences have been realized to their full extent, the status
group evolves into a closed 'caste.' Status distinctions are then guaranteed
not merely by conventions and laws, but also by *rituals*. This occurs in such
a way that every physical contact with a member of any caste that is considered to be 'lower' by the members of a 'higher' caste is considered as making
for a ritualistic impurity and to be a stigma which must be expiated by a religious act. Individual castes develop quite distinct cults and gods.

In general, however, the status structure reaches such extreme consequences only where there are underlying differences which are held to be
'ethnic.' The 'caste' is, indeed, the normal form in which ethnic communities usually live side by side in a 'societalized' manner. These ethnic
communities believe in blood relationship and exclude exogamous marriage
and social intercourse. Such a caste situation is part of the phenomenon of
'pariah' peoples and is found all over the world. These people form communities, acquire specific occupational traditions of handicrafts or of other arts,
and cultivate a belief in their ethnic community. They live in a 'diaspora'
strictly segregated from all personal intercourse, except that of an unavoidable sort, and their situation is legally precarious. Yet, by virtue of their
economic indispensability, they are tolerated, indeed, frequently privileged,
and they live in interspersed political communities. The Jews are the most
impressive historical example.

A 'status' segregation grown into a 'caste' differs in its structure from a mere
'ethnic' segregation: the caste structure transforms the horizontal and uncon-
nected coexistences of ethnically segregated groups into a vertical social
system of super- and subordination. Correctly formulated: a comprehensive
societalization integrates the ethnically divided communities into specific
political and communal action. In their consequences they differ precisely in
this way: ethnic coexistences condition a mutual repulsion and disdain but
allow each ethnic community to consider its own honor as the highest one;
the caste structure brings about a social subordination and an acknowledg-
ment of 'more honor' in favor of the privileged caste and status groups. This

is due to the fact that in the caste structure ethnic distinctions as such have become 'functional' distinctions within the political societalization (warriors, priests, artisans that are politically important for war and for building, and so on). But even pariah people who are most despised are usually apt to continue cultivating in some manner that which is equally peculiar to ethnic and to status communities: the belief in their own specific 'honor.' This is the case with the Jews.

Only with the negatively privileged status groups does the 'sense of dignity' take a specific deviation. A sense of dignity is the precipitation in individuals of social honor and of conventional demands which a positively privileged status group raises for the deportment of its members. The sense of dignity that characterizes positively privileged status groups is naturally related to their 'being' which does not transcend itself, that is, it is to their 'beauty and excellence.' Their kingdom is 'of this world.' They live for the present and by exploiting their great past. The sense of dignity of the negatively privileged strata naturally refers to a future lying beyond the present, whether it is of this life or of another. In other words, it must be nurtured by the belief in a providential 'mission' and by a belief in a specific honor before God. The 'chosen people's' dignity is nurtured by a belief either that in the beyond 'the last will be the first,' or that in this life a Messiah will appear to bring forth into the light of the world which has cast them out the hidden honor of the pariah people. This simple state of affairs, and not the 'resentment' which is so strongly emphasized in Nietzsche's much admired construction in the *Genealogy of Morals,* is the source of the religiosity cultivated by pariah status groups. In passing, we may note that resentment may be accurately applied only to a limited extent; for one of Nietzsche's main examples, Buddhism, it is not at all applicable.

Incidentally, the development of status groups from ethnic segregations is by no means the normal phenomenon. On the contrary, since objective 'racial differences' are by no means basic to every subjective sentiment of an ethnic community, the ultimately racial foundation of status structure is rightly and absolutely a question of the concrete individual case. Very frequently a status group is instrumental in the production of a thoroughbred anthropological type. Certainly a status group is to a high degree effective in producing extreme types, for they select personally qualified individuals (e.g. the Knighthood selects those who are fit for warfare, physically and psychically). But selection is far from being the only, or the predominant, way in which status groups are formed: Political membership or class situation has at all times been at least as frequently decisive. And today the class situation is by far the predominant factor, for of course the possibility of a style of life expected for members of a status group is usually conditioned economically.

Status Privileges

For all practical purposes, stratification by status goes hand in hand with a monopolization of ideal and material goods or opportunities, in a manner we have come to know as typical. Besides the specific status honor, which always rests upon distance and exclusiveness, we find all sorts of material monopolies. Such honorific preferences may consist of the privilege of wearing special costumes, of eating special dishes taboo to others, of carrying arms—which is most obvious in its consequences—the right to pursue certain non-professional dilettante artistic practices, e.g. to play certain musical instruments. Of course, material monopolies provide the most effective motives for the exclusiveness of a status group; although, in themselves, they are rarely sufficient, almost always they come into play to some extent. Within a status circle there is the question of intermarriage: the interest of the families in the monopolization of potential bridegrooms is at least of equal importance and is parallel to the interest in the monopolization of daughters. The daughters of the circle must be provided for. With an increased inclosure of the status group, the conventional preferential opportunities for special employment grow into a legal monopoly of special offices for the members. Certain goods become objects for monopolization by status groups. In the typical fashion these include 'entailed estates' and frequently also the possessions of serfs or bondsmen and, finally, special trades. This monopolization occurs positively when the status group is exclusively entitled to own and to manage them; and negatively when, in order to maintain its specific way of life, the status group must *not* own and manage them.

The decisive role of a 'style of life' in status 'honor' means that status groups are the specific bearers of all 'conventions.' In whatever way it may be manifest, all 'stylization' of life either originates in status groups or is at least conserved by them. Even if the principles of status conventions differ greatly, they reveal certain typical traits, especially among those strata which are most privileged. Quite generally, among privileged status groups there is a status disqualification that operates against the performance of common physical labor. This disqualification is now 'setting in' in America against the old tradition of esteem for labor. Very frequently every rational economic pursuit, and especially 'entrepreneurial activity,' is looked upon as a disqualification of status. Artistic and literary activity is also considered as degrading work as soon as it is exploited for income, or at least when it is connected with hard physical exertion. An example is the sculptor working like a mason in his dusty smock as over against the painter in his salon-like 'studio' and those forms of musical practice that are acceptable to the status group.

ECONOMIC CONDITIONS AND EFFECTS OF STATUS STRATIFICATION

The frequent disqualification of the gainfully employed as such is a direct result of the principle of status stratification peculiar to the social order, and of course, of this principle's opposition to a distribution of power which is regulated exclusively through the market. These two factors operate along with various individual ones, which will be touched upon below.

We have seen above that the market and its processes 'knows no personal distinctions': 'functional' interests dominate it. It knows nothing of 'honor.' The status order means precisely the reverse, viz.: stratification in terms of 'honor' and of styles of life peculiar to status groups as such. If mere economic acquisition and naked economic power still bearing the stigma of its extra-status origin could bestow upon anyone who has won it the same honor as those who are interested in status by virtue of style of life claim for themselves, the status order would be threatened at its very root. This is the more so as, given equality of status honor, property *per se* represents an addition even if it is not overtly acknowledged to be such. Yet if such economic acquisition and power gave the agent any honor at all, his wealth would result in his attaining more honor than those who successfully claim honor by virtue of style of life. Therefore all groups having interests in the status order react with special sharpness precisely against the pretensions of purely economic acquisition. In most cases they react the more vigorously the more they feel themselves threatened. Calderon's respectful treatment of the peasant, for instance, as opposed to Shakespeare's simultaneous and ostensible disdain of the *canaille* illustrates the different way in which a firmly structured status order reacts as compared with a status order that has become economically precarious. This is an example of a state of affairs that recurs everywhere. Precisely because of the rigorous reactions against the claims of property *per se*, the 'parvenu' is never accepted, personally and without reservation, by the privileged status groups, no matter how completely his style of life has been adjusted to theirs. They will only accept his descendants who have been educated in the conventions of their status group and who have never besmirched its honor by their own economic labor.

As to the general *effect* of the status order, only one consequence can be stated, but it is a very important one: the hindrance of the free development of the market occurs first for those goods which status groups directly withheld from free exchange by monopolization. This monopolization may be effected either legally or conventionally. For example, in many Hellenic cities during the epoch of status groups, and also originally in Rome, the inherited estate (as is shown by the old formula for indication against spendthrifts) was monopolized just as were the estates of knights, peasants, priests, and especially the clientele of the craft and merchant guilds. The market is restricted, and the power of naked property *per se*, which gives its stamp to 'class formation,' is pushed into the background. The results of this process can be most varied. Of course, they do not necessarily weaken the contrasts in the economic situation. Frequently they strengthen these contrasts, and in any case, where stratification by status permeates a community as strongly as was the case in all political communities of antiquity and of the Middle Ages, one can never speak of a genuinely free market competition as we understand it today. There are wider effects than this direct exclusion of special goods from the market. From the contrariety between the status order and the purely economic order mentioned above, it follows that in most instances the notion of honor peculiar to status absolutely abhors that which is essential to the market: higgling. Honor abhors higgling among peers and occasionally it taboos higgling for the members of a status group in general. Therefore, everywhere some status groups, and usually the most influential, consider almost any kind of overt participation in economic acquisition as absolutely stigmatizing.

With some over-simplification, one might thus say that 'classes' are stratified according to their relations to the production and acquisition of goods; whereas 'status groups' are stratified according to the principles of their *consumption* of goods as represented by special 'styles of life.'

An 'occupational group' is also a status group. For normally, it successfully claims social honor only by virtue of the special style of life which may be determined by it. The differences between classes and status groups frequently overlap. It is precisely those status communities most strictly segregated in terms of honor (viz. the Indian castes) who today show, although within very rigid limits, a relatively high degree of indifference to pecuniary income. However, the Brahmins seek such income in many different ways.

As to the general economic conditions making for the predominance of stratification by 'status,' only very little can be said. When the bases of the acquisition and distribution of goods are relatively stable, stratification by status is favored. Every technological repercussion and economic transformation threatens stratification by status and pushes the class situation into the foreground. Epochs and countries in which the naked class situation is of predominant significance are regularly the periods of technical and economic transformations. And every slowing down of the shifting of economic stratifications leads, in due course, to the growth of status structures and makes for a resuscitation of the important role of social honor.

PARTIES

Whereas the genuine place of 'classes' is within the economic order, the place of 'status groups' is within the social order, that is, within the sphere of the distribution of 'honor.' From within these spheres, classes and status groups influence one another and they influence the legal order and are in turn influenced by it. But 'parties' live in a house of 'power.'

Their action is oriented toward the acquisition of social 'power,' that is to say, toward influencing a communal action no matter what its content may be. In principle, parties may exist in a social 'club' as well as in a 'state.' As over against the actions of classes and status groups, for which this is not necessarily the case, the communal actions of 'parties' always mean a societalization. For party actions are always directed toward a goal which is striven for in planned manner. This goal may be a 'cause' (the party may aim at realizing a program for ideal or material purposes), or the goal may be 'personal' (sinecures, power, and from these, honor for the leader and the followers of the party). Usually the party action aims at all these simultaneously. Parties are, therefore, only possible within communities that are societalized, that is, which have some rational order and a staff of persons available who are ready to enforce it. For parties aim precisely at influencing this staff, and if possible, to recruit it from party followers.

In any individual case, parties may represent interests determined through 'class situation' or 'status situation,' and they may recruit their following respectively from one or the other. But they need be neither purely 'class' nor purely 'status' parties. In most cases they are partly class parties and partly status parties, but sometimes they are neither. They may represent ephemeral or enduring structures. Their means of attaining power may be quite varied, ranging from naked violence of any sort to canvassing for votes with coarse or subtle means: money, social influence, the force of speech, suggestion, clumsy hoax, and so on to the rougher or more artful tactics of obstruction in parliamentary bodies.

The sociological structure of parties differs in a basic way according to the kind of communal action which they struggle to influence. Parties also differ according to whether or not the community is stratified by status or by classes. Above all else, they vary according to the structure of domination within the community. For their leaders normally deal with the conquest of a community. They are, in the general concept which is maintained here, not only products of specially modern forms of domination. We shall also designate as parties the ancient and medieval 'parties,' despite the fact that their structure differs basically from the structure of modern parties. By virtue of these structural differences of domination it is impossible to say anything about the structure of parties without discussing the structural forms of social domination *per se*. Parties, which are always structures struggling for domination, are very frequently organized in a very strict 'authoritarian' fashion. . . .

Concerning 'classes,' 'status groups,' and 'parties,' it must be said in general that they necessarily presuppose a comprehensive societalization, and especially a political framework of communal action, within which they operate. This does not mean that parties would be confined by the frontiers of any individual political community. On the contrary, at all times it has been the order of the day that the societalization (even when it aims at the use of military force in common) reaches beyond the frontiers of politics. This has been the case in the solidarity of interests among the Oligarchs and among the democrats in Hellas, among the Guelfs and among Ghibellines in the Middle Ages, and within the Calvinist party during the period of religious struggles. It has been the case up to the solidarity of the landlords (international congress of agrarian landlords), and has continued among princes (holy alliance, Karlsbad decrees), socialist workers, conservatives (the longing of Prussian conservatives for Russian intervention in 1850). But their aim is not necessarily the establishment of new international political, i.e. *territorial*, dominion. In the main they aim to influence the existing dominion.[2]

NOTES

[1] *Wirtschaft und Gesellschaft,* part III, chap. 4, pp. 631–40. The first sentence in paragraph one and the several definitions in this chapter which are in brackets do not appear in the original text. They have been taken from other contexts of *Wirtschaft und Gesellschaft.*

[2] The posthumously published text breaks off here. We omit an incomplete sketch of types of 'warrior estates.'

5

THE DIVISION OF LABOR
IN SOCIETY

Emile Durkheim

♦♦♦

In *The Division of Labor in Society,* we emphasise the state of legal and moral anomie in which economic life exists at the present time. In fact, in this particular sphere of activity, professional ethics only exist in a very rudimentary state. There are professional ethics for the lawyer and magistrate, the soldier and professor, the doctor and priest, etc. Yet if we attempted to express in somewhat more precise terms contemporary ideas of what should be the relationship between employer and white-collar worker, between the industrial worker and the factory boss, between industrialists in competition with one another or between industrialists and the public, how imprecise

Emile Durkheim, *The Division of Labor in Society,* with an introduction by Lewis A. Coser, and translated by W. D. Halls, pp. xxxi, xxxii, xxxv, xxxix–xl, xlii–xlv, l–lv, lviii–lix. Introduction copyright 1984 by Lewis A. Coser. Translation copyright 1984 by The Higher & Further Education Division, Macmillan Publishers, Ltd. Reprinted with the permission of The Free Press, a Division of Simon and Schuster, Inc. The text excerpted here was altered in minor ways to make the transition between sections smoother.

would be the statements that we could formulate! Some vague generalities about the loyalty and commitment that employees of every kind owe to those who employ them, or about the moderation that employers should manifest in exercising their economic superiority, a certain condemnation of any competition that is too blatantly unfair, or of any too glaring exploitation of the consumer: this is almost the sum total of what the ethical consciousness of these professions comprises. Moreover, most of these precepts lack any juridical character. They are backed only by public opinion and not by the law—and it is well known how indulgent that opinion shows itself to be about the way in which such vague obligations are fulfilled. Those actions most blameworthy are so often excused by success that the boundary between the permissible and the prohibited, between what is just and what is unjust, is no longer fixed in any way, but seems capable of being shifted by individuals in an almost arbitrary fashion. So vague a morality, one so inconsistent, cannot constitute any kind of discipline. The upshot is that this entire sphere of collective life is for the most part removed from the moderating action of any rules.

It is to this state of anomie that must be attributed the continually recurring conflicts and disorders of every kind of which the economic world affords so sorry a spectacle. For, since nothing restrains the forces present from reacting together, or prescribes limits for them that they are obliged to respect, they tend to grow beyond all bounds, each clashing with the other, each warding off and weakening the other. . . .

Political society as a whole, or the state, clearly cannot draw up the system of rules that is now lacking. Economic life, because it is very special and is daily becoming increasingly specialised, lies outside their authority and sphere of action. Activity within a profession can only be effectively regulated through a group close enough to that profession to be thoroughly cognisant of how it functions, capable of perceiving all its needs and following every fluctuation in them. The sole group that meets these conditions is that constituted by all those working in the same industry, assembled together and organised in a single body. This is what is termed a corporation, or professional group.

Yet in the economic field the professional group no more exists than does a professional ethic. Since the last century when, *not without reason,* the ancient corporations were dissolved, hardly more than fragmentary and incomplete attempts have been made to reconstitute them on a different basis. Doubtless, individuals who are busy in the same trade are in contact with one another by the very fact that their activities are similar. Competition with one another engenders mutual relationships. But these are in no way regular; depending upon chance meetings, they are very often entirely of an individual nature. One industrialist finds himself in contact with another, but the body of industrialists in some particular speciality do not meet to act in concert. Exceptionally, we do see all members of the same profession come together at a conference to deal with some problem of common interest. But such conferences last only a short while: they do not survive the particular circumstances that gave rise to them. Consequently the collective life for which they provided an opportunity dies more or less entirely with them. . . .

Can we legitimately believe that corporative organisation is called upon to play in contemporary societies a more considerable part? If we deem it indispensable it is not because of the services it might render the economy, but on account of the moral influence it could exercise. What we particularly see in the professional grouping is a moral force capable of curbing individual egoism, nurturing among workers a more envigorated feeling of their common solidarity, and preventing the law of the strongest from being applied too brutally in industrial and commercial relationships. Yet such a grouping is deemed unfit for such a role. Because it springs from temporal interests, it can seemingly only serve utilitarian ends, and the memories that survive of the corporations during the *ancien régime* only confirm this impression. We incline to visualise them in the future as they were towards the end of their former existence, intent above all on maintaining or increasing their privileges and monopolies. We fail to see how such narrow vocational concerns might have any beneficial effect upon the morality of the corporation or its members.

However, we should refrain from extending to the entire corporative system what may have been true of certain corporations during a very short period in their development. Far from the system having been, because of its very constitution, infected by a kind of moral sickness, during the greater part of its existence it played above all a moral role. This is especially evident with the Roman corporation. 'Among the Romans,' declares Walzing, 'the corporations of artisans were far from having so pronounced a professional character as in the Middle Ages. We come across no regulations concerning methods, no obligatory apprenticeship, and no monopoly. Nor was their purpose to accumulate the capital necessary to exploit an industry.'[1] Doubtless their associating together gave them more power to safeguard the common interest, when the need arose. But this was only one of the useful by-products that the institution engendered. It was not the justification for its existence, nor its main function. Above all else, the corporation was a collegiate religious body. Each one possessed its own particular god, who, when the means were available, was worshipped in a special temple. Just as every family had its *Lar familiaris* and every city its *Genius publicus,* so every collegiate body had its protecting divinity, the *Genius collegii.* Naturally this professional form of worship was not without its festivities, and sacrifices and banquets were celebrated in common together. Moreover, all kinds of circumstances would serve as the occasion for festive gatherings; distribution of food and money was often made at the expense of the community. . . .

The facts cited adequately demonstrate that a professional grouping is not at all incapable of exerting a moral effect. The very important place that religion held in its life highlights very particularly the true nature of its functions, for in such times every religious community constituted a moral environment, just as every kind of moral discipline necessarily tended to take on a religious form. Moreover, this characteristic of corporative organisation is due to the effect of very general causes which we can see at work in different circumstances. Within a political society, as soon as a certain number of individuals find they hold in common ideas, interests, sentiments and occupations which the rest of the population does not share in, it is inevitable that, under the influence of these similarities, they should be attracted to one another. They will seek one another out, enter into relationships and associate together. Thus a restricted group is gradually formed within society as a whole, with its own special features. Once such a group is formed, a moral life evolves within it which naturally bears the distinguishing mark of the special conditions in which it has developed. It is impossible for men to live together and be in regular contact with one another without their acquiring some feeling for the group which they constitute through having united together, without their becoming attached to it, concerning themselves with its interests and taking it into account in their behaviour. And this attachment to something that transcends the individual, this subordination of the particular to the general interest, is the very well-spring of all moral activity. Let this sentiment only crystallise and grow more determinate, let it be translated into well-defined formulas by being applied to the most common circumstances of life, and we see gradually being constituted a corpus of moral rules.

Domestic morality did not arise any differently. Because of the prestige that the family retains in our eyes, if it appears to us to have been and continue to be a school of altruism and abnegation, the highest seat of morality, it is through the very special characteristics it is privileged to possess, ones that could not be found at any level elsewhere. We like to believe that in blood kinship there exists an extraordinarily powerful reason for moral identification with others. But, as we have often had occasion to show,[2] blood kinship has in no way the extraordinary effectiveness attributed to it. The proof of this is that in a large number of societies relations not linked by the blood tie are very numerous in a family. Thus so-called artificial kinship is entered into very readily and has all the effects of natural kinship. Conversely, very frequently those closely knit by ties of blood are morally and legally strangers to one another. For example, this is true of blood kin in the Roman family. Thus the family does not derive its whole strength from unity of descent. Quite simply, it is a group of individuals who have drawn close to one another within the body politic through a very specially close community of ideas, feelings and interests. Blood kinship was able to make such a concentration of individuals easier, for it naturally tends to have the effect of bringing different consciousnesses together. Yet many other factors have also intervened: physical proximity, solidarity of interest, the need to unite to fight a common danger, or simply to unite, have been causes of a different kind which have made people come together.

Such causes are not peculiar to the family but are to be found, although in different forms, within the corporation. Thus if the former group has played so important a role in the moral history of humanity, why should not also the latter be capable of so doing? Undoubtedly one difference will always exist between them, inasmuch as family members share in common their entire existence, whereas the members of a corporation share only their professional concerns. The family is a kind of complete society whose influence extends to economic activity as well as to that of religion, politics, and science, etc. Everything of any importance that we do, even outside the home, has repercussions upon it and sparks off an appropriate reaction. In one sense the corporation's sphere of influence is more limited. Yet we must not forget the ever more important place that our profession assumes in our lives as work becomes increasingly segmented. . . .

What past experience demonstrates above all is that the organisational framework of the professional group should always be related to that of economic life. It is because this condition was not fulfilled that the system of corporations disappeared. Thus, since the market, from being municipal as it once was, has become national and international, the corporation should assume the same dimensions. Instead of being restricted exclusively to the artisans of one town, it must grow so as to include all the members of one profession scattered over the whole country,[3] for in whatever region they may be, whether they live in town or countryside, they are all linked to one another and share a common life. Since this common life is in certain respects independent of any territorial boundaries, a suitable organism must be created to give expression to this life and to regulate its functions. Because of the dimensions that it assumes, such an organism should necessarily be closely in contact and directly linked with the central organism of the life of the collectivity. Events important enough to affect a whole category of industrial enterprises within a country necessarily have wide repercussions of which the state cannot fail to be aware. This impels it to intervene. Thus for good reason the royal power tended instinctively not to leave large-scale industry outside its ambit as soon as it appeared. It could not fail to take an interest in a form of activity which by its very nature is always liable to affect society as a whole. Yet such regulatory action, although necessary, should not degenerate into utter subordination, as happened in the seventeenth and eighteenth centuries. The two organisms, although in contact with each other, should remain distinct and autonomous; each has functions that it alone can perform. If it falls to political assemblies to lay down the general principles for industrial legislation, they are not capable of diversifying them according to the various types of industry. It is this diversification that is the corporation's proper task.[4] A unitary organisation over a whole country also in no way precludes the formation of secondary organisations which include similar workers in the same region or locality. Their role could be to spell out even more specifically, in accordance with local or regional needs, the regulations for a profession. Thus economic activity could be regulated and demarcated without losing any of its diversity.

Moreover, we must reject the belief that the corporation's sole role should consist in laying down and applying rules. It is undoubtedly true that wherever a group is formed, a moral discipline is also formed. But the institution of that discipline is only one of the numerous ways in which any collective activity manifests itself. A group is not only a moral authority regulating the life of its members, but also a source of life *sui generis*. From it there arises a warmth that quickens or gives fresh life to each individual, which makes him disposed to empathise, causing selfishness to melt away. Thus in the past the family has been responsible for legislating a code of law and morality whose severity has often been carried to an extreme of harshness. But it has also been the environment where, for the first time, men have learnt to appreciate the outpouring of feeling. We have likewise seen how the corporation, both in Rome and during the Middle Ages, created these same needs and sought to satisfy them. The corporations of the future will be assigned even greater and more complex functions, because of their increased scope. Around their purely professional functions will be grouped others which at present are exercised by the communes and private associations. Among these are functions of mutual assistance which, in order to be entirely fulfilled, assume between helpers and helped feelings of solidarity as well as a certain homogeneity of intellect and morals, such as that readily engendered by the exercise of the same profession. Many educational activities (technical education, adult education, etc.) should also, it seems, find in the corporation their natural habitat. The same is also true for a certain type of artistic activity. It would seem in accordance with the nature of things that such a noble form of diversion and recreation should develop alongside the more serious aspects of life, acting as a balancing and restorative influence. In fact we now already see trade unions acting at the same time as friendly societies, and others are setting up communal centres where courses are organised, and concerts and dramatic performances held. Hence the activity of a corporation can take on the most varied forms.

We may even reasonably suppose that the corporation will be called upon to become the foundation, or one of the essential foundations, of our political organisation. We have seen that, although it first began outside the social system, it tended to become more and more closely involved in it as economic life developed. We have therefore every reason to anticipate that, if progress continues on the same lines, the corporation is destined to assume an ever more central and preponderant place in society. It was once the elementary division of communal organisation. Now that the commune, from being the autonomous unit that it once was, has been absorbed into the state just as the municipal market was absorbed into the national market, may we not legitimately think that the corporation should also undergo a corresponding transformation and become the elementary division of the state, the basic political unit? Society, instead of remaining what it is today—a conglomerate of land masses juxtaposed together—would become a vast system of national corporations. The demand is raised in various quarters for electoral colleges to be constituted by professions and not by territorial constituencies. Certainly in this way political assemblies would more accurately reflect the diversity of social interests and their interconnections. They would more exactly epitomise social life as a whole. Yet if we state that the country, in order to become conscious of itself, should be grouped by professions, is not this to acknowledge that the organised profession or the corporation should become the essential organ of public life?

In this way a serious gap in the structure of European societies, and in our own in particular, would be filled. We shall see how, as history unfolds, an organisation based on territorial groupings (village, town, district or province, etc.) becomes progressively weaker. There is no doubt that we each belong to a commune or a *département,* but the ties binding us to them become daily more loose and tenuous. These geographical divisions are in the main artificial, and no longer arouse deep emotions within us. The provincial spirit has vanished beyond recall. 'Parish pump' patriotism has become an anachronism that cannot be restored at will. Strictly local or *département* matters hardly affect or enthrall us either any longer, save in so far as they go hand in hand with matters relating to our profession. Our activity extends much beyond these groups, which are too narrow for it; moreover, much of what happens within them leaves us indifferent. Thus what might be described as the spontaneous collapse of the old social structure has occurred. But this internal organisation cannot disappear without something taking its place. A society made up of an extremely large mass of unorganised individuals, which an overgrown state attempts to limit and restrain, constitutes a veritable sociological monstrosity. For collective activity is always too complex to be capable of finding expression in the one single organ of the state. Moreover, the state is too remote from individuals, its connections with them too superficial and irregular, to be able to penetrate the depths of their consciousness and socialise them from within. This is why, when the state constitutes the sole environment in which men can fit themselves for the business of living in common, they inevitably 'contract out,' detaching themselves from one another, and thus society disintegrates to a corresponding extent. A nation cannot be maintained unless, between the state and individuals, a whole range of secondary groups are interposed. These must be close enough to the individual to attract him strongly to their activities and, in so doing, to absorb him into the mainstream of social life. We have just demonstrated how professional groupings are fitted to perform this role, and how indeed everything marks them out for it. Hence we can comprehend how important it is, particularly in the economic sphere, that they should emerge from that inchoate and disorganised state in which they have lain for a century, since professions of this kind today absorb the greater part of the energies of society.[5]

NOTES

[1] Waltzing, *Etude historique sur les corporations profession chez les Romains,* vol. I, p. 194.

[2] Cf. especially *Année sociologique,* vol. I, pp. 313 ff.

[3] We need not discuss the international organisation which, because of the international character of the market, would necessarily develop at a level above that of the national organisation. For at present the latter alone can constitute a legal entity. In the present state of European law the former can only result from arrangements freely concluded between national corporations.

[4] This specialisation could not occur without the help of elected assemblies charged with representing the corporation. In the present state of industry, these assemblies, as well as those tribunals entrusted with the task of applying the regulations of an occupation, should clearly include representatives of employees and employers, as is already the case with the industrial arbitration tribunals. The proportion of each should correspond to the respective importance attributed by public opinion to these two factors of production. But if it is necessary for both sides to meet on the governing councils of the corporation it is no less indispensable for them to constitute distinct and independent groups at the lower level of corporative organisation, because too often their interests vie with one another and are opposing. To feel that they exist freely, they must be aware of their separate existence. The two bodies so constituted can then appoint their representatives to the common assemblies.

[5] Moreover, we do not mean that territorial constituencies are destined to disappear completely, but only that they will fade into the background. Old institutions never vanish in the face of new ones to such an extent that they leave no trace of themselves. They persist not only by the mere fact of survival, but also because there persists some trace of the needs to which they corresponded. Material proximity will always constitute a link between men. Consequently the political and social organisation based on territory will certainly subsist. But it will no longer enjoy its present predominance, precisely because that link is losing some of its force. What is more, we have shown above that, even at the base of the corporation will still be found geographical divisions. Moreover, between the various corporations from a same locality or region there will necessarily be special relationships of solidarity which will, from time to time, demand an appropriate organisation.

6

EQUALITY AND INEQUALITY IN MODERN SOCIETY, OR SOCIAL STRATIFICATION REVISITED

Talcott Parsons

◆◆◆

Sociological interest has tended to focus on inequality and its forms, causes, and justifications. There has been, however, for several centuries now, a trend to the institutionalization of continually extending bases of equality. This came to an important partial culmination in the eighteenth century, which happened to be the founding period of the politically independent American variant of Western society. Such cultural influences as the conceptions of natural rights or the rights of man had a profound effect on the normative definition of the nature of the new society and received a particularly important embodiment in the Bill of Rights, which was built into

Talcott Parsons, "Equality and Inequality in Modern Society, or Social Stratification Revisited," in *Social Stratification: Research and Theory for the 1970s*, edited by Edward O. Laumann, pp. 14–15, 22–25, 70. Copyright 1970 by Bobbs-Merrill Company.

the United States Constitution as the first ten amendments. The egalitarian focus of this system of "rights" was unmistakable. It was also, however, closely associated with the nearly contemporary emphases of the French Revolution on the concept of citizenship. In the United States this could, to a degree impossible in the Europe of that time, be dissociated from religious and ethnic bases of the solidarity of societal communities, since the pattern of separation of church and state and denominational pluralism in the religious sphere was already well launched. This "liberalizing" tendency was reinforced by the beginnings of the attenuation of the assumption that the new American societal community was "essentially" Anglo-Saxon. Though English remained the common language for the whole society, the ethnic and religious diversity of the elements entering the society by immigration strongly reinforced the pluralistic potentials which were present in the cultural tradition. Indeed, the Negro, recently the most difficult element to include, has, after a long and tragic history, begun to change status quite markedly in the direction of equality. Though there is a good deal of skepticism on this score, the indications of the trend point, in my judgment, to broadly successful inclusion after much further tension and struggle over a protracted period. Thus we can say that two of the most deep-seated ascriptive bases of inequality, religion and ethnicity, have lost much of their force in a society which in both respects has become notably pluralistic in composition.

EQUALITY AND SOCIAL CLASS

In spite of its "oversimplification," the Marxian conception remains a very useful point of reference. It was not fully accurate, even in 1838, and has certainly become progressively less so for the principal modern societies. But what have been the principal changes? On the kinship side, the most important one has been the attenuation of lineages with their intergeneration solidarity, leading to an increased "isolation" of the nuclear family. The most important single shift has been from total or virtual "arrangement" of marriages to a situation of relatively high degree of individual freedom of marriage choice, not without ascriptive "preferences," but still allowing much more mixing across ascriptive lines than before. This in turn has been associated with the loosening of the ties of the family to the other three ascriptive contexts, namely, religious affiliation—indexed by the increase of "mixed" marriages—ethnicity, and local particularism. These more specific bases of class identification have tended to be replaced by more generalized "style of life" patterns related to income levels and access to consumers' goods.

On the "property" side, we can clearly no longer speak of a "capitalistic" propertied class which has replaced the earlier "feudal" landed class. The changes are principally of two types. One concerns the immense extent to which household income has come from occupational rather than property sources, extending upward in status terms from the proletarian wage worker to the very top of the occupational scale. This clearly leaves the problem of the relation of the income-receiver to the employing organization problematical, but it clearly cannot be simply dichotomized into the case of the classical "worker," who is simply paid by those who control the means of production, and the "owner," who, if he has a salary, essentially must be conceived to "pay himself." The second type of change is the relative dissociation of rights to property income from effective control of the means of production. Thus most of the recipients of corporate dividends have no more control of the enterprises in which they invest than do customers over those from which they buy.

The Marxian synthesis essentially asserted the *codetermination* of class status by economic *and* political factors—ownership of economic facilities giving *control*, in a political sense, of the firm as an organization. This in turn was conceived to be synthesized with the kinship system in its lineage aspect. The process of differentiation in modern society has, however, broken down this double synthesis, insofar as it existed at all, in classical nineteenth-century "capitalism." In consequence, not only has the mobility of economic and political resources been greatly enhanced but the door has been opened to the involvement of factors other than the classical three of kinship solidarity, proprietorship, and political power in private organizations. One effect is to make it possible for other ascriptive factors to have a continued or even revived existence, in the enhanced independence of "minority" religious and ethnic solidarities, and also relative to the "microascription" of which Mayhew (1968) speaks. But the main macrosocial structure has moved much farther away from ascriptive foci, even that of class, than the Marxian analysis would have it.

At the same time, the "property" complex has become much more highly differentiated. Not only have the ownership component as claim to income and the political power component as right to control become differentiated

from each other, but the variegated occupational system has developed a
wide range of qualitatively different types. The most important new element
is probably the injection, on a scale not even vaguely envisioned by Marx, of
many kinds of trained competence as factors in effective occupational performance. This has established a set of links between the occupational system
and that of education, especially higher education, which did not exist before. The growth of a vast range of white-collar occupations for which
secondary education is prerequisite is one major consequence, but perhaps
the most important is the emergence into a new prominence of the professions, dependent as these are on university level training.

Occupation rather than property having become the primary focus of
household status, both through the prestige value of occupational positions
and functions themselves and through the income and style of life they
ground, there is neither a simple dichotomy nor a single neat hierarchical
continuum in the status system—and least of all is there such a continuum
hinging on ownership as distinguished from employed status. There is, of
course, an hierarchical dimension to the occupational system; but, especially
in the upper ranges, it is only one of several dimensions of differentiation. It
is particularly important that there is no clear-cut break between an upper
and a lower "class"; even the famous line between manual and nonmanual
work has ceased to be of primary significance.[1]

In the light of these developments, we may suggest the usefulness of di-
vorcing the concept of social class from its historic relation to both kinship
and property as such; to define *class status*, for the unit of social structure, as
position on the hierarchical dimension of the differentiation of the societal
system; and to consider *social class* as an aggregate of such units, individual
and/or collective, that in their own estimation and those of others in the society occupy position of approximately equal status in this respect.

Certainly for the male individual as unit, the two primary foci of class status are occupation and kinship. The former is articulated with a variety of
the other predominantly universalistic and functionally specific structures of
the society, particularly the market system, with special reference to the very
complex phenomena of the labor market and the structure of power and authority especially in specific-function organizations, and the educational
system and other foci of the institutionalization of differences of kind and
level of competence.

Kinship, on the other hand, is for both the individual member and the social system, diffuse in function; it is the most important residual basis of

diffuse solidarity and personal security. It, then, is articulated with the other principal bases of diffuse solidarity, which include the massive historic ones of ethnicity and religion and the relations between household and more extended kinship groupings, as well as those of residential neighborhood and, extending from this, a complex variety of solidarities associated with territorial localism, extending up to the societal community itself. Class status, for the unit, must include the whole complex of membership in diffusely solidary collectivities.

Diffuse solidarities, in this sense, constitute the structure of modern "communities." It is important to our general argument to be clear that there is no one community in a sociologically relevant sense but that a modern society is a very complex composite of differentiated and articulating—sometimes conflicting—units of community. This is one of the two primary respects in which such societies are "pluralistic." The typical individual participates not in one, but in several of them. He is, of course, a family member; but there are two typical family memberships for each individual, not one. Both his ethnic and his religious identification may be in part independent of family membership—e.g., he may "intermarry" both ethnically and religiously. In even modestly high-status neighborhoods, he probably lives in one which is "mixed" from such points of view, as well as heterogeneous by occupational roles. Even at the level of the societal community as a whole there is major variation, e.g., as to the degrees to which people have transnational affiliations, on the basis of kinship, occupation, or other grounds.

The other primary respect in which modern societies are pluralistic has to do with the functionally specific roles of which occupation is prototypical. Besides occupation itself, which is, like marriage, in the normal case a one-at-a-time involvement, this pluralism has above all to do with memberships in more or less formalized voluntary associations, which, for the participating individual, have immensely varying modes and levels of significance.

NOTE

[1] It is well known that, in Communist countries, the higher nonmanual occupations, including those of industrial managers and scientists, are classified as belonging to the "intelligentsia," which is explicitly said to be part of the "working class." Of course theoretically in such societies there is no longer a "bourgeois" class.

REFERENCE

Mayhew, Leon. 1968. "Ascription in Modern Societies." *Sociological Inquiry* (Spring): 105–120.

7

THE POWER ELITE

C. Wright Mills

◆◆◆

The powers of ordinary men are circumscribed by the everyday worlds in which they live, yet even in these rounds of job, family, and neighborhood they often seem driven by forces they can neither understand nor govern. 'Great changes' are beyond their control, but affect their conduct and outlook none the less. The very framework of modern society confines them to projects not their own, but from every side, such changes now press upon the men and women of the mass society, who accordingly feel that they are without purpose in an epoch in which they are without power.

But not all men are in this sense ordinary. As the means of information and of power are centralized, some men come to occupy positions in American society from which they can look down upon, so to speak, and by their decisions mightily affect, the everyday worlds of ordinary men and women. They are not made by their jobs; they set up and break down jobs for thousands of others; they are not confined by simple family responsibilities; they can escape. They may live in many hotels and houses, but they are bound by no one community. They need not merely 'meet the demands of the day and hour'; in some part, they create these demands, and cause others to meet them. Whether or not they profess their power, their technical and political experience of it far transcends that of the underlying population. What Jacob Burckhardt said of 'great men,' most Americans might well say of their elite: 'They are all that we are not.'[1]

The power elite is composed of men whose positions enable them to transcend the ordinary environments of ordinary men and women; they are in positions to make decisions having major consequences. Whether they do or do not make such decisions is less important than the fact that they do occupy such pivotal positions: their failure to act, their failure to make decisions, is itself an act that is often of greater consequence than the decisions they do make. For they are in command of the major hierarchies and organizations of modern society. They rule the big corporations. They run the machinery of the state and claim its prerogatives. They direct the military establishment. They occupy the strategic command posts of the social structure, in which are now centered the effective means of the power and the wealth and the celebrity which they enjoy.

The power elite are not solitary rulers. Advisers and consultants, spokesmen and opinion-makers are often the captains of their higher thought and decision. Immediately below the elite are the professional politicians of the middle levels of power, in the Congress and in the pressure groups, as well as among the new and old upper classes of town and city and region. Mingling with them in curious ways are those professional celebrities who live by being continually displayed but are never, so long as they remain celebrities, displayed enough. If such celebrities are not at the head of any dominating hierarchy, they do often have the power to distract the attention of the public or afford sensations to the masses, or, more directly, to gain the ear of those who do occupy positions of direct power. More or less unattached, as critics of morality and technicians of power, as spokesmen of God and creators of mass sensibility, such celebrities and consultants are part of the immediate scene in which the drama of the elite is enacted. But that drama itself is centered in the command posts of the major institutional hierarchies.

I

The truth about the nature and the power of the elite is not some secret which men of affairs know but will not tell. Such men hold quite various theories about their own roles in the sequence of event and decision. Often they are uncertain about their roles, and even more often they allow their fears and their hopes to affect their assessment of their own power. No matter how great their actual power, they tend to be less acutely aware of it than of the resistances of others to its use. Moreover, most American men of affairs have learned well the rhetoric of public relations, in some cases even to the point of using it when they are alone, and thus coming to believe it. The personal awareness of the actors is only one of the several sources one must examine in order to understand the higher circles. Yet many who believe that there is no elite, or at any rate none of any consequence, rest their argument upon what men of affairs believe about themselves, or at least assert in public.

There is, however, another view: those who feel, even if vaguely, that a compact and powerful elite of great importance does now prevail in America often base that feeling upon the historical trend of our time. They have felt, for example, the domination of the military event, and from this they infer that generals and admirals, as well as other men of decision influenced by them, must be enormously powerful. They hear that the Congress has again abdicated to a handful of men decisions clearly related to the issue of war or peace. They know that the bomb was dropped over Japan in the name of the United States of America, although they were at no time consulted about the matter. They feel that they live in a time of big decisions; they know that they are not making any. Accordingly, as they consider the present as history, they infer that at its center, making decisions or failing to make them, there must be an elite of power.

On the one hand, those who share this feeling about big historical events assume that there is an elite and that its power is great. On the other hand, those who listen carefully to the reports of men apparently involved in the great decisions often do not believe that there is an elite whose powers are of decisive consequence.

Both views must be taken into account, but neither is adequate. The way to understand the power of the American elite lies neither solely in recognizing the historic scale of events nor in accepting the personal awareness reported by men of apparent decision. Behind such men and behind the events of history, linking the two, are the major institutions of modern society. These hierarchies of state and corporation and army constitute the means of power; as such they are now of a consequence not before equaled in human history—and at their summits, there are now those command posts of modern society which offer us the sociological key to an understanding of the role of the higher circles in America.

Within American society, major national power now resides in the economic, the political, and the military domains. Other institutions seem off to the side of modern history, and, on occasion, duly subordinated to these. No family is as directly powerful in national affairs as any major corporation; no church is as directly powerful in the external biographies of young men in America today as the military establishment; no college is as powerful in the shaping of momentous events as the National Security Council. Religious, educational, and family institutions are not autonomous centers of national power; on the contrary, these decentralized areas are increasingly shaped by the big three, in which developments of decisive and immediate consequence now occur. . . .

Within each of the big three, the typical institutional unit has become enlarged, has become administrative, and, in the power of its decisions, has become centralized. Behind these developments there is a fabulous technology, for as institutions, they have incorporated this technology and guide it, even as it shapes and paces their developments.

The economy—once a great scatter of small productive units in autonomous balance—has become dominated by two or three hundred giant corporations, administratively and politically interrelated, which together hold the keys to economic decisions.

The political order, once a decentralized set of several dozen states with a weak spinal cord, has become a centralized, executive establishment which has taken up into itself many powers previously scattered, and now enters into each and every cranny of the social structure.

The military order, once a slim establishment in a context of distrust fed by state militia, has become the largest and most expensive feature of government, and, although well versed in smiling public relations, now has all the grim and clumsy efficiency of a sprawling bureaucratic domain.

In each of these institutional areas, the means of power at the disposal of decision-makers have increased enormously; their central executive powers have been enhanced; within each of them modern administrative routines have been elaborated and tightened up.

As each of these domains becomes enlarged and centralized, the consequences of its activities become greater, and its traffic with the others increases. The decisions of a handful of corporations bear upon military and political as well as upon economic developments around the world. The decisions of the military establishment rest upon and grievously affect political life as well as the very level of economic activity. The decisions made within the political domain determine economic activities and military programs. There is no longer, on the one hand, an economy, and, on the other hand, a political order containing a military establishment unimportant to politics and to money-making. There is a political economy linked, in a thousand ways, with military institutions and decisions. On each side of the world-split running through central Europe and around the Asiatic rimlands, there is an ever-increasing interlocking of economic, military, and political structures.[2] If there is government intervention in the corporate economy, so is there corporate intervention in the governmental process. In the structural sense, this triangle of power is the source of the interlocking directorate that is most important for the historical structure of the present.

The fact of the interlocking is clearly revealed at each of the points of crisis of modern capitalist society—slump, war, and boom. In each, men of decision are led to an awareness of the interdependence of the major institutional orders. In the nineteenth century, when the scale of all institutions was smaller, their liberal integration was achieved in the automatic economy, by an autonomous play of market forces, and in the automatic political domain, by the bargain and the vote. It was then assumed that out of the imbalance and friction that followed the limited decisions then possible a new equilibrium would in due course emerge. That can no longer be assumed, and it is not assumed by the men at the top of each of the three dominant hierarchies.

For given the scope of their consequences, decisions—and indecisions—in any one of these ramify into the others, and hence top decisions tend either to become co-ordinated or to lead to a commanding indecision. It has not always been like this. When numerous small entrepreneurs made up the economy, for example, many of them could fail and the consequences still remain local; political and military authorities did not intervene. But now, given political expectations and military commitments, can they afford to allow key units of the private corporate economy to break down in slump? Increasingly, they do intervene in economic affairs, and as they do so, the controlling decisions in each order are inspected by agents of the other two, and economic, military, and political structures are interlocked.

At the pinnacle of each of the three enlarged and centralized domains, there have arisen those higher circles which make up the economic, the political, and the military elites. At the top of the economy, among the corporate rich, there are the chief executives; at the top of the political order, the members of the political directorate; at the top of the military establishment, the elite of soldier-statesmen clustered in and around the Joint Chiefs of Staff and the upper echelon. As each of these domains has coincided with the others, as decisions tend to become total in their consequence, the leading men in each of the three domains of power—the warlords, the corporation chieftains, the political directorate—tend to come together, to form the power elite of America.

2

The higher circles in and around these command posts are often thought of in terms of what their members possess: they have a greater share than other people of the things and experiences that are most highly valued. From this point of view, the elite are simply those who have the most of what there is to have, which is generally held to include money, power, and prestige—as well as all the ways of life to which these lead.[3] But the elite are not simply those who have the most, for they could not 'have the most' were it not for their positions in the great institutions. For such institutions are the necessary bases of power, of wealth, and of prestige, and at the same time, the chief means of exercising power, of acquiring and retaining wealth, and of cashing in the higher claims for prestige.

By the powerful we mean, of course, those who are able to realize their will, even if others resist it. No one, accordingly, can be truly powerful unless he has access to the command of major institutions, for it is over these institutional means of power that the truly powerful are, in the first instance, powerful. Higher politicians and key officials of government command such institutional power; so do admirals and generals, and so do the major owners and executives of the larger corporations. Not all power, it is true, is anchored in and exercised by means of such institutions, but only within and through them can power be more or less continuous and important. . . .

If we took the one hundred most powerful men in America, the one hundred wealthiest, and the one hundred most celebrated away from the institutional positions they now occupy, away from their resources of men and women and money, away from the media of mass communication that are now focused upon them—then they would be powerless and poor and uncelebrated. For power is not of a man. Wealth does not center in the person of the wealthy. Celebrity is not inherent in any personality. To be celebrated, to be wealthy, to have power requires access to major institutions, for the institutional positions men occupy determine in large part their chances to have and to hold these valued experiences.

3

The people of the higher circles may also be conceived as members of a top social stratum, as a set of groups whose members know one another, see one another socially and at business, and so, in making decisions, take one another into account. The elite, according to this conception, feel themselves *actors* to be, and are felt by others to be, the inner circle of 'the upper social classes.'[4] They form a more or less compact social and psychological entity; they have become self-conscious members of a social class. People are either accepted into this class or they are not, and there is a qualitative split, rather than merely a numerical scale, separating them from those who are not elite. They are more or less aware of themselves as a social class and they behave toward one another differently from the way they do toward members of other classes. They accept one another, understand one another, marry one another, tend to work and to think if not together at least alike.

Now, we do not want by our definition to prejudge whether the elite of the command posts are conscious members of such a socially recognized class, or whether considerable proportions of the elite derive from such a clear and distinct class. These are matters to be investigated. Yet in order to be able to recognize what we intend to investigate, we must note something that all biographies and memoirs of the wealthy and the powerful and the eminent make clear: no matter what else they may be, the people of these higher circles are involved in a set of overlapping 'crowds' and intricately connected 'cliques.' There is a kind of mutual attraction among those who 'sit on the same terrace'—although this often becomes clear to them, as well as to others, only at the point at which they feel the need to draw the line; only when, in their common defense, they come to understand what they have in common, and so close their ranks against outsiders.

The idea of such ruling stratum implies that most of its members have similar social origins, that throughout their lives they maintain a network of informal connections, and that to some degree there is an interchangeability of position between the various hierarchies of money and power and celebrity. We must, of course, note at once that if such an elite stratum does exist, its social visibility and its form, for very solid historical reasons, are quite different from those of the noble cousinhoods that once ruled various European nations.

That American society has never passed through a feudal epoch is of decisive importance to the nature of the American elite, as well as to American society as a historic whole. For it means that no nobility or aristocracy, established before the capitalist era, has stood in tense opposition to the higher bourgeoisie. It means that this bourgeoisie has monopolized not only wealth but prestige and power as well. It means that no set of noble families has commanded the top positions and monopolized the values that are generally held in high esteem; and certainly that no set has done so explicitly by inherited right. It means that no high church dignitaries or court nobilities, no entrenched landlords with honorific accouterments, no monopolists of high army posts have opposed the enriched bourgeoisie and in the name of birth and prerogative successfully resisted its self-making.

But this does *not* mean that there are no upper strata in the United States. That they emerged from a 'middle class' that had no recognized aristocratic superiors does not mean they remained middle class when enormous increases in wealth made their own superiority possible. Their origins and their newness may have made the upper strata less visible in America than elsewhere. But in America today there are in fact tiers and ranges of wealth and power of which people in the middle and lower ranks know very little and may not even dream. There are families who, in their well-being, are quite insulated from the economic jolts and lurches felt by the merely prosperous and those farther down the scale. There are also men of power who in quite small groups make decisions of enormous consequence for the underlying population.

The American elite entered modern history as a virtually unopposed bourgeoisie. No national bourgeoisie, before or since, has had such opportunities and advantages. Having no military neighbors, they easily occupied an isolated continent stocked with natural resources and immensely inviting to a willing labor force. A framework of power and an ideology for its justification were already at hand. Against mercantilist restriction, they inherited the principle of *laissez-faire;* against Southern planters, they imposed the principle of industrialism. The Revolutionary War put an end to colonial pretensions to nobility, as loyalists fled the country and many estates were broken up. The Jacksonian upheaval with its status revolution put an end to pretensions to monopoly of descent by the old New England families. The

Civil War broke the power, and so in due course the prestige, of the antebellum South's claimants for the higher esteem. The tempo of the whole capitalist development made it impossible for an inherited nobility to develop and endure in America.

No fixed ruling class, anchored in agrarian life and coming to flower in military glory, could contain in America the historic thrust of commerce and industry, or subordinate to itself the capitalist elite—as capitalists were subordinated, for example, in Germany and Japan. Nor could such a ruling class anywhere in the world contain that of the United States when industrialized violence came to decide history. Witness the fate of Germany and Japan in the two world wars of the twentieth century; and indeed the fate of Britain herself and her model ruling class, as New York became the inevitable economic, and Washington the inevitable political capital of the western capitalist world.

4

The elite who occupy the command posts may be seen as the possessors of power and wealth and celebrity; they may be seen as members of the upper stratum of a capitalistic society. They may also be defined in terms of psychological and moral criteria, as certain kinds of selected individuals. So defined, the elite, quite simply, are people of superior character and energy.

The humanist, for example, may conceive of the 'elite' not as a social level or category, but as a scatter of those individuals who attempt to transcend themselves, and accordingly, are more noble, more efficient, made out of better stuff. It does not matter whether they are poor or rich, whether they hold high position or low, whether they are acclaimed or despised; they are elite because of the kind of individuals they are. The rest of the population is mass, which, according to this conception, sluggishly relaxes into uncomfortable mediocrity.[5]

This is the sort of socially unlocated conception which some American writers with conservative yearnings have recently sought to develop. But most moral and psychological conceptions of the elite are much less sophisticated, concerning themselves not with individuals but with the stratum as a whole. Such ideas, in fact, always arise in a society in which some people possess more than do others of what there is to possess. People with advantages are loath to believe that they just happen to be people with advantages.

They come readily to define themselves as inherently worthy of what they possess; they come to believe themselves 'naturally' elite; and, in fact, to imagine their possessions and their privileges as natural extensions of their own elite selves. In this sense, the idea of the elite as composed of men and women having a finer moral character is an ideology of the elite as a privileged ruling stratum, and this is true whether the ideology is elite-made or made up for it by others.

In eras of equalitarian rhetoric, the more intelligent or the more articulate among the lower and middle classes, as well as guilty members of the upper, may come to entertain ideas of a counter-elite. In western society, as a matter of fact, there is a long tradition and varied images of the poor, the exploited, and the oppressed as the truly virtuous, the wise, and the blessed. Stemming from Christian tradition, this moral idea of a counter-elite composed of essentially higher types condemned to a lowly station, may be and has been used by the underlying population to justify harsh criticism of ruling elites and to celebrate utopian images of a new elite to come.

The moral conception of the elite, however, is not always merely an ideology of the overprivileged or a counter-ideology of the underprivileged. It is often a fact: having controlled experiences and select privileges, many individuals of the upper stratum do come in due course to approximate the types of character they claim to embody. Even when we give up—as we must—the idea that the elite man or woman is born with an elite character, we need not dismiss the idea that their experiences and trainings develop in them characters of a specific type. . . .

5

These several notions of the elite, when appropriately understood, are intricately bound up with one another, and we shall use them all in this examination of American success. We shall study each of several higher circles as offering candidates for the elite, and we shall do so in terms of the major institutions making up the total society of America; within and between each of these institutions, we shall trace the interrelations of wealth and power and prestige. But our main concern is with the power of those who now occupy the command posts, and with the role which they are enacting in the history of our epoch.

Such an elite may be conceived as omnipotent, and its powers thought of as a great hidden design. Thus, in vulgar Marxism, events and trends are explained by reference to 'the will of the bourgeoisie'; in Nazism, by reference to 'the conspiracy of the Jews'; by the petty right in America today, by reference to 'the hidden force' of Communist spies. According to such notions of the omnipotent elite as historical cause, the elite is never an entirely visible agency. It is, in fact, a secular substitute for the will of God, being realized in a sort of providential design, except that usually non-elite men are thought capable of opposing it and eventually overcoming it.

The opposite view—of the elite as impotent—is now quite popular among liberal-minded observers. Far from being omnipotent, the elites are thought to be so scattered as to lack any coherence as a historical force. Their invisibility is not the invisibility of secrecy but the invisibility of the multitude. Those who occupy the formal places of authority are so check-mated—by other elites exerting pressure, or by the public as an electorate, or by constitutional codes—that, although there may be upper classes, there is no ruling class; although there may be men of power, there is no power elite; although there may be a system of stratification, it has no effective top. In the extreme, this view of the elite, as weakened by compromise and dis-united to the point of nullity, is a substitute for impersonal collective fate; for, in this view, the decisions of the visible men of the higher circles do not count in history.

Internationally, the image of the omnipotent elite tends to prevail. All good events and pleasing happenings are quickly imputed by the opinion-makers to the leaders of their own nation; all bad events and unpleasant experiences are imputed to the enemy abroad. In both cases, the omnipotence of evil rulers or of virtuous leaders is assumed. Within the nation, the use of such rhetoric is rather more complicated: when men speak of the power of their own party or circle, they and their leaders are, of course, impotent; only 'the people' are omnipotent. But, when they speak of the power of their opponent's party or circle, they impute to them omnipotence; 'the people' are now powerlessly taken in.

More generally, American men of power tend, by convention, to deny that they are powerful. No American runs for office in order to rule or even govern, but only to serve; he does not become a bureaucrat or even an official, but a public servant. And nowadays, as I have already pointed out, such postures have become standard features of the public-relations programs of all men of power. So firm a part of the style of power-wielding have they become that conservative writers readily misinterpret them as indicating a trend toward an 'amorphous power situation.'

But the 'power situation' of America today is less amorphous than is the perspective of those who see it as a romantic confusion. It is less a flat, momentary 'situation' than a graded, durable structure. And if those who occupy its top grades are not omnipotent, neither are they impotent. It is the form and the height of the gradation of power that we must examine if we would understand the degree of power held and exercised by the elite.

If the power to decide such national issues as are decided were shared in an absolutely equal way, there would be no power elite; in fact, there would be no *gradation* of power, but only a radical homogeneity. At the opposite extreme as well, if the power to decide issues were absolutely monopolized by one small group, there would be no gradation of power; there would simply be this small group in command, and below it, the undifferentiated, dominated masses. American society today represents neither the one nor the other of these extremes, but a conception of them is none the less useful: it makes us realize more clearly the question of the structure of power in the United States and the position of the power elite within it.

Within each of the most powerful institutional orders of modern society there is a gradation of power. The owner of a roadside fruit stand does not have as much power in any area of social or economic or political decision as the head of a multi-million-dollar fruit corporation; no lieutenant on the line is as powerful as the Chief of Staff in the Pentagon; no deputy sheriff carries as much authority as the President of the United States. Accordingly, the problem of defining the power elite concerns the level at which we wish to draw the line. By lowering the line, we could define the elite out of existence; by raising it, we could make the elite a very small circle indeed. In a preliminary and minimum way, we draw the line crudely, in charcoal as it were: By the power elite, we refer to those political, economic, and military circles which as an intricate set of overlapping cliques share decisions having at least national consequences. In so far as national events are decided, the power elite are those who decide them. . . .

6

It is not my thesis that for all epochs of human history and in all nations, a creative minority, a ruling class, an omnipotent elite, shape all historical events. Such statements, upon careful examination, usually turn out to be mere tautologies,[6] and even when they are not, they are so entirely general as to be useless in the attempt to understand the history of the present. The minimum definition of the power elite as those who decide whatever is decided of major consequence, does not imply that the members of this elite are always and necessarily the history-makers; neither does it imply that they never are. We must not confuse the conception of the elite, which we wish to define, with one theory about their role: that they are the history-makers of our time. To define the elite, for example, as 'those who rule America' is less to define a conception than to state one hypothesis about the role and power of that elite. No matter how we might define the elite, the extent of its members' power is subject to historical variation. If, in a dogmatic way, we try to include that variation in our generic definition, we foolishly limit the use of a needed conception. If we insist that the elite be defined as a strictly coordinated class that continually and absolutely rules, we are closing off from our view much to which the term more modestly defined might open to our observation. In short, our definition of the power elite cannot properly contain dogma concerning the degree and kind of power that ruling groups everywhere have. Much less should it permit us to smuggle into our discussion a theory of history.

During most of human history, historical change has not been visible to the people who were involved in it, or even to those enacting it. Ancient Egypt and Mesopotamia, for example, endured for some four hundred generations with but slight changes in their basic structure. That is six and a half times as long as the entire Christian era, which has only prevailed some sixty generations; it is about eighty times as long as the five generations of the United States' existence. But now the tempo of change is so rapid, and the means of observation so accessible, that the interplay of event and decision seems often to be quite historically visible, if we will only look carefully and from an adequate vantage point.

When knowledgeable journalists tell us that 'events, not men, shape the big decisions,' they are echoing the theory of history as Fortune, Chance, Fate, or the work of The Unseen Hand. For 'events' is merely a modern word for these older ideas, all of which separate men from history-making, because all of them lead us to believe that history goes on behind men's backs. History is drift with no mastery; within it there is action but no deed; history is mere happening and the event intended by no one.[7]

The course of events in our time depends more on a series of human decisions than on any inevitable fate. The sociological meaning of 'fate' is simply this: that, when the decisions are innumerable and each one is of small consequence, all of them add up in a way no man intended—to history as fate. But not all epochs are equally fateful. As the circle of those who decide is narrowed, as the means of decision are centralized and the consequences of decisions become enormous, then the course of great events often rests upon the decisions of determinable circles. This does not necessarily mean that the same circle of men follow through from one event to another in such a way that all of history is merely their plot. The power of the elite does not necessarily mean that history is not also shaped by a series of small decisions, none of which are thought out. It does not mean that a hundred small arrangements and compromises and adaptations may not be built into the going policy and the living event. The idea of the power elite implies nothing about the process of decision-making as such: it is an attempt to delimit the social areas within which that process, whatever its character, goes on. It is a conception of who is involved in the process.

The degree of foresight and control of those who are involved in decisions that count may also vary. The idea of the power elite does not mean that the estimations and calculated risks upon which decisions are made are not often wrong and that the consequences are sometimes, indeed often, not those intended. Often those who make decisions are trapped by their own inadequacies and blinded by their own errors.

Yet in our time the pivotal moment does arise, and at that moment, small circles do decide or fail to decide. In either case, they are an elite of power. The dropping of the A-bombs over Japan was such a moment; the decision on Korea was such a moment; the confusion about Quemoy and Matsu, as well as before Dienbienphu were such moments; the sequence of maneuvers which involved the United States in World War II was such a 'moment.' Is it not true that much of the history of our times is composed of such moments? And is not that what is meant when it is said that we live in a time of big decisions, of decisively centralized power?

Most of us do not try to make sense of our age by believing in a Greek-like, eternal recurrence, nor by a Christian belief in a salvation to come, nor by any steady march of human progress. Even though we do not reflect upon such matters, the chances are we believe with Burckhardt that we live in a mere succession of events; that sheer continuity is the only principle of history. History is merely one thing after another; history is meaningless in that it is not the realization of any determinate plot. It is true, of course, that our sense of continuity, our feeling for the history of our time, is affected by crisis. But we seldom look beyond the immediate crisis or the crisis felt to be just ahead. We believe neither in fate nor providence; and we assume, without talking about it, that 'we'—as a nation—can decisively shape the future but that 'we' as individuals somehow cannot do so.

Any meaning history has, 'we' shall have to give to it by our actions. Yet the fact is that although we are all of us within history we do not all possess equal powers to make history. To pretend that we do is sociological non-sense and political irresponsibility. It is nonsense because any group or any individual is limited, first of all, by the technical and institutional means of power at its command; we do not all have equal access to the means of power that now exist, nor equal influence over their use. To pretend that 'we' are all history-makers is politically irresponsible because it obfuscates any attempt to locate responsibility for the consequential decisions of men who do have access to the means of power.

From even the most superficial examination of the history of the western society we learn that the power of decision-makers is first of all limited by the level of technique, by the *means* of power and violence and organization that prevail in a given society. In this connection we also learn that there is a fairly straight line running upward through the history of the West; that the means of oppression and exploitation, of violence and destruction, as well as the means of production and reconstruction, have been progressively en-larged and increasingly centralized.

As the institutional means of power and the means of communications that tie them together have become steadily more efficient, those now in command of them have come into command of instruments of rule quite unsurpassed in the history of mankind. And we are not yet at the climax of their development. We can no longer lean upon or take soft comfort from the historical ups and downs of ruling groups of previous epochs. In that sense, Hegel is correct: we learn from history that we cannot learn from it.

NOTES

¹ Jacob Burckhardt, *Force and Freedom* (New York: Pantheon Books, 1943), pp. 303 ff.

² Cf. Hans Gerth and C. Wright Mills, *Character and Social Structure* (New York: Harcourt, Brace, 1953), pp. 457 ff.

³ The statistical idea of choosing some value and calling those who have the most of it an elite derives, in modern times, from the Italian economist, Pareto, who puts the central point in this way: 'Let us assume that in every branch of human activity each individual is given an index which stands as a sign of his capacity, very much the way grades are given in the various subjects in examinations in school. The highest type of lawyer, for instance, will be given 10. The man who does not get a client will be given 1—reserving zero for the man who is an out-and-out idiot. To the man who has made his millions—honestly or dishonestly as the case may be—we will give 10. To the man who has earned his thousands we will give 6; to such as

just manage to keep out of the poor-house, 1, keeping zero for those who get in . . . So let us make a class of people who have the highest indices in their branch of activity, and to that class give the name of *elite.*' Vilfredo Pareto, *The Mind and Society* (New York: Harcourt, Brace, 1935), par. 2027 and 2031. Those who follow this approach end up not with one elite, but with a number corresponding to the number of values they select. Like many rather abstract ways of reasoning, this one is useful because it forces us to think in a clear-cut way. For a skillful use of this approach, see the work of Harold D. Lasswell, in particular, *Politics: Who Gets What, When, How* (New York: McGraw-Hill, 1936); and for a more systematic use, H. D. Lasswell and Abraham Kaplan, *Power and Society* (New Haven: Yale University Press, 1950).

[4] The conception of the elite as members of a top social stratum, is, of course, in line with the prevailing common-sense view of stratification. Technically, it is closer to 'status group' than to 'class,' and has been very well stated by Joseph A. Schumpeter, 'Social Classes in an Ethically Homogeneous Environment,' *Imperialism and Social Classes* (New York: Augustus M. Kelley, Inc., 1951), pp. 133 ff., especially pp. 137–47. Cf. also his *Capitalism, Socialism and Democracy,* 3rd ed. (New York: Harper, 1950), Part II. For the distinction between class and status groups, see *From Max Weber: Essays in Sociology* (trans. and ed. by Gerth and Mills (New York: Oxford University Press, 1946). For an analysis of Pareto's conception of the elite compared with Marx's conception of classes, as well as data on France, see Raymond Aron, 'Social Structure and Ruling Class,' *British Journal of Sociology,* vol. I, nos. 1 and 2 (1950).

[5] The most popular essay in recent years which defines the elite and the mass in terms of a morally evaluated character-type is probably José Ortega y Gasset's, *The Revolt of the Masses,* 1932 (New York: New American Library, Mentor Edition, 1950), esp. pp. 91 ff.

[6] As in the case, quite notably, of Gaetano Mosca, *The Ruling Class* (New York: McGraw-Hill, 1939). For a sharp analysis of Mosca, see Fritz Morstein Marx, 'The Bureaucratic State,' *Review of Politics,* vol. I, 1939, pp. 457 ff. Cf. also Mills, 'On Intellectual Craftsmanship,' April 1952, mimeographed, Columbia College, February 1955.

[7] Cf. Karl Löwith, *Meaning in History* (Chicago: University of Chicago Press, 1949), pp. 125 ff. for concise and penetrating statements of several leading philosophies of history.

8

JOBLESS POVERTY

A NEW FORM OF SOCIAL DISLOCATION
IN THE INNER-CITY GHETTO

William Julius Wilson

◆◆◆

In September 1996 my book, *When Work Disappears: The World of the New Urban Poor,* was published. It describes a new type of poverty in our nation's metropolises: poor, segregated neighborhoods in which a majority of adults are either unemployed or have dropped out of the labor force altogether. What is the effect of these "jobless ghettos" on individuals, families, and neighborhoods? What accounts for their existence? I suggest several factors and conclude with policy recommendations: a mix of public-and-private sector projects is more effective than relying on a strategy of employer subsidies.

William Julius Wilson, "Jobless Poverty: A New Form of Social Dislocation in the Inner-City Ghetto," in *A Nation Divided: Diversity, Inequality, and Community in American Society,* edited by Phyllis Moen, Donna Dempster-McClain, and Henry A. Walker, pp. 133–145, 149–150. Copyright 1999 by Cornell University.

The Research Studies

When Work Disappears was based mainly on three research studies conducted in Chicago between 1986 and 1993. The first of these three studies included a variety of data: a random survey of nearly 2,500 poor and nonpoor African American, Latino, and white residents in Chicago's poor neighborhoods; a more focused survey of 175 participants who were reinterviewed and answered open-ended questions; a survey of 179 employers selected to reflect distribution of employment across industry and firm size in the Chicago metropolitan areas; and comprehensive ethnographic research, including participant-observation research and life-history interviews by ten research assistants in a representative sample of inner-city neighborhoods.

The first of the two remaining projects also included extensive data: a survey of a representative sample of 546 black mothers and up to two of their adolescent children (aged eleven to sixteen—or 887 adolescents) in working-class, middle-class, and high-poverty neighborhoods; a survey of a representative sample of 500 respondents from two high-joblessness neighborhoods on the South Side of Chicago; and six focus-group discussions involving the residents and former residents of these neighborhoods.

Jobless Ghettos

The jobless poverty of today stands in sharp contrast to previous periods. In 1950, a substantial portion of the urban black population was poor but they were working. Urban poverty was quite extensive but people held jobs. However, as we entered the 1990s most adults in many inner-city ghetto neighborhoods were not working. For example, in 1950 a significant majority of adults held jobs in a typical week in the three neighborhoods that represent the historic core of the Black Belt in Chicago—Douglas, Grand Boulevard, and Washington Park. But by 1990, only four in ten in Douglas worked in a typical week, one in three in Washington Park, and one in four in Grand Boulevard.[1] In 1950, 69 percent of all males aged fourteen and older who lived in these three neighborhoods worked in a typical week, and in 1960, 64 percent of this group were so employed. However, by 1990 only 37 percent of all males aged sixteen and over held jobs in a typical week in these three neighborhoods.

The disappearance of work has had negative effects not only on individuals and families, but on the social life of neighborhoods as well. Inner-city joblessness is a severe problem that is often overlooked or obscured when the focus is mainly on poverty and its consequences. Despite increases in the concentration of poverty since 1970, inner cities have always featured high levels of poverty. But the levels of inner-city joblessness reached during the first half of the 1990s were unprecedented.

Joblessness versus Informal Work Activity

I should note that when I speak of "joblessness" I am not solely referring to official unemployment. The unemployment rate represents only the percentage of workers in the *official* labor force—that is, those who are *actively* looking for work. It does not include those who are outside of or have dropped out of the labor market, including the nearly six million males aged twenty-five to sixty who appeared in the census statistics but were not recorded in the labor market statistics in 1990 (Thurow 1990).

These uncounted males in the labor market are disproportionately represented in the inner-city ghettos. Accordingly, in *When Work Disappears,* I use a more appropriate measure of joblessness, a measure that takes into account both official unemployment and non–labor-force participation. That measure is the employment-to-population ratio, which corresponds to the percentage of adults aged sixteen and older who are working. Using the employment-to-population ratio we find, for example, that in 1990 only one in three adults aged sixteen and older held a job in the ghetto poverty areas of Chicago, areas representing roughly 425,000 men, women, and children. And in the ghetto tracts of the nation's one hundred largest cities, for every ten adults who did not hold a job in a typical week in 1990 there were only six employed persons (Kasarda 1993).

The consequences of high neighborhood joblessness are more devastating than those of high neighborhood poverty. A neighborhood in which people are poor but employed is much different than a neighborhood in which people are poor and jobless. *When Work Disappears* shows that many of today's problems in the inner-city ghetto neighborhoods—crime, family dissolution, welfare, low levels of social organization, and so on—are fundamentally a consequence of the disappearance of work.

It should be clear that when I speak of the disappearance of work, I am referring to the declining involvement in or lack of attachment to the formal labor market. It could be argued that, in the general sense of the term, "job-lessness" does not necessarily mean "nonwork." In other words, to be officially unemployed or officially outside the labor market does not mean that one is totally removed from all forms of work activity. Many people who are officially jobless are nonetheless involved in informal kinds of work activity, ranging from unpaid housework to work that draws income from the informal or illegal economies.

Housework is work, baby-sitting is work, even drug dealing is work. However, what contrasts work in the formal economy with work activity in the informal and illegal economies is that work in the formal economy is characterized by, indeed calls for, greater regularity and consistency in schedules and hours. Work schedules and hours are formalized. The demands for discipline are greater. It is true that some work activities outside the formal economy also call for discipline and regular schedules. Several studies reveal that the social organization of the drug industry is driven by discipline and a work ethic, however perverse.[2] However, as a general rule, work in the informal and illegal economies is far less governed by norms or expectations that place a premium on discipline and regularity. For all these reasons, when I speak of the disappearance of work, I mean work in the formal economy, work that provides a framework for daily behavior because of the discipline, regularity, and stability that it imposes.

Effect of Joblessness on Routine and Discipline

In the absence of regular employment, a person lacks not only a place in which to work and the receipt of regular income but also a coherent organization of the present—that is, a system of concrete expectations and goals. Regular employment provides the anchor for the spatial and temporal aspects of daily life. It determines where you are going to be and when you are going to be there. In the absence of regular employment, life, including family life, becomes less coherent. Persistent unemployment and irregular employment hinder rational planning in daily life, a necessary condition of adaptation to an industrial economy (Bourdieu 1965).

Thus, a youngster who grows up in a family with a steady breadwinner and in a neighborhood in which most of the adults are employed will tend to develop some of the disciplined habits associated with stable or steady employment—habits that are reflected in the behavior of his or her parents and of other neighborhood adults. These might include attachment to a routine, a recognition of the hierarchy found in most work situations, a sense of personal efficacy attained through the routine management of financial affairs, endorsement of a system of personal and material rewards associated with dependability and responsibility, and so on. Accordingly, when this youngster enters the labor market, he or she has a distinct advantage over the youngsters who grow up in households without a steady breadwinner and in neighborhoods that are not organized around work—in other words, a milieu in which one is more exposed to the less disciplined habits associated with casual or infrequent work.

With the sharp recent rise of solo-parent families, black children who live in inner-city households are less likely to be socialized in a work environment for two main reasons. Their mothers, saddled with child-care responsibilities, can prevent a slide deeper into poverty by accepting welfare. Their fathers, removed from family responsibilities and obligations, are more likely to become idle as a response to restricted employment opportunities, which further weakens their influence in the household and attenuates their contact with the family. In short, the social and cultural responses to joblessness are reflected in the organization of family life and patterns of family formation; there they have implications for labor-force attachment as well.

Given the current policy debates that assign blame to the personal shortcomings of the jobless, we need to understand their behavior as responses and adaptations to chronic subordination, including behaviors that have evolved into cultural patterns. The social actions of the jobless—including their behavior, habits, skills, styles, orientations, attitudes—ought not to be analyzed as if they are unrelated to the broader structure of their opportunities and constraints that have evolved over time. This is not to argue that individuals and groups lack the freedom to make their own choices, engage in certain conduct, and develop certain styles and orientations; but I maintain that their decisions and actions occur within a context of constraints and opportunities that are drastically different from those in middle-class society.

EXPLANATIONS OF THE GROWTH OF JOBLESS GHETTOS

What accounts for the growing proportion of jobless adults in inner-city communities? An easy explanation would be racial segregation. However, a race-specific argument is not sufficient to explain recent changes in such neighborhoods. After all, these historical Black Belt neighborhoods were *just as segregated by skin color in 1950* as they are today, yet the level of employment was much higher then. One has to account for the ways in which racial segregation interacts with other changes in society to produce the recent escalating rates of joblessness. Several factors stand out: the decreasing demand for low-skilled labor, the suburbanization of jobs, the social deterioration of ghetto neighborhoods, and negative employer attitudes. I discuss each of these factors next.

Decreasing Demand for Low-Skilled Labor

The disappearance of work in many inner-city neighborhoods is in part related to the nationwide decline in the fortunes of low-skilled workers. The sharp decline in the relative demand for unskilled labor has had a more adverse effect on blacks than on whites because a substantially larger proportion of African Americans are unskilled. Although the number of skilled blacks (including managers, professionals, and technicians) has increased sharply in the last several years, the proportion of those who are unskilled remains large, because the black population, burdened by cumulative experiences of racial restrictions, was overwhelmingly unskilled just several decades ago (Schwartzman 1997).[3]

The factors involved in the decreased relative demand for unskilled labor include changes in skill-based technology, the rapid growth in college enrollment that increased the supply and reduced the relative cost of skilled labor, and the growing internationalization of economic activity, including trade liberalization policies, which reduced the price of imports and raised the output of export industries (Schwartzman 1997). The increased output of export industries aids skilled workers, simply because they are heavily represented in export industries. But increasing imports, especially those from developing countries that compete with labor-intensive industries (for example, apparel, textile, toy, footwear, and some manufacturing industries), hurts unskilled labor (Schwartzman 1997).

Accordingly, inner-city blacks are experiencing a more extreme form of the economic marginality that has affected most unskilled workers in America since 1980. Unfortunately, there is a tendency among policy makers, black leaders, and scholars alike to separate the economic problems of the ghetto from the national and international trends affecting American families and neighborhoods. If the economic problems of the ghetto are defined solely in racial terms they can be isolated and viewed as only requiring race-based solutions as proposed by those on the left, or as only requiring narrow political solutions with subtle racial connotations (such as welfare reform), as strongly proposed by those on the right.

Overemphasis on Racial Factors

Race continues to be a factor that aggravates inner-city black employment problems as we shall soon see. But the tendency to overemphasize the racial factors obscures other more fundamental forces that have sharply increased inner-city black joblessness. As the late black economist Vivian Henderson put it several years ago, "[I]t is as if racism having put blacks in their economic place steps aside to watch changes in the economy destroy that place" (Henderson 1975, 54). To repeat, the concentrated joblessness of the inner-city poor represents the most dramatic form of the growing economic dislocations among the unskilled stemming in large measure from changes in the organization of the economy, including the global economy.

Suburbanization of Jobs

But inner-city workers face an additional problem: the growing suburbanization of jobs. Most ghetto residents cannot afford an automobile and therefore have to rely on public transit systems that make the connection between inner-city neighborhoods and suburban job locations difficult and time consuming.

Although studies based on data collected before 1970 showed no consistent or convincing effects on black employment as a consequence of this spatial mismatch, the employment of inner-city blacks relative to suburban blacks has clearly deteriorated since then. Recent research (conducted mainly by urban labor economists) strongly shows that the decentralization of employment is continuing and that employment in manufacturing, most of which is already suburbanized, has decreased in central cities, particularly in the Northeast and Midwest (Holzer 1996).

Blacks living in central cities have less access to employment (as measured by the ratio of jobs to people and the average travel time to and from work) than do central-city whites. Moreover, unlike most other groups of workers across the urban-suburban divide, less-educated central-city blacks receive lower wages than suburban blacks who have similar levels of education. And the decline in earnings of central-city blacks is related to the decentralization

of employment—that is, the movement of jobs from the cities to the suburbs—in metropolitan areas (Holzer 1996).

Social Deterioration of Ghetto Neighborhoods

Changes in the class, racial, and demographic composition of inner-city
neighborhoods have also contributed to the high percentage of jobless adults
in these neighborhoods. Because of the steady out-migration of more advantaged families, the proportion of nonpoor families and prime-age working
adults has decreased sharply in the typical inner-city ghetto since 1970 (Wilson 1987). In the face of increasing and prolonged joblessness, the declining
proportion of nonpoor families and the overall depopulation has made it increasingly difficult to sustain basic neighborhood institutions or to achieve
adequate levels of social organization. The declining presence of working-
and middle-class blacks has also deprived ghetto neighborhoods of key structural and cultural resources. Structural resources include residents with
income high enough to sustain neighborhood services, and cultural resources
include conventional role models for neighborhood children.

On the basis of our research in Chicago, it appears that what many high jobless neighborhoods have in common is a relatively high degree of social
integration (high levels of local neighboring while being relatively isolated
from contacts in the broader mainstream society) and low levels of informal social control (feelings that they have little control over their immediate
environment, including the environment's negative influences on their children). In such areas, not only are children at risk because of the lack of
informal social controls, they are also disadvantaged because the social interaction among neighbors tends to be confined to those whose skills, styles,
orientations, and habits are not as conducive to promoting positive social outcomes (academic success, pro-social behavior, employment in the formal labor
market, etc.) as those in more stable neighborhoods. Although the close interaction among neighbors in such areas may be useful in devising strategies,
disseminating information, and developing styles of behavior that are helpful
in a ghetto milieu (teaching children to avoid eye-to-eye contact with strangers
and to develop a tough demeanor in the public sphere for self-protection), they
may be less effective in promoting the welfare of children in society at large.

Despite being socially integrated, the residents in Chicago's ghetto neighborhoods shared a feeling that they had little informal social control over the
children in their environment. A primary reason is the absence of a strong or-

ganizational capacity or an institutional resource base that would provide an extra layer of social organization in their neighborhoods. It is easier for parents to control the behavior of the children in their neighborhoods when a strong institutional resource base exists and when the links between community institutions such as churches, schools, political organizations, businesses, and civic clubs are strong or secure. The higher the density and stability of formal organizations, the less illicit activities such as drug trafficking, crime, prostitution, and the formation of gangs can take root in the neighborhood.

Few Community Institutions

A weak institutional resource base is what distinguishes high jobless inner-city neighborhoods from stable middle-class and working-class areas. As one resident of a high jobless neighborhood on the South Side of Chicago put it, "Our children, you know, seems to be more at risk than any other children there is, because there's no library for them to go to. There's not a center they can go to, there's no field house that they can go into. There's nothing. There's nothing at all." Parents in high jobless neighborhoods have a much more difficult task controlling the behavior of their adolescents and preventing them from getting involved in activities detrimental to pro-social development. Given the lack of organizational capacity and a weak institutional base, some parents choose to protect their children by isolating them from activities in the neighborhood, including avoiding contact and interaction with neighborhood families. Wherever possible, and often with great difficulty when one considers the problems of transportation and limited financial resources, they attempt to establish contacts and cultivate relations with individuals, families, and institutions, such as church groups, schools, and community recreation programs, outside their neighborhood. A note of caution is necessary, though. It is just as indefensible to treat inner-city residents as super heroes who overcome racist oppression as it is to view them as helpless victims. We should, however, appreciate the range of choices, including choices representing cultural influences, that are available to inner-city residents who live under constraints that most people in the larger society do not experience.

Effect of Joblessness on Marriage and Family

It is within the context of labor-force attachment that the public policy discussion on welfare reform and family values should be couched. The research that we have conducted in Chicago suggests that as employment prospects recede, the foundation for stable relationships becomes weaker over time. More permanent relationships such as marriage give way to temporary liaisons that result in broken unions, out-of-wedlock pregnancies, and, to a lesser extent, separation and divorce. The changing norms concerning marriage in the larger society reinforce the movement toward temporary liaisons in the inner city, and therefore economic considerations in marital decisions take on even greater weight. Many inner-city residents have negative outlooks toward marriage, outlooks that are developed in and influenced by an environment featuring persistent joblessness.

The disrupting effect of joblessness on marriage and family causes poor inner-city blacks to be even more disconnected from the job market and discouraged about their role in the labor force. The economic marginality of the ghetto poor is cruelly reinforced, therefore, by conditions in the neighborhoods in which they live.

Negative Employer Attitudes

In the eyes of employers in metropolitan Chicago, the social conditions in the ghetto render inner-city blacks less desirable as workers, and therefore many are reluctant to hire them. One of the three studies that provided the empirical foundation for *When Work Disappears* included a representative sample of employers in the greater Chicago area who provided entry-level jobs. An overwhelming majority of these employers, both white and black, expressed negative views about inner-city ghetto workers, and many stated that they were reluctant to hire them. For example, a president of an inner-city manufacturing firm expressed a concern about employing residents from certain inner-city neighborhoods:

> If somebody gave me their address, uh, Cabrini Green I might unavoidably have some concerns.
>
> *Interviewer:* What would your concerns be?
>
> That the poor guy probably would be frequently unable to get to work and . . . I probably would watch him more carefully even if it wasn't fair, than I would with somebody else. I know what I should do though is recognize that here's a guy that is trying to get out of his situation and probably will work harder than somebody else who's already out of there and he might be the best one around here. But I,

I think I would have to struggle accepting that premise at the beginning. (Wilson 1996, field notes)

In addition to qualms about the neighborhood milieu of inner-city residents, the employers frequently mentioned concerns about applicants' language skills and educational training. An employer from a computer software firm in Chicago expressed the view "that in many businesses the ability to meet the public is paramount and you do not talk street talk to the buying public. Almost all your black welfare people talk street talk. And who's going to sit them down and change their speech patterns?" (Wilson 1996, field notes) A Chicago real estate broker made a similar point:

> A lot of times I will interview applicants who are black, who are sort of lower class. . . . They'll come to me and I cannot hire them because their language skills are so poor. Their speaking voice for one thing is poor . . . they have no verbal facility with the language . . . and these . . . you know, they just don't know how to speak and they'll say "salesmens" instead of "salesmen" and that's a problem. . . . They don't know punctuation, they don't know how to use correct grammar, and they cannot spell. And I can't hire them. And I feel bad about that and I think they're being very disadvantaged by the Chicago Public School system. (Wilson 1996, field notes)

Another respondent defended his method of screening out most job applicants on the telephone on the basis of their use of "grammar and English":

> I have every right to say that that's a requirement for this job. I don't care if you're pink, black, green, yellow or orange, I demand someone who speaks well. You want to tell me that I'm a bigot, fine, call me a bigot. I know blacks, you don't even know they're black. (Wilson 1996, field notes)

Finally, an inner-city banker claimed that many blacks in the ghetto "simply cannot read. When you're talking our type of business, that disqualifies them immediately, we don't have a job here that doesn't require that somebody have minimum reading and writing skills" (Wilson 1996, field notes).

How should we interpret the negative attitudes and actions of employers? To what extent do they represent an aversion to blacks *per se* and to what degree do they reflect judgments based on the job-related skills and training of inner-city blacks in a changing labor market? I should point out that the statements made by the African American employers concerning the qualifications of inner-city black workers did not differ significantly from those of the white employers. Whereas 74 percent of all the white employers who responded to the open-ended questions expressed negative views of the job-related traits of inner-city blacks, 80 percent of the black employers did so as well.

This raises a question about the meaning and significance of race in certain situations—in other words, how race intersects with other factors. A key hypothesis in this connection is that given the recent shifts in the economy, employers are looking for workers with a broad range of abilities: "hard" skills (literacy, numerical ability, basic mechanical ability, and other testable attributes) and "soft" skills (personalities suitable to the work environment, good grooming, group-oriented work behaviors, etc.). While hard skills are the product of education and training—benefits that are apparently in short supply in inner-city schools—soft skills are strongly tied to culture, and are therefore shaped by the harsh environment of the inner-city ghetto. For example, our research revealed that many parents in the inner-city ghetto neighborhoods of Chicago wanted their children not to make eye-to-eye contact with strangers and to develop a tough demeanor when interacting with people on the streets. While such behaviors are helpful for survival in the ghetto, they hinder successful interaction in mainstream society.

Statistical Discrimination

If employers are indeed reacting to the difference in skills between white and black applicants, it becomes increasingly difficult to discuss the motives of employers: are they rejecting inner-city black applicants out of overt racial discrimination or on the basis of qualifications?

Nonetheless, many of the selective recruitment practices do represent what economists call "statistical discrimination": employers make assumptions about the inner-city black workers *in general* and reach decisions based on those assumptions before they have had a chance to review systematically the qualifications of an individual applicant. The net effect is that many black inner-city applicants are never given the chance to prove their qualifications on an individual level because they are systematically screened out by the selective recruitment process.

Statistical discrimination, although representing elements of class bias against poor workers in the inner city, is clearly a matter of race both directly and indirectly. Directly, the selective recruitment patterns effectively screen out far more black workers from the inner city than Hispanic or white workers from the same types of backgrounds. But indirectly, race is also a factor, even in those decisions to deny employment to inner-city black workers on the basis of objective and thorough evaluations of their qualifications. The hard and soft skills among inner-city blacks that do not match the current needs of the labor market are products of racially segregated communities, communities that have historically featured widespread social constraints and restricted opportunities.

Thus the job prospects of inner-city workers have diminished not only because of the decreasing relative demand for low-skilled labor in the United States economy, the suburbanization of jobs, and the social deterioration of ghetto neighborhoods, but also because of negative employer attitudes. This combination of factors presents a real challenge to policy makers. Indeed, considering the narrow range of social policy options in the "balance-the-budget" political climate, how can we immediately alleviate the inner-city jobs problem—a problem which will undoubtedly grow when the new welfare reform bill takes full effect and creates a situation that will be even more harmful to inner-city children and adolescents?

PUBLIC POLICY DILEMMAS

What are the implications of these studies on public policy? A key issue is public-sector employment. If firms in the private sector cannot hire or refuse to hire low-skilled adults who are willing to take minimum-wage jobs, then policy makers should consider a policy of public-sector employment-of-last-resort. Indeed, until current changes in the labor market are reversed or until the skills of the next generation of workers can be upgraded before they enter the labor market, many workers, especially those who are not in the official labor force, will not be able to find jobs unless the government becomes an employer-of-last-resort (Danziger and Gottschalk 1995). This argument applies especially to low-skilled inner-city black workers. It is bad enough that they face the problem of shifts in labor-market demand shared by all low-skilled workers; it is even worse that they confront negative employer perceptions about their work-related skills and attitudes.

For all these reasons, the passage of the 1996 welfare reform bill, which did not include a program of job creation, could have very negative social consequences in the inner city. Unless something is done to enhance the employment opportunities of inner-city welfare recipients who reach the time limit for the receipt of welfare, they will flood a pool already filled with low-skilled, jobless workers. . . .

West Virginia, a state that has been plagued with a severe shortage of work opportunities, has provided community service jobs to recipients of welfare for several years. In Wisconsin, Governor Thompson's welfare reform plan envisions community service jobs for many parents in the more depressed areas of the state, and the New Hope program in Milwaukee provides community service jobs for those unable to find employment in the private sector (Center on Budget and Policy Priorities 1996). It is especially important that this mixed strategy include a plan to make *adequate* monies available to localities or communities with high jobless and welfare dependency rates.

Obviously, as more people become employed and gain work experience, they will have a better chance of finding jobs in the private sector when jobs become available. The attitudes of employers toward inner-city workers could change, in part because they would be dealing with job applicants who have steady work experience and who could furnish references from their previous supervisors. Children are more likely to be socialized in a work-oriented environment and to develop the job readiness skills that are seen as important even for entry-level jobs.

Thus, given the recent welfare reform legislation, *adequate* strategies to enhance the employment opportunities of inner-city residents should be contemplated, strategies that would be adequately financed and designed to address the employment problems of low-skilled workers not only in periods of tight labor markets, but, even more important, in periods when the labor market is slack.

Notes

[1] The figures on adult employment are based on calculations from data provided by the 1990 U.S. Bureau of the Census (1993) and the *Local Community Fact Book for Chicago—1950* (1953) and the *Local Community Fact Book for Chicago—1960* (1963). The adult employment rates represent the number of employed individuals (aged fourteen and older in 1950 and sixteen and older in 1990) among the total number of adults in a given area. Those who are not employed include both the individuals who are members of the labor force but are not working and those who have dropped out or are not part of the labor force.

[2] See, for example, Bourgois (1995) and Venkatesh (1996).

[3] The economist David Schwartzman defines "unskilled workers to include operators, fabricators, and laborers, and those in service occupations, including private household workers, those working in protective service occupations, food service, and cleaning and building service." On the basis of this definition he estimates that 80 percent of all black workers and 38 percent of all white workers were unskilled in 1950. By 1990, 46 percent of black workers and 27 percent of white workers were employed in unskilled occupations (Schwartzman 1997).

BIBLIOGRAPHY

Bourdieu, Pierre. 1965. *Travail et Travailleurs en Algerie.* Paris: Editions Mouton.

Bourgois, Philippe. 1995. *In Search of Respect: Selling Crack in El Barrio.* New York: Cambridge University Press.

Center on Budget and Policy Priorities. 1996. *The Administration's $3 Billion Jobs Proposal.* Washington, DC: Center on Budget and Policy Priorities.

Danziger, Sheldon H., and Peter Gottschalk. 1995. *America Unequal.* Cambridge, MA: Harvard University Press.

Henderson, Vivian. 1975. "Race, Economics, and Public Policy." *Crisis* 83 (Fall):50–55.

Holzer, Harry J. 1996. *What Employers Want: Job Prospects for Less-Educated Workers.* New York: Russell Sage.

Kasarda, John D. 1993. "Inner-City Concentrated Poverty and Neighborhood Distress: 1970–1990." *Housing Policy Debate* 4(3): 253–302.

Local Community Fact Book for Chicago—1950. 1953. Chicago: Community Inventory, University of Chicago.

Local Community Fact Book for Chicago—1960. 1963. Chicago: Community Inventory, University of Chicago.

Schwartzman, David. 1997. *Black Unemployment: Part of Unskilled Unemployment.* Westport, CT: Greenwood.

Thurow, Lester. 1990. "The Crusade That's Killing Prosperity." *American Prospect* March/April:54–59.

U.S. Bureau of the Census. 1993. *Census of Population: Detailed Characteristics of the Population.* Washington, DC: U.S. Government Printing Office.

Venkatesh, Sudhir. 1996. "Private Lives, Public Housing: An Ethnography of the Robert Taylor Homes." Ph.D. dissertation., University of Chicago.

Wilson, William Julius. 1987. *The Truly Disadvantaged: The Inner City, the Underclass, and Public Policy.* Chicago: University of Chicago Press.

———. 1996. *When Work Disappears: The World of the New Urban Poor.* New York: Alfred A. Knopf.

9

AMERICAN APARTHEID

SEGREGATION AND THE MAKING
OF THE UNDERCLASS

Douglas S. Massey and Nancy A. Denton

◆◆◆

It is quite simple. As soon as there is a group area then all your uncertainties are removed and that is, after all, the primary purpose of this Bill [requiring racial segregation in housing].

> —Minister of the Interior, Union of
> South Africa legislative debate on
> the Group Areas Act of 1950

During the 1970s and 1980s a word disappeared from the American vocabulary.[1] It was not in the speeches of politicians decrying the multiple ills besetting American cities. It was not spoken by government officials responsible for administering the nation's social programs. It was not mentioned by journalists reporting on the rising tide of homelessness, drugs,

Douglas S. Massey and Nancy A. Denton, *American Apartheid: Segregation and the Making of the Underclass* (Cambridge, Mass.: Harvard University Press, 1993), pp. 1–9, 12–16, 239–241. Copyright 1993 by the President and Fellows of Harvard University Press.

and violence in urban America. It was not discussed by foundation executives and think-tank experts proposing new programs for unemployed parents and unwed mothers. It was not articulated by civil rights leaders speaking out against the persistence of racial inequality; and it was nowhere to be found in the thousands of pages written by social scientists on the urban underclass. The word was segregation.

Most Americans vaguely realize that urban America is still a residentially segregated society, but few appreciate the depth of black segregation or the degree to which it is maintained by ongoing institutional arrangements and contemporary individual actions. They view segregation as an unfortunate holdover from a racist past, one that is fading progressively over time. If racial residential segregation persists, they reason, it is only because civil rights laws passed during the 1960s have not had enough time to work or because many blacks still prefer to live in black neighborhoods. The residential segregation of blacks is viewed charitably as a "natural" outcome of impersonal social and economic forces, the same forces that produced Italian and Polish neighborhoods in the past and that yield Mexican and Korean areas today.

But black segregation is not comparable to the limited and transient segregation experienced by other racial and ethnic groups, now or in the past. No group in the history of the United States has ever experienced the sustained high level of residential segregation that has been imposed on blacks in large American cities for the past fifty years. This extreme racial isolation did not just happen; it was manufactured by whites through a series of self-conscious actions and purposeful institutional arrangements that continue today. Not only is the depth of black segregation unprecedented and utterly unique compared with that of other groups, but it shows little sign of change with the passage of time or improvements in socioeconomic status.

If policymakers, scholars, and the public have been reluctant to acknowledge segregation's persistence, they have likewise been blind to its consequences for American blacks. Residential segregation is not a neutral fact; it systematically undermines the social and economic well-being of blacks in the United States. Because of racial segregation, a significant share of black America is condemned to experience a social environment where poverty and joblessness are the norm, where a majority of children are born out of wedlock, where most families are on welfare, where educational failure prevails, and where social and physical deterioration abound. Through prolonged exposure to such an environment, black chances for social and economic success are drastically reduced.

Deleterious neighborhood conditions are built into the structure of the black community. They occur because segregation concentrates poverty to build a set of mutually reinforcing and self-feeding spirals of decline into black neighborhoods. When economic dislocations deprive a segregated group of employment and increase its rate of poverty, socioeconomic deprivation inevitably becomes more concentrated in neighborhoods where that group lives. The damaging social consequences that follow from increased poverty are spatially concentrated as well, creating uniquely disadvantaged environments that become progressively isolated—geographically, socially, and economically—from the rest of society.

The effect of segregation on black well-being is structural, not individual. Residential segregation lies beyond the ability of any individual to change; it constrains black life chances irrespective of personal traits, individual motivations, or private achievements. For the past twenty years this fundamental fact has been swept under the rug by policymakers, scholars, and theorists of the urban underclass. Segregation is the missing link in prior attempts to understand the plight of the urban poor. As long as blacks continue to be segregated in American cities, the United States cannot be called a race-blind society.

THE FORGOTTEN FACTOR

The present myopia regarding segregation is all the more startling because it once figured prominently in theories of racial inequality. Indeed, the ghetto was once seen as central to black subjugation in the United States. In 1944 Gunnar Myrdal wrote in *An American Dilemma* that residential segregation "is basic in a mechanical sense. It exerts its influence in an indirect and impersonal way: because Negro people do not live near white people, they cannot . . . associate with each other in the many activities founded on common neighborhood. Residential segregation . . . becomes reflected in uni-racial schools, hospitals, and other institutions" and creates "an artificial city . . . that permits any prejudice on the part of public officials to be freely vented on Negroes without hurting whites."[2]

Kenneth B. Clark, who worked with Gunnar Myrdal as a student and later applied his research skills in the landmark *Brown v. Topeka* school integration case, placed residential segregation at the heart of the U.S. system of racial oppression. In *Dark Ghetto,* written in 1965, he argued that "the dark ghetto's invisible walls have been erected by the white society, by those who have power, both to confine those who have *no* power and to perpetuate their powerlessness. The dark ghettos are social, political, educational, and—above all—economic colonies. Their inhabitants are subject peoples, victims of the greed, cruelty, insensitivity, guilt, and fear of their masters."[3]

Public recognition of segregation's role in perpetuating racial inequality was galvanized in the late 1960s by the riots that erupted in the nation's ghettos. In their aftermath, President Lyndon B. Johnson appointed a commission chaired by Governor Otto Kerner of Illinois to identify the causes of the violence and to propose policies to prevent its recurrence. The Kerner Commission released its report in March 1968 with the shocking admonition that the United States was "moving toward two societies, one black, one white—separate and unequal."[4] Prominent among the causes that the commission identified for this growing racial inequality was residential segregation.

In stark, blunt language, the Kerner Commission informed white Americans that "discrimination and segregation have long permeated much of American life; they now threaten the future of every American."[5] "Segregation and poverty have created in the racial ghetto a destructive environment totally unknown to most white Americans. What white Americans have never fully understood—but what the Negro can never forget—is that white society is deeply implicated in the ghetto. White institutions created it, white institutions maintain it, and white society condones it."[6]

The report argued that to continue present policies was "to make permanent the division of our country into two societies; one, largely Negro and poor, located in the central cities; the other, predominantly white and affluent, located in the suburbs."[7] Commission members rejected a strategy of ghetto enrichment coupled with abandonment of efforts to integrate, an approach they saw "as another way of choosing a permanently divided country."[8] Rather, they insisted that the only reasonable choice for America was "a policy which combines ghetto enrichment with programs designed to encourage integration of substantial numbers of Negroes into the society outside the ghetto."[9]

America chose differently. Following the passage of the Fair Housing Act in 1968, the problem of housing discrimination was declared solved, and residential segregation dropped off the national agenda. Civil rights leaders stopped pressing for the enforcement of open housing, political leaders increasingly debated employment and educational policies rather than housing integration, and academicians focused their theoretical scrutiny on everything from culture to family structure, to institutional racism, to federal welfare systems. Few people spoke of racial segregation as a problem or acknowledged its persisting consequences. By the end of the 1970s residential segregation became the forgotten factor in American race relations.[10]

While public discourse on race and poverty became more acrimonious and more focused on divisive issues such as school busing, racial quotas, welfare, and affirmative action, conditions in the nation's ghettos steadily deteriorated.[11] By the end of the 1970s, the image of poor minority families mired in an endless cycle of unemployment, unwed childbearing, illiteracy, and dependency had coalesced into a compelling and powerful concept: the urban underclass.[12] In the view of many middle-class whites, inner cities had come to house a large population of poorly educated single mothers and jobless men—mostly black and Puerto Rican—who were unlikely to exit poverty and become self-sufficient. In the ensuing national debate on the causes for this persistent poverty, four theoretical explanations gradually emerged: culture, racism, economics, and welfare.

Cultural explanations for the underclass can be traced to the work of Oscar Lewis, who identified a "culture of poverty" that he felt promoted patterns of behavior inconsistent with socioeconomic advancement.[13] According to Lewis, this culture originated in endemic unemployment and chronic social immobility, and provided an ideology that allowed poor people to cope with feelings of hopelessness and despair that arose because their chances for socioeconomic success were remote. In individuals, this culture was typified by a lack of impulse control, a strong present-time orientation, and little ability to defer gratification. Among families, it yielded an absence of childhood, an early initiation into sex, a prevalence of free marital unions, and a high incidence of abandonment of mothers and children.

Although Lewis explicitly connected the emergence of these cultural patterns to structural conditions in society, he argued that once the culture of poverty was established, it became an independent cause of persistent poverty. This idea was further elaborated in 1965 by the Harvard sociologist and then Assistant Secretary of Labor Daniel Patrick Moynihan, who in a confidential report to the President focused on the relationship between male unemployment, family instability, and the intergenerational transmission of poverty, a process he labeled a "tangle of pathology."[14] He warned that because of the structural absence of employment in the ghetto, the black family was disintegrating in a way that threatened the fabric of community life.

When these ideas were transmitted through the press, both popular and scholarly, the connection between culture and economic structure was somehow lost, and the argument was popularly perceived to be that "people were poor because they had a defective culture." This position was later explicitly adopted by the conservative theorist Edward Banfield, who argued that lower-class culture—with its limited time horizon, impulsive need for gratification, and psychological self-doubt—was primarily responsible for persistent urban poverty.[15] He believed that these cultural traits were largely imported, arising primarily because cities attracted lower-class migrants.

The culture-of-poverty argument was strongly criticized by liberal theorists as a self-serving ideology that "blamed the victim."[16] In the ensuing wave of reaction, black families were viewed not as weak but, on the contrary, as resilient and well-adapted survivors in an oppressive and racially prejudiced society.[17] Black disadvantages were attributed not to a defective culture but to the persistence of institutional racism in the United States. According to theorists of the underclass such as Douglas Glasgow and Alphonso Pinkney, the black urban underclass came about because deeply imbedded racist practices within American institutions—particularly schools and the economy—effectively kept blacks poor and dependent.[18]

As the debate on culture versus racism ground to a halt during the late 1970s, conservative theorists increasingly captured public attention by focusing on a third possible cause of poverty: government welfare policy. According to Charles Murray, the creation of the underclass was rooted in the liberal welfare state.[19] Federal antipoverty programs altered the incentives governing the behavior of poor men and women, reducing the desirability of marriage, increasing the benefits of unwed childbearing, lowering the attractiveness of menial labor, and ultimately resulted in greater poverty.

A slightly different attack on the welfare state was launched by Lawrence Mead, who argued that it was not the generosity but the permissiveness of the U.S. welfare system that was at fault.[20] Jobless men and unwed mothers should be required to display "good citizenship" before being supported by the state. By not requiring anything of the poor, Mead argued, the welfare state undermined their independence and competence, thereby perpetuating their poverty.

This conservative reasoning was subsequently attacked by liberal social scientists, led principally by the sociologist William Julius Wilson, who had long been arguing for the increasing importance of class over race in under-standing the social and economic problems facing blacks.[21] In his 1987 book *The Truly Disadvantaged,* Wilson argued that persistent urban poverty stemmed primarily from the structural transformation of the inner-city economy.[22] The decline of manufacturing, the suburbanization of employment, and the rise of a low-wage service sector dramatically reduced the number of city jobs that paid wages sufficient to support a family, which led to high rates of joblessness among minorities and a shrinking pool of "marriageable" men (those financially able to support a family). Marriage thus became less attractive to poor women, unwed childbearing increased, and female-headed families proliferated. Blacks suffered disproportionately from these trends because, owing to past discrimination, they were concentrated in locations and occupations particularly affected by economic restructuring.

Wilson argued that these economic changes were accompanied by an increase in the spatial concentration of poverty within black neighborhoods. This new geography of poverty, he felt, was enabled by the civil rights revolution of the 1960s, which provided middle-class blacks with new opportunities outside the ghetto.[23] The out-migration of middle-class families from ghetto areas left behind a destitute community lacking the institutions, resources, and values necessary for success in post-industrial society. The urban underclass thus arose from a complex interplay of civil rights policy, economic restructuring, and a historical legacy of discrimination.

Theoretical concepts such as the culture of poverty, institutional racism, welfare disincentives, and structural economic change have all been widely debated. None of these explanations, however, considers residential segregation to be an important contributing cause of urban poverty and the underclass. In their principal works, Murray and Mead do not mention segregation at all;[24] and Wilson refers to racial segregation only as a historical legacy from the past, not as an outcome that is institutionally supported and actively created today.[25] Although Lewis mentions segregation sporadically in his writings, it is not assigned a central role in the set of structural factors responsible for the culture of poverty, and Banfield ignores it entirely. Glasgow, Pinkney, and other theorists of institutional racism mention the ghetto frequently, but generally call not for residential desegregation but for race-specific policies to combat the effects of discrimination in the schools and labor markets. In general, then, contemporary theorists of urban poverty do not see high levels of black-white segregation as particularly relevant to understanding the underclass or alleviating urban poverty.[26]

The purpose of this book is to redirect the focus of public debate back to issues of race and racial segregation, and to suggest that they should be fundamental to thinking about the status of black Americans and the origins of the urban underclass. Our quarrel is less with any of the prevailing theories of urban poverty than with their systematic failure to consider the important role that segregation has played in mediating, exacerbating, and ultimately amplifying the harmful social and economic processes they treat.

We join earlier scholars in rejecting the view that poor urban blacks have an autonomous "culture of poverty" that explains their failure to achieve socioeconomic success in American society. We argue instead that residential segregation has been instrumental in creating a structural niche within which a deleterious set of attitudes and behaviors—a culture of segregation—has arisen and flourished. Segregation created the structural conditions for the emergence of an oppositional culture that devalues work, schooling, and marriage and that stresses attitudes and behaviors that are antithetical and often hostile to success in the larger economy. Although poor black neighborhoods still contain many people who lead conventional, productive lives, their example has been overshadowed in recent years by a growing concentration of poor, welfare-dependent families that is an inevitable result of residential segregation.

We readily agree with Douglas, Pinkney, and others that racial discrimination is widespread and may even be institutionalized within large sectors of American society, including the labor market, the educational system, and the welfare bureaucracy. We argue, however, that this view of black subjugation is incomplete without understanding the special role that residential segregation plays in enabling all other forms of racial oppression. Residential segregation is the institutional apparatus that supports other racially discriminatory processes and binds them together into a coherent and uniquely effective system of racial subordination. Until the black ghetto is dismantled as a basic institution of American urban life, progress ameliorating racial inequality in other arenas will be slow, fitful, and incomplete.

We also agree with William Wilson's basic argument that the structural transformation of the urban economy undermined economic supports for the black community during the 1970s and 1980s.[27] We argue, however, that in the absence of segregation, these structural changes would not have produced the disastrous social and economic outcomes observed in inner cities during these decades. Although rates of black poverty were driven up by the economic dislocations Wilson identifies, it was segregation that confined the increased deprivation to a small number of densely settled, tightly packed, and geographically isolated areas.

Wilson also argues that concentrated poverty arose because the civil rights revolution allowed middle-class blacks to move out of the ghetto. Although we remain open to the possibility that class-selective migration did occur,[28] we argue that concentrated poverty would have happened during the 1970s with or without black middle-class migration. Our principal objection to Wilson's focus on middle-class out-migration is not that it did not occur, but that it is misdirected: focusing on the flight of the black middle class deflects attention from the real issue, which is the limitation of black residential options through segregation.

Middle-class households—whether they are black, Mexican, Italian, Jewish, or Polish—always try to escape the poor. But only blacks must attempt their escape within a highly segregated, racially segmented housing market. Because of segregation, middle-class blacks are less able to escape than other groups, and as a result are exposed to more poverty. At the same time, because of segregation no one will move into a poor black neighborhood except other poor blacks. Thus both middle-class blacks and poor blacks lose compared with the poor and middle class of other groups: poor blacks live under unrivaled concentrations of poverty and affluent blacks live in neighborhoods that are far less advantageous than those experienced by the middle class of other groups.

Finally, we concede Murray's general point that federal welfare policies are linked to the rise of the urban underclass, but we disagree with his specific hypothesis that generous welfare payments, by themselves, discouraged employment, encouraged unwed childbearing, undermined the strength of the family, and thereby caused persistent poverty.[29] We argue instead that welfare payments were only harmful to the socioeconomic well-being of groups that were residentially segregated. As poverty rates rose among blacks in response to the economic dislocations of the 1970s and 1980s, so did the use of welfare programs. Because of racial segregation, however, the higher levels of welfare receipt were confined to a small number of isolated, all-black neighborhoods. By promoting the spatial concentration of welfare use, therefore, segregation created a residential environment within which welfare dependency was the norm, leading to the intergenerational transmission and broader perpetuation of urban poverty.

COMING TO TERMS WITH AMERICAN APARTHEID

Our fundamental argument is that racial segregation—and its characteristic institutional form, the black ghetto—are the key structural factors responsible for the perpetuation of black poverty in the United States. Residential segregation is the principal organizational feature of American society that is responsible for the creation of the urban underclass. . . . It can be shown that any increase in the poverty rate of a residentially segregated group leads to an immediate and automatic increase in the geographic concentration of poverty. When the rate of minority poverty is increased under conditions of high segregation, all of the increase is absorbed by a small number of neighborhoods. When the same increase in poverty occurs in an integrated group, the added poverty is spread evenly throughout the urban area, and the neighborhood environment that group members face does not change much.

During the 1970s and 1980s, therefore, when urban economic restructuring and inflation drove up rates of black and Hispanic poverty in many urban areas, underclass communities were created only where increased minority poverty coincided with a high degree of segregation—principally in older metropolitan areas of the northeast and the midwest. Among Hispanics, only Puerto Ricans developed underclass communities, because only they were highly segregated; and this high degree of segregation is directly attributable to the fact that a large proportion of Puerto Ricans are of African origin.

The interaction of intense segregation and high poverty leaves black neighborhoods extremely vulnerable to fluctuations in the urban economy, because any dislocation that causes an upward shift in black poverty rates will also produce a rapid change in the concentration of poverty and, hence, a dramatic shift in the social and economic composition of black neighborhoods. The concentration of poverty, for example, is associated with the wholesale withdrawal of commercial institutions and the deterioration or elimination of goods and services distributed through the market.

Neighborhoods, of course, are dynamic and constantly changing, and given the high rates of residential turnover characteristic of contemporary American cities, their well-being depends to a great extent on the characteristics and actions of their residents. Decisions taken by one actor affect the subsequent decisions of others in the neighborhood. In this way isolated actions affect the well-being of the community and alter the stability of the neighborhood.

Because of this feedback between individual and collective behavior, neighborhood stability is characterized by a series of thresholds, beyond which various self-perpetuating processes of decay take hold. Above these thresholds, each actor who makes a decision that undermines neighborhood well-being makes it increasingly likely that other actors will do the same. Each property owner who decides not to invest in upkeep and maintenance, for example, lowers the incentive for others to maintain their properties. Likewise, each new crime promotes psychological and physical withdrawal from public life, which reduces vigilance within the neighborhood and undermines the capacity for collective organization, making additional criminal activity more likely.

Segregation increases the susceptibility of neighborhoods to these spirals of decline. During periods of economic dislocation, a rising concentration of black poverty is associated with the simultaneous concentration of other negative social and economic conditions. Given the high levels of racial segregation characteristic of American urban areas, increases in black poverty such as those observed during the 1970s can only lead to a concentration of housing abandonment, crime, and social disorder, pushing poor black neighborhoods beyond the threshold of stability.

By building physical decay, crime, and social disorder into the residential structure of black communities, segregation creates a harsh and extremely disadvantaged environment to which ghetto blacks must adapt. In concentrating poverty, moreover, segregation also concentrates conditions such as drug use, joblessness, welfare dependency, teenage childbearing, and unwed parenthood, producing a social context where these conditions are not only common but the norm. By adapting to this social environment, ghetto dwellers evolve a set of behaviors, attitudes, and expectations that are sharply at variance with those common in the rest of American society.

As a direct result of the high degree of racial and class isolation created by segregation, for example, Black English has become progressively more distant from Standard American English, and its speakers are at a clear disadvantage in U.S. schools and labor markets. Moreover, the isolation and intense poverty of the ghetto provides a supportive structural niche for the emergence of an "oppositional culture" that inverts the values of middle-class society. Anthropologists have found that young people in the ghetto experience strong peer pressure not to succeed in school, which severely limits their prospects for social mobility in the larger society. Quantitative research shows that growing up in a ghetto neighborhood increases the likelihood of dropping out of high school, reduces the probability of attending college, lowers the likelihood of employment, reduces income earned as an adult, and increases the risk of teenage childbearing and unwed pregnancy.

Segregation also has profound political consequences for blacks, because it so isolates them geographically that they are the only ones who benefit from public expenditures in their neighborhoods. The relative integration of most ethnic groups means that jobs or services allocated to them will generally benefit several other groups at the same time. Integration thus creates a basis for political coalitions and pluralist politics, and most ethnic groups that seek public resources are able to find coalition partners because other groups can anticipate sharing the benefits. That blacks are the only ones to benefit from resources allocated to the ghetto—and are the only ones harmed when resources are removed—makes it difficult for them to find partners for political coalitions. Although segregation paradoxically makes it easier for blacks to elect representatives, it limits their political influence and marginalizes them within the American polity. Segregation prevents blacks from participating in pluralist politics based on mutual self-interest.

Because of the close connection between social and spatial mobility, segregation also perpetuates poverty. One of the primary means by which individuals improve their life chances—and those of their children—is by moving to neighborhoods with higher home values, safer streets, higher-quality schools, and better services. As groups move up the socioeconomic ladder, they typically move up the residential hierarchy as well, and in doing so they not only improve their standard of living but also enhance their chances for future success. Barriers to spatial mobility are barriers to social mobility, and by confining blacks to a small set of relatively disadvantaged neighborhoods, segregation constitutes a very powerful impediment to black socioeconomic progress.

Despite the obvious deleterious consequences of black spatial isolation, policymakers have not paid much attention to segregation as a contributing cause of urban poverty and have not taken effective steps to dismantle the ghetto. Indeed, for most of the past two decades public policies tolerated and even supported the perpetuation of segregation in American urban areas. Although many political initiatives were launched to combat discrimination and prejudice in the housing and banking industries, each legislative or judicial act was fought tenaciously by a powerful array of people who believed in or benefited from the status quo.

Although a comprehensive open housing bill finally passed Congress under unusual circumstances in 1968, it was stripped of its enforcement provisions as its price of enactment, yielding a Fair Housing Act that was structurally flawed and all but doomed to fail. As documentation of the law's defects accumulated in multiple congressional hearings, government reports, and scholarly studies, little was done to repair the situation until 1988, when a series of scandals and political errors by the Reagan administration finally enabled a significant strengthening of federal antidiscrimination law.

Yet even more must be done to prevent the permanent bifurcation of the United States into black and white societies that are separate and unequal. As of 1990, levels of racial segregation were still extraordinarily high in the nation's large urban areas, particularly those of the north. Segregation has remained high because fair housing enforcement relies too heavily on the private efforts of individual victims of discrimination. Whereas the processes that perpetuate segregation are entrenched and institutionalized, fair housing enforcement is individual, sporadic, and confined to a small number of isolated cases.

As long as the Fair Housing Act is enforced individually rather than systemically, it is unlikely to be effective in overcoming the structural arrangements that support segregation and sustain the ghetto. Until the government throws its considerable institutional weight behind efforts to dismantle the ghetto, racial segregation will persist. . . .

Ultimately, however, dismantling the ghetto and ending the long reign of racial segregation will require more than specific bureaucratic reforms; it requires a moral commitment that white America has historically lacked. The segregation of American blacks was no historical accident; it was brought about by actions and practices that had the passive acceptance, if not the active support, of most whites in the United States. Although America's apartheid may not be rooted in the legal strictures of its South African relative, it is no less effective in perpetuating racial inequality, and whites are no less culpable for the socioeconomic deprivation that results.

As in South Africa, residential segregation in the United States provides a firm basis for a broader system of racial injustice. The geographic isolation of Africans within a narrowly circumscribed portion of the urban environment—whether African townships or American ghettos—forces blacks to live under extraordinarily harsh conditions and to endure a social world where poverty is endemic, infrastructure is inadequate, education is lacking, families are fragmented, and crime and violence are rampant.[30] Moreover, segregation confines these unpleasant by-products of racial oppression to an isolated portion of the urban geography far removed from the experience of most whites. Resting on a foundation of segregation, apartheid not only denies blacks their rights as citizens but forces them to bear the social costs of their own victimization.

Although Americans have been quick to criticize the apartheid system of South Africa, they have been reluctant to acknowledge the consequences of their own institutionalized system of racial separation. The topic of segregation has virtually disappeared from public policy debates; it has vanished from the list of issues on the civil rights agenda; and it has been ignored by social scientists spinning endless theories of the underclass. Residential segregation has become the forgotten factor of American race relations, a minor footnote in the ongoing debate on the urban underclass. Until policymakers, social scientists, and private citizens recognize the crucial role of America's own apartheid in perpetuating urban poverty and racial injustice, the United States will remain a deeply divided and very troubled society.[31]

NOTES

[1] Epigraph from Edgar H. Brookes, *Apartheid: A Documentary Study of Modern South Africa* (London: Routledge and Kegan Paul, 1968), p. 142.

[2] Gunnar Myrdal, *An American Dilemma*, vol. 1 (New York: Harper and Brothers, 1944), p. 618; see also Walter A. Jackson, *Gunnar Myrdal and America's Conscience* (Chapel Hill: University of North Carolina Press, 1990), pp. 88–271.

[3] Kenneth B. Clark, *Dark Ghetto: Dilemmas of Social Power* (New York: Harper and Row, 1965), p. 11.

[4] U.S. National Advisory Commission on Civil Disorders, *The Kerner Report* (New York: Pantheon Books, 1988), p. 1.

[5] Ibid.

[6] Ibid., p. 2.

[7] Ibid., p. 22.

[8] Ibid.

[9] Ibid.

[10] A few scholars attempted to keep the Kerner Commission's call for desegregation alive, but their voices have largely been unheeded in the ongoing debate. Thomas Pettigrew has continued to assert the central importance of residential segregation, calling it the "linchpin" of American race relations; see "Racial Change and Social Policy," *Annals of the American Academy of Political and Social Science* 441 (1979):114–31. Gary Orfield has repeatedly pointed out segregation's deleterious effects on black prospects for education, employment, and socioeconomic mobility; see "Separate Societies: Have the Kerner Warnings Come True?" in Fred R. Harris and Roger W. Wilkins, eds., *Quiet Riots: Race and Poverty in the United States* (New York: Pantheon Books, 1988), pp. 100–122; and "Ghettoization and Its Alternatives," in Paul E. Peterson, ed., *The New Urban Reality* (Washington, D.C.: Brookings Institution, 1985), pp. 161–96.

[11] See Thomas B. Edsall and Mary D. Edsall, *Chain Reaction: The Impact of Race, Rights, and Taxes on American Politics* (New York: Norton, 1991).

[12] For an informative history of the evolution of the concept of the underclass, see Michael B. Katz, *The Undeserving Poor: From the War on Poverty to the War on Welfare* (New York: Pantheon, 1989), pp. 185–235.

[13] Oscar Lewis, *La Vida: A Puerto Rican Family in the Culture of Poverty—San Juan and New York* (New York: Random House, 1965); "The Culture of Poverty," *Scientific American* 215 (1966): 19–25; "The Culture of Poverty," in Daniel P. Moynihan, ed., *On Understanding Poverty: Perspectives from the Social Sciences* (New York: Basic Books, 1968), pp. 187–220.

[14] The complete text of this report is reprinted in Lee Rainwater and William L. Yancey, *The Moynihan Report and the Politics of Controversy* (Cambridge: MIT Press, 1967), pp. 39–125.

[15] Edward C. Banfield, *The Unheavenly City* (Boston: Little, Brown, 1970).

[16] William Ryan, *Blaming the Victim* (New York: Random House, 1971).

[17] Carol Stack, *All Our Kin: Strategies of Survival in a Black Community* (New York: Harper and Row, 1974).

[18] Douglas C. Glasgow, *The Black Underclass: Poverty, Unemployment, and Entrapment of Ghetto Youth* (New York: Vintage, 1981), p. 11; Alphonso Pinkney, *The Myth of Black Progress* (Cambridge: Cambridge University Press, 1984), pp. 78–80.

[19] Charles Murray, *Losing Ground: American Social Policy, 1950–1980* (New York: Basic Books, 1984).

[20] Lawrence M. Mead, *Beyond Entitlement: The Social Obligations of Citizenship* (New York: Free Press, 1986).

[21] William Julius Wilson, *The Declining Significance of Race: Blacks and Changing American Institutions* (Chicago: University of Chicago Press, 1978).

[22] William Julius Wilson, *The Truly Disadvantaged: The Inner City, the Underclass, and Public Policy* (Chicago: University of Chicago Press, 1987), pp. 1–108.

[23] Ibid., pp. 49–62.

[24] The subject indices of *Losing Ground* and *Beyond Entitlement* contain no references at all to residential segregation.

[25] The subject index of *The Truly Disadvantaged* contains two references to pre1960s Jim Crow segregation.

[26] Again with the exception of Thomas Pettigrew and Gary Orfield.

[27] We have published several studies documenting how the decline of manufacturing, the suburbanization of jobs, and the rise of low-wage service employment eliminated high-paying jobs for manual workers, drove up rates of black male unemployment, and reduced the attractiveness of marriage to black women, thereby contributing to a proliferation of female-headed families and persistent poverty. See Mitchell L. Eggers and Douglas S. Massey, "The Structural Determinants of Urban Poverty," *Social Science Research* 20 (1991): 217–55; Mitchell L. Eggers and Douglas S. Massey, "A Longitudinal Analysis of Urban Poverty: Blacks in U.S. Metropolitan Areas between 1970 and 1980," *Social Science Research* 21 (1992): 175–203.

[28] The evidence on the extent of middle-class out-migration from ghetto areas is inconclusive. Because racial segregation does not decline with rising socioeconomic status, out-movement from poor black neighborhoods certainly has not been to white areas. When Kathryn P. Nelson measured rates of black out-migration from local "zones" within forty metropolitan areas, however, she found higher rates of out-movement for middle- and upper-class blacks compared with poor blacks; but her "zones" contained more than 100,000 inhabitants, making them considerably larger than neighborhoods (see "Racial Segregation, Mobility, and

Poverty Concentration," paper presented at the annual meetings of the Population Association of America, Washington, D.C., March 19–23, 1991). In contrast, Edward Gramlich and
Deborah Laren found that poor and middle-class blacks displayed about the same likelihood
of out-migration from poor census tracts (see "Geographic Mobility and Persistent Poverty,"
Department of Economics, University of Michigan, Ann Arbor, 1990).

[29] See Eggers and Massey, "A Longitudinal Analysis of Urban Poverty."

[30] See International Defense and Aid Fund for Southern Africa, *Apartheid: The Facts* (London: United Nations Centre against Apartheid, 1983), pp. 15–26.

[31] We are not the first to notice the striking parallel between the institutionalized system of
racial segregation in U.S. cities and the organized, state-sponsored system of racial repression
in South Africa. See John H. Denton, *Apartheid American Style* (Berkeley, Calif.: Diablo Press,
1967); James A. Kushner, "Apartheid in America: An Historical and Legal Analysis of Contemporary Racial Residential Segregation in the United States," *Howard Law Journal* 22
(1979):547–60.

10

A THEORY OF
ETHNIC ANTAGONISM

THE SPLIT LABOR MARKET

Edna Bonacich

◆◆◆

Societies vary considerably in their degree of ethnic and racial antagonism. Such territories as Brazil, Mexico, and Hawaii are generally acknowledged to be relatively low on this dimension; while South Africa, Australia, and the United States are considered especially high. Literally hundreds of variables have been adduced to account for these differences, ranging from religions of dominant groups, to whether the groups who migrate are dominant or subordinate, to degrees of difference in skin color, to an irreducible "tradition" of ethnocentrism. While some writers have attempted to synthesize or systematize some subset of these (e.g., Lieberson, 1961; Mason, 1970; Noel, 1968; Schermerhorn, 1970; van den Berghe, 1966), one is generally struck by the absence of a developed theory accounting for variations in ethnic antagonism.

Edna Bonacich, "A Theory of Ethnic Antagonism: The Split Labor Market," *American Sociological Review* (October 1972), pp. 547–559. Copyright 1972 by the American Sociological Association. Used by permission of the American Sociological Association and the author.

One approach to this problem is to consider an apparent anomaly, namely that ethnic antagonism has taken two major, seemingly antithetical forms: exclusion movements, and so-called caste systems.[1] An example of the former is the "white Australia" policy; while South Africa's color bar illustrates the latter. The United States has shown both forms, with a racial caste system in the South and exclusion of Asian and "new" immigrants[2] from the Pacific and eastern seaboards respectively. Apart from manifesting antagonism between ethnic elements, exclusion and caste seem to have little in common. In the one, an effort is made to prevent an ethnically different group from being part of the society. In the other, an ethnically different group is essential to the society: it is an exploited class supporting the entire edifice. The Deep South felt it could not survive without its black people; the Pacific coast could not survive with its Japanese. This puzzle may be used as a touchstone for solving the general problem of ethnic antagonism, for to be adequate a theory must be able to explain it.

The theory presented here is, in part, a synthesis of some of the ideas used by Oliver Cox to explain the Japanese-white conflict on the U.S. Pacific coast (Cox, 1948:408–22), and by Marvin Harris to analyze the difference between Brazil and the deep south in rigidity of the "color line" (Harris, 1964:79–94). It stresses the role of a certain kind of economic competition in the development of ethnic antagonism. Economic factors have, of course, not gone unnoticed, though until recently sociological literature has tended to point them out briefly, then move on to more "irrational" factors (even such works as *The Economics of Discrimination*, Becker, 1957). A resurgence of Marxian analysis (e.g. Blauner, 1969; Reich, 1971) has thrust economic considerations to the fore, but I shall argue that even this approach cannot adequately deal with the problem posed by exclusion movements and caste systems. In addition, both Marxist and non-Marxist writers assume that racial and cultural differences in themselves prompt the development of ethnic antagonism. This theory challenges that assumption, suggesting that economic processes are more fundamental.

No effort is made to prove the accuracy of the following model. Such proof depends on a lengthier exposition. Historical illustrations are presented to support it.

ETHNIC ANTAGONISM

"Ethnic" rather than "racial" antagonism was selected as the dependent variable because the former is seen to subsume the latter. Both terms refer to groups defined socially as sharing a common ancestry in which membership is therefore inherited or ascribed, whether or not members are currently physically or culturally distinctive.[3] The difference between race and ethnicity lies in the size of the locale from which a group stems, races generally coming from continents, and ethnicities from national subsections of continents. In the past the term "race" has been used to refer to both levels, but general usage today has reversed this practice (e.g. Schermerhorn, 1970; Shibutani and Kwan, 1965). Ethnicity has become the generic term.

Another reason for choosing this term is that exclusion attempts and caste-like arrangements are found among national groupings within a racial category. For example, in 1924 whites (Europeans) attempted to exclude whites of different national backgrounds from the United States by setting up stringent immigration quotas.

The term "antagonism" is intended to encompass all levels of intergroup conflict, including ideologies and beliefs (such as racism and prejudice), behaviors (such as discrimination, lynchings, riots), and institutions (such as laws perpetuating segregation). Exclusion movements and caste systems may be seen as the culmination of many pronouncements, actions, and enactments, and are continuously supported by more of the same. "Antagonism" was chosen over terms like prejudice and discrimination because it carries fewer moralistic and theoretical assumptions (see Schermerhorn, 1970:6–9). For example, both of these terms see conflict as emanating primarily from one side: the dominant group. Antagonism allows for the possibility that conflict is mutual; i.e. a product of interaction.

THE SPLIT LABOR MARKET

The central hypothesis is that ethnic antagonism first germinates in a labor market split along ethnic lines. To be split, a labor market must contain at least two groups of workers whose price of labor differs for the same work, or would differ if they did the same work. The concept "price of labor" refers to labor's total cost to the employer, including not only wages, but the cost of recruitment, transportation, room and board, education, health care (if the employer must bear these), and the costs of labor unrest. The degree of worker "freedom" does not interfere with this calculus; the cost of a slave can be estimated in the same monetary units as that of a wage earner, from his purchase price, living expenses, policing requirements, and so on.

	Free Man (White)			Prisoner (White)			Coolie (Indian)		
	£	s.	d.	£	s.	d.	£	s.	d.
Rations	16	18	0	13	14	4	9	6	4
Clothing	--	--	--	3	3	0	1	1	8
Wages	25	0	0	--	--	--	6	0	0
Passage from India	--	--	--	--	--	--	2	0	0
Total per Annum	41	18	0	16	17	4	18	8	0

From Yarwood (1968:13)

Table 10.1   Estimated Cost of Three Types of Labor to Be Shepherds in New South Wales, 1841

The price of a group of workers can be roughly calculated in advance and comparisons made even though two groups are not engaged in the same activity at the same time. Thus in 1841 in the colony of New South Wales, the Legislative Council's Committee on Immigration estimated the relative costs of recruiting three groups of laborers to become shepherds. Table 10.1 shows their findings. The estimate of free white labor, for example, was based on what it would take to attract these men from competing activities.

FACTORS AFFECTING THE INITIAL PRICE OF LABOR

Labor markets that are split by the entrance of a new group develop a dynamic which may in turn affect the price of labor. One must therefore distinguish initial from later price determinants. The initial factors can be divided into two broad categories: resources and motives.

1. Resources

Three types of resources are important price determinants. These are:

a. Level of Living, or Economic Resources.   The ethnic groups forming the labor market in a contact situation derive from different economic systems, either abroad or within a conquered territory. For members of an ethnic group to be drawn into moving, they must at least raise their wage

level. In general, the poorer the economy of the recruits, the less the inducement needed for them to enter the new labor market. Crushing poverty may
drive them to sell their labor relatively cheaply. For example, Lind
(1968:199) describes the effect of the living level on the wage scale received
by immigrant workers to Hawaii:

> In every case [of labor importations] the superior opportunities for
> gaining a livelihood have been broadcast in regions of surplus man-
> power, transportation facilities have been provided, and finally a
> monetary return larger than that already received has been offered to the
> prospective laborer. The monetary inducement has varied considerably,
> chiefly according to the plane of living of the population being re-
> cruited, and the cheapest available labor markets have, of course, been
> most extensively drawn upon.

Workers need not accept the original wage agreement for long after they
have immigrated, since other opportunities may exist; for instance, there
may be ample, cheap land available for individual farming. One capitalist device for keeping wages low at least for a time is to bind immigrants to
contracts before they leave the old economy. The Indian indenture system,
for example, rested on such an arrangement (Gillion, 1962:19–38).

b. Information.   Immigrants may be pushed into signing contracts out of
ignorance. They may agree to a specific wage in their homeland not know-
ing the prevailing wage in the new country, or having been beguiled by a
false account of life and opportunity there. Williams (1944:11), for example,
describes some of the false promises made to draw British and Germans as
workers to West Indian sugar plantations before the advent of African slavery. Chinese labor to Australia was similarly "obtained under 'false and
specious pretences'" (Willard, 1967:9).

The possibilities for defrauding a population lacking access to the truth are
obvious. In general, the more people know about conditions obtaining in the
labor market to which they are moving, the better can they protect themselves against disadvantageous wage agreements.

c. Political Resources.   By political resources I mean the benefits to a
group of organizing. Organization can exist at the level of labor, or it can occur at higher levels, for example, in a government that protects them. These

levels are generally related in that a strong government can help organize its emigrants. There are exceptions, however: strong emigrant governments tend not to extend protection to their deported convicts or political exiles; and some highly organized groups, like the Jews in the United States, have not received protection from the old country.

Governments vary in the degree to which they protect their emigrants. Japan kept close watch over the fate of her nationals who migrated to Hawaii and the Pacific coast; and the British colonial government in India tried to guard against abuses of the indenture system (for example, by refusing to permit Natal to import Indian workers for their sugar plantations until satisfactory terms had been agreed to; cf. Ferguson-Davie, 1952:4–10). In contrast Mexican migrant workers to the United States have received little protection from their government, and African states were unable to intervene on behalf of slaves brought to America. Often the indigenous populations of colonized territories have been politically weak following conquest. Thus African nations in South Africa have been unable to protect their migrant workers in the cities.

In general, the weaker a group politically, the more vulnerable it is to the use of force, hence to an unfavorable wage bargain (or to no wage bargain at all, as with slavery). The price of a labor group varies inversely with the amount of force that can be used against it, which in turn depends on its political resources.

2. Motives

Two motives affect the price of labor, both related to the worker's intention of not remaining permanently in the labor force. Temporary workers tend to cost less than permanent workers for two reasons. First, they are more willing to put up with undesirable work conditions since these need not be endured forever. If they are migrants, this tolerance may extend to the general standard of living. Often migrant temporary workers are males who have left the comforts of home behind and whose employers need not bear the cost of housing and educating their families. Even when families accompany them, such workers tend to be willing to accept a lower standard of living since it is only short term.

Second, temporary workers avoid involvement in lengthy labor disputes. Since they will be in the labor market a short while, their main concern is immediate employment. They may be willing to undercut wage standards if need be to get a job and are therefore ripe candidates for strikebreaking. Permanent workers also stand to lose from lengthy conflict, but they hope for benefits to their progeny. If temporary workers are from elsewhere, they have no such interest in future business-labor relations. Altogether, temporary workers have little reason to join the organizations and unions of a permanent work force, and tend not to do so.

a. Fixed or Supplementary Income Goal. Some temporary workers enter the market either to supplement family income, or to work toward a specific purchase. The worker's standard of living does not, therefore, depend on his earnings on the job in question, since his central source of employment or income lies elsewhere. Examples of this phenomenon are to be found throughout Africa:

> ... the characteristic feature of the labor market in most of Africa has always been the massive circulation of Africans between their villages and paid employment outside. In some places villagers engage in wage-earning seasonally. More commonly today they work for continuous though short-term periods of roughly one to three years, after which they return to the villages. ... the African villager, the potential migrant into paid employment, has a relatively low, clearly-defined and rigid income goal; he wants money to pay head and hut taxes, to make marriage payments required of prospective bridegrooms, or to purchase some specific consumer durable (a bicycle, a rifle, a sewing machine, a given quantity of clothing or textiles, etc.) (Berg, 1966:116–8).

Such a motive produces the "backward-sloping labor supply function" characteristic of many native peoples in colonized territories. In addition to the general depressing effects on wages of being temporary, this motive leads to a fairly rapid turnover in personnel, making organization more difficult and hindering the development of valuable skills which could be used for bargaining. If wages were to rise, workers would reach their desired income and withdraw more quickly from the market, thereby lessening their chances of developing the political resources necessary to raise their wages further.

b. Fortune Seeking. Many groups, commonly called sojourners (see Siu, 1952), migrate long distances to seek their fortune, with the ultimate intention of improving their position in their homeland. Such was the case with

Japanese immigrants on the west coast and Italian immigrants in the east. Such workers stay longer in the labor market, and can develop political resources. However, since they are temporary they have little incentive to join the organizations of the settled population. Instead they tend to create competing organizations composed of people who will play a part in their future in the homeland, i.e. members of the same ethnic group.

Sojourner laborers have at least three features which affect the price of labor: lower wages, longer hours, and convenience to the employer. The Japanese show all three. Millis (1915:45) cites the U.S. Immigration Commission on the question of relative wages:

> The Japanese have usually worked for a lower wage than the members of any other race save the Chinese and the Mexican. In the salmon canneries the Chinese have been paid higher wages than the Japanese engaged in the same occupations. In the lumber industry, all races, including the East Indian, have been paid higher wages than the Japanese doing the same kind of work. As section hands and laborers in railway shops they have been paid as much or more than the Mexicans, but as a rule less than the white men of many races.

And so on. The lower wage level of Japanese workers reflects both a lower standard of living, and a desire to get a foothold in the labor market. As Iwata (1962:27) puts it: "Their willingness to accept even lower wages than laborers of other races enabled the Japanese to secure employment readily."

Millis (1915:155) describes a basket factory in Florin, California, where Japanese workers had displaced white female workers because the latter were unwilling to work more than ten hours a day or on weekends. The Japanese, anxious to return to Japan as quickly as possible, were willing to work twelve to fourteen hours per day and on weekends, thereby saving their employers the costs of a special overtime work force.

The Japanese immigrants developed political resources through a high degree of community organization. This could be used for the convenience of the employer, by solving his recruitment problems, seeing that work got done, and providing workers with board and lodging. In the case of seasonal labor, the Japanese community could provide for members during the off-season by various boarding arrangements and clubs, and by transporting labor to areas of demand (Ichihashi, 1932:172–6; Millis, 1915:44–5). These conveniences saved the employer money.[4]

As the reader may have noted, I have omitted a factor usually considered vital in determining the price of labor, i.e. differences in skills. I would contend, however, that this does not in itself lead to that difference in price for the same work which distinguishes a split labor market. While a skilled worker may be able to get a higher paying job, an unskilled laborer of another ethnicity may be trained to fill that job for the same wage. Skills are only indirectly important in that they can be used to develop political resources, which in turn may lead to a difference in wage level for the same work.

PRICE OF LABOR AND ETHNICITY

Ethnic differences need not always produce a price differential. Thus, if several ethnic groups who are approximately equal in resources and/or goals enter the same economic system, a split labor market will not develop. Alternatively, in a two-group contact situation, if one ethnic group occupies the position of a business elite and has no members in the labor force (or in a class that could easily be pushed into the labor force, e.g. low-capital farmers) then regardless of the other group's price, the labor market will not be split. This statement is a generalization of the point made by Harris (1964) that the critical difference in race relations between the deep south and Brazil was that the former had a white yeomanry in direct competition with ex-slaves, while the Portuguese only occupied the role of a business elite (plantation owners).

Conversely, a split labor force does not only stem from ethnic differences. For example, prison and female labor have often been cheaper than free male labor in Western societies. Prison labor has been cheap because prisoners lack political resources, while women often labor for supplementary incomes (cf. Hutchinson, 1968:59–61; Heneman and Yoder, 1965:543–4).

That initial price discrepancies in labor should ever fall along ethnic lines is a function of two forces. First, the original wage agreement arrived at between business and new labor often takes place in the labor group's point of origin. This is more obviously a feature of immigrant labor, but also occurs within a territory when conquered peoples enter their conquerors' economy. In other words, the wage agreement is often concluded within a national context, these nationalities coming to comprise the ethnic elements of the new labor market. One would thus expect the initial wages of co-nationals to be similar.

Second, nations or peoples that have lived relatively separately from one another are likely to have developed different employment motives and levels of resources (wealth, organization, communication channels). In other words, the factors that affect the price of labor are likely to differ grossly between nations, even though there may be considerable variation within each nation, and overlap between nations. Color differences in the initial price of labor only seem to be a factor because resources have historically been roughly correlated with color around the world.[5] When color and resources are not correlated in the "expected" way, then I would predict that price follows resources and motives rather than color.

In sum, the prejudices of business do not determine the price of labor, darker skinned or culturally different persons being paid less because of them. Rather, business tries to pay as little as possible for labor, regardless of ethnicity, and is held in check by the resources and motives of labor groups. Since these often vary by ethnicity, it is common to find ethnically split labor markets.

THE DYNAMICS OF SPLIT LABOR MARKETS

In split labor markets, conflict develops between three key classes: business, higher paid labor, and cheaper labor. The chief interests of these classes are as follows:

1. Business or Employers

This class aims at having as cheap and docile a labor force as possible to compete effectively with other businesses. If labor costs are too high (owing to such price determinants as unions), employers may turn to cheaper sources, importing overseas groups or using indigenous conquered populations. In the colony of Queensland in Australia, for example, it was believed that cotton farming would be the most suitable economic enterprise:

> However, such plantations (being too large) could not be worked, much less cleared, by their owners; neither could the work be done by European laborers because sufficient numbers of these were not available—while even had there been an adequate supply, the high rates of wages would have been prohibitive. This was a consideration which assumed vast importance when it was realized that cotton would have to be cultivated in

Queensland at a considerably lower cost than in the United States in order to compensate for the heavier freights from Queensland—the more
distant country from England. It seemed then that there was no possibility of successful competition with America unless the importation of
some form of cheap labor was permitted. (Moles, 1968:41)

Cheaper labor may be used to create a new industry having substantially
lower labor costs than the rest of the labor market, as in Queensland. Or they
may be used as strikebreakers or replacements to undercut a labor force trying to improve its bargaining position with business. If cheap labor is
unavailable, business may turn to mechanization, or try to relocate firms in
areas of the world where the price of labor is lower.

2. Higher Paid Labor

This class is very threatened by the introduction of cheaper labor into the
market, fearing that it will either force them to leave the territory or reduce
them to its level. If the labor market is split ethnically, the class antagonism
takes the form of ethnic antagonism. It is my contention (following Cox,
1948:411n) that, while much rhetoric of ethnic antagonism concentrates on
ethnicity and race, it really in large measure (though probably not entirely)
expresses this class conflict.

The group comprising higher paid labor may have two components. First,
it may include current employees demanding a greater share of the profits or
trying to maintain their position in the face of possible cuts. A second element is the small, independent, entrepreneur, like the subsistence farmer or
individual miner. The introduction of cheaper labor into these peoples' line
can undermine their position, since the employer of cheaper labor can produce at lower cost. The independent operator is then driven into the labor
market. The following sequence occurs in many colonies: settlement by
farmers who work their own land, the introduction of intensive farming using cheaper labor, a rise in land value and a consequent displacement of
independent farmers. The displaced class may move on (as occurred in many
of the West Indies when African slave labor was introduced to raise sugar),
but if it remains, it comes to play the role of higher paid labor.

The presence of cheaper labor in areas of the economy where higher paid
labor is not currently employed is also threatening to the latter, since the former attract older industries. The importance of potential competition
cannot be over-stressed. Oftentimes writers assert the irrationality of ethnic

antagonism when direct economic competition is not yet in evidence owing to few competitors having entered the labor market, or to competitors having concentrated in a few industries. Thus Daniels (1966:29) belittles the role of trade unions in the Asiatic Exclusion League by describing one of the major contributors as "an organization whose members, like most trade unionists in California, were never faced with job competition from Japanese." It does not take direct competition for members of a higher priced labor group to see the possible threat to their well-being, and to try to prevent its materializing. If they have reason to believe many more low-priced workers are likely to follow an initial "insignificant trickle" (as Daniels, 1966:1, describes the Japanese immigration, failing to mention that it was insignificant precisely because a larger anticipated flow had been thwarted, and diverted to Brazil), or if they see a large concentration of cheaper labor in a few industries which could easily be used to undercut them in their own, they will attempt to forestall undercutting.

Lest you think this fear misguided, take note that, when business could override the interests of more expensive labor, the latter have indeed been displaced or undercut. In British Guiana the local labor force, composed mainly of African ex-slaves, called a series of strikes in 1842 and 1847 against planters' attempts to reduce their wages. Plantation owners responded by using public funds to import over 50,000 cheaper East Indian indentured workers (Despres, 1969). A similar situation obtained in Mississippi, where Chinese were brought in to undercut freed blacks. Loewen (1971:23) describes the thinking of white land-owners: "the 'Chinaman' would not only himself supply a cheaper and less troublesome work force but in addition his presence as a threatening alternative would intimidate the Negro into resuming his former docile behavior." Such displacement has occurred not only to nonwhite more expensive labor, but, as the effects of slavery in the West Indies show, to whites by white capitalists.

3. Cheaper Labor

The employer uses this class partly to undermine the position of more expensive labor, through strikebreaking and undercutting. The forces that make the cheaper group cost less permit this to occur. In other words, either they lack the resources to resist an offer or use of force by business, or they seek a quick return to another economic and social base.

With the possible exception of sojourners, cheaper labor does not intentionally undermine more expensive labor; it is paradoxically its weakness that makes it so threatening, for business can more thoroughly control it. Cox makes this point (1948:417–8) in analyzing why Pacific coast white and Asian workers could not unite in a coalition against business:

> . . . the first generation of Asiatic workers is ordinarily very much under the control of labor contractors and employers, hence it is easier for the employer to frustrate any plans for their organization. Clearly this cultural bar helped antagonize white workers against the Asiatics. The latter were conceived of as being in alliance with the employer. It would probably have taken two or three generations before, say, the East Indian low-caste worker on the Coast became sufficiently Americanized to adjust easily to the policies and aims of organized labor.

Ethnic antagonism is specifically produced by the competition that arises from a price differential. An oversupply of equal-priced labor does not produce such antagonism, though it too threatens people with the loss of their job. However, hiring practices will not necessarily fall along ethnic lines, there being no advantage to the employer in hiring workers of one or another ethnicity. All workingmen are on the same footing, competing for scarce jobs (cf. Blalock, 1967:84–92, who uses this model of labor competition). When one ethnic group is decidedly cheaper than another (i.e. when the labor market is split) the higher paid worker faces more than the loss of his job; he faces the possibility that the wage standard in all jobs will be undermined by cheaper labor.

VICTORY FOR MORE EXPENSIVE LABOR

If an expensive labor group is strong enough (strength generally depending on the same factors that influence price), they may be able to resist being displaced. Both exclusion and caste systems represent such victories for higher paid labor.

1. Exclusion

Exclusion movements generally occur when the majority of a cheaper labor group resides outside a given territory but desires to enter it (often at the request of business groups). The exclusion movement tries to prevent the physical presence of cheaper labor in the employment area, thereby preserving a non-split, higher priced labor market.

There are many examples of exclusion attempts around the world. In Australia, for instance, a group of white workers was able to prevent capitalists from importing cheaper labor from India, China, Japan, and the Pacific Islands. Attempts at importation were met with strikes, boycotts, petitions, and deputations (Willard, 1967:51–7). Ultimately, organized white labor pressed for strong exclusion measures, and vigilantly ensured their enforcement. As Yarwood (1964:151–2) puts it: "A comparison of the records of various governments during our period [1896–1923] leaves no doubt as to the special role of the Labour Party as the guardian of the ports." In other words, a white Australia policy (i.e. the exclusion of Asian and Polynesian immigrants) appears to have sprung from a conflict of interests between employers who wanted to import cheap labor, and a labor force sufficiently organized to ward off such a move.

California's treatment of Chinese and Japanese labor is another example of exclusion. A socialist, Cameron H. King, Jr., articulates the threatened labor group's position:

> Unskilled labor has felt this competition [from the Japanese] for some time being compelled to relinquish job after job to the low standard of living it could not endure. The unskilled laborers are largely unorganized and voiceless. But as the tide rises it is reaching the skilled laborers and the small merchants. These are neither unorganized nor voiceless, and viewing the menace to their livelihood they loudly demand protection of their material interests. We of the Pacific Coast certainly know that exclusion is an effective solution. In the seventh decade of the nineteenth century the problem arose of the immigration of Chinese laborers. The Republican and Democratic parties failed to give heed to the necessities of the situation and the Workingman's party arose and swept the state with the campaign cry of "The Chinese must go." Then the two old parties woke up and have since realized that to hold the labor vote they must stand for Asiatic exclusion. (King, 1908:665–6)

King wrote this around the time of the Gentlemen's Agreement, an arrangement of the U.S. and Japanese governments to prevent further immigration of Japanese labor to the Pacific Coast (Bailey, 1934). The Agreement was aimed specifically at labor and not other Japanese immigrants, suggesting that economic and not racial factors were at issue.

Exclusion movements clearly serve the interests of higher paid labor. Its standards are protected, while the capitalist class is deprived of cheaper labor.

2. Caste

If cheaper labor is present in the market, and cannot be excluded, then higher paid labor will resort to a caste arrangement, which depends on exclusiveness rather than exclusion. Caste is essentially an aristocracy of labor (a term borrowed from Lenin, e.g. 1964), in which higher paid labor deals with the undercutting potential of cheaper labor by excluding them from certain types of work. The higher paid group controls certain jobs exclusively and gets paid at one scale of wages, while the cheaper group is restricted to another set of jobs and is paid at a lower scale. The labor market split is submerged because the differentially priced workers ideally never occupy the same position.

Ethnically distinct cheaper groups (as opposed to women, for example, who face a caste arrangement in many Western societies) may reside in a territory for two reasons: either they were indigenous or they were imported early in capitalist-labor relations, when the higher paid group could not prevent the move. Two outstanding examples of labor aristocracies based on ethnicity are South Africa, where cheaper labor was primarily indigenous, and the U.S. South, where they were imported as slaves.

Unlike exclusion movements, caste systems retain the underlying reality of a price differential, for if a member of the subordinate group were to occupy the same position as a member of the stronger labor group he would be paid less. Hence, caste systems tend to become rigid and vigilant, developing an elaborate battery of laws, customs, and beliefs aimed to prevent undercutting. The victory has three facets. First, the higher paid group tries to ensure its power in relation to business by monopolizing the acquisition of certain essential skills, thereby ensuring the effectiveness of strike action, or by controlling such important resources as purchasing power. Second, it tries to prevent the immediate use of cheaper labor as undercutters and strikebreakers by denying them access to general education thereby making their training as quick replacements more difficult, or by ensuring through such devices as "influx control" that the cheaper group will retain a base in their traditional economies. The latter move ensures a backward-sloping labor supply function (cf. Berg, 1966) undesirable to business. Third, it tries to weaken the cheaper group politically, to prevent their pushing for those resources that would make them useful as undercutters. In other words, the solution to the devastating potential of weak, cheap labor is, paradoxically, to weaken them further, until it is no longer in business' immediate interest to use them as replacements.

South Africa is perhaps the most extreme modern example of an ethnic caste system. A split labor market first appeared there in the mining industry. With the discovery of diamonds in 1869, a white working class emerged.[6] At first individual whites did the searching, but, as with the displacement of small farms by plantations, they were displaced by consolidated, high-capital operations, and became employees of the latter (Doxey, 1961:18). It was this class together with imported skilled miners from Cornwall (lured to Africa by high wages) which fought the capitalists over the use of African labor. Africans were cheaper because they came to the mines with a fixed income goal (e.g. the price of a rifle) and did not view the mines as their main source of livelihood. By contrast, European workers remained in the mines and developed organizations to further their interests.

Clearly, it would have been to the advantage of businessmen, once they knew the skills involved, to train Africans to replace the white miners at a fraction of the cost; but this did not happen. The mining companies accepted a labor aristocracy, not out of ethnic solidarity with the white workers but:

> (as was to be the case throughout the later history of mining) they had little or no choice because of the collective strength of the white miners. . . . The pattern which was to emerge was that of the Europeans showing every sign of preparedness to use their collective strength to ensure their exclusive supremacy in the labour market. Gradually the concept of trade unionism, and, for that matter, of socialism, became accepted in the minds of the European artisans as the means of maintaining their own position against non-white inroads. (Doxey, 1961:23–4)

The final showdown between mine owners and white workers occurred in the 1920s when the owners tried to substitute cheaper non-white labor for white labor in certain semi-skilled occupations. This move precipitated the "Rand Revolt," a general strike of white workers on the Witwatersrand, countered by the calling in of troops and the declaration of martial law. The result was a coalition between Afrikaner nationalists (predominantly workers and small-scale farmers being pushed off the land by larger, British-owned farms) and the English-speaking Labor Party (Van der Horst, 1965:117–8). The Revolt "showed the lengths to which white labour was prepared to go to defend its privileged position. From that time on, mine managements have never directly challenged the colour-bar in the mining industry" (Van der Horst, 1965:118).

The legislative history of much of South Africa (and of the post-bellum Deep South) consists in attempts by higher priced white labor to ward off undercutting by cheaper groups, and to entrench its exclusive control of certain jobs.[7]

This interpretation of caste contrasts with the Marxist argument that the capitalist class purposefully plays off one segment of the working class against the other (e.g. Reich, 1971). Business, I would contend, rather than desiring to protect a segment of the working class supports a liberal or laissez-faire ideology that would permit all workers to compete freely in an open market. Such open competition would displace higher paid labor. Only under duress does business yield to labor aristocracy, a point made in *Deep South*, a book written when the depression had caused the displacement of white tenant farmers and industrial workers by blacks:

> The economic interests of these groups [employers] would also demand that cheaper colored labor should be employed in the "white collar" jobs in business offices, governmental offices, stores, and banks. In this field, however, the interests of the employer group conflict not only with those of the lower economic group of whites but also with those of the more literate and aggressive middle group of whites. A white store which employed colored clerks, for example, would be boycotted by both these groups. The taboo upon the employment of colored workers in such fields is the result of the political and purchasing power of the white middle and lower groups. (Davis, *et. al.*, 1941:480)

In sum, exclusion and caste are similar reactions to a split labor market. They represent victories for higher paid labor. The victory of exclusion is more complete in that cheaper labor is less available to business. For this reason I would hypothesize that a higher paid group prefers exclusion to caste, even though exclusion means they have to do the dirty work. Evidence for this comes from Australia where, in early attempts to import Asian labor, business tried to buy off white labor's opposition by offering to form them into a class of "mechanics" and foremen over the "coolies" (Yarwood, 1968:16, 42). The offer was heartily rejected in favor of exclusion. Apartheid in South Africa can be seen as an attempt to move from caste to the exclusion of the African work force.

Most of our examples have contained a white capitalist class, a higher paid white labor group, and a cheaper, non-white labor group. Conditions in

Europe and around the world, and not skin color, yield such models. White capitalists would gladly dispense with and undercut their white working-class brethren if they could, and have done so whenever they had the opportunity. In the words of one agitator for excluding Chinese from the U.S. Pacific coast: "I have seen men . . . American born, who certainly would, if I may use a strong expression, employ devils from Hell if the devils would work for 25 cents less than a white man" (cited in Daniels and Kitano, 1970:43).

In addition, cases have occurred of white workers playing the role of cheap labor, and facing the same kind of ethnic antagonism as non-white workers. Consider the riots against Italian strikebreakers in the coal fields of Pennsylvania in 1874 (Higham, 1965:47–8). In the words of one writer: "Unions resented the apparently inexhaustible cheap and relatively docile labor supply which was streaming from Europe obviously for the benefit of their employers" (Wittke, 1953:10).

Even when no ethnic differences exist, split labor markets may produce ethnic-like antagonism. Carey McWilliams (1945:82–3) describes an instance:

> During the depression years, "Old Stock"—that is, white, Protestant, Anglo-Saxon Americans, from Oklahoma, Arkansas, and Texas—were roundly denounced in California as "interlopers." The same charges were made against them that were made against the Japanese: they were "dirty"; they had "enormous families"; they engaged in unfair competition; they threatened to "invade" the state and to "undermine" its institutions. During these turgid years (1930–1938) California attempted *to exclude*, by various extra-legal devices, those yeoman farmers just as it had excluded the Chinese and Japanese. "Okies" were "inferior" and "immoral." There was much family discord when Okie girl met California boy, and vice versa. . . . The prejudice against the Okies was obviously not "race" prejudice; yet it functioned in much the same manner.

CONCLUSION

Obviously, this type of three-way conflict is not the only important factor in ethnic relations. But it does help explain some puzzles, including, of course, the exclusion-caste anomaly. For example, Philip Mason (1970:64) develops

Category		
Domination	Paternalism	Competition
	Situations	
South Africa	Nigeria	Britain
(1960)	(1952)	(1968)
1–4	1–2000	50–1
U. S. South	Nyasaland	U.S. North
(1960)	(1966)	(1960)
4–1	1–570	15–1
Rhodesia	Tanganyika	New Zealand
(1960)		
1–16	1–450	13–1
	Uganda	
	1–650	
Adapted from Mason (1970:64)		

Table 10.2   Numerical Proportion of Dominant to Subordinate Ethnic Groups

a typology of race relations and finds that it relates to numerical proportions without being able to explain the dynamic behind this correlation. Table 10.2 presents a modified version of his chart. My theory can explain these relationships. Paternalism arises in situations where the cleavage between business and labor corresponds to an ethnic difference. A small business elite rules a large group of workers who entered the labor market at approximately the same price or strength. No split labor market existed, hence no ethnic caste system arises. The higher proportion of the dominant ethnicity under "Domination" means that part of the dominant group must be working class. A labor element that shares ethnicity with people who have sufficient resources to become the business elite is generally likely to come from a fairly wealthy country and have resources of its own. Such systems are likely to develop split labor markets. Finally, competition has under it societies whose cheaper labor groups have not been a major threat because the indigenous population available as cheap labor has been small and/or exclusion has effectively kept business groups from importing cheap labor in large numbers.

This theory helps elucidate other observations. One is the underlying similarity in the situation of blacks and women. Another is the history of political sympathy between California and the South. And, a third is the conservatism of the American white working class, or what Daniels and Kitano (1970:45) consider to be an "essential paradox of American life: [that]

movements for economic democracy have usually been violently opposed to a thorough-going ethnic democracy." Without having to resort to psychological constructs like "authoritarianism," this theory is able to explain the apparent paradox.

In sum, in comparing those countries with the most ethnic antagonism with those having the least, it is evident that the difference does not lie in the fact that the former are Protestant and the latter Catholic: Protestants are found in all three of Mason's types, and Hawaii is a Protestant-dominated territory. It does not lie in whether the dominant or subordinate group moves: South Africa and the Deep South show opposite patterns of movement. It is evident that some of the most antagonistic territories have been British colonies, but not all British colonies have had this attribute. The characteristic that those British colonies and other societies high on ethnic antagonism share is that they all have a powerful white, or more generally higher paid, working class.

Notes

[1] I do not wish to enter the debate over the applicability of the term "caste" to race relations (cf. Cox, 1948; Davis, et al., 1941). It is used here only for convenience and implies no particular theoretical bent.

[2] The term "exclusion" has not usually been applied to immigrant quotas imposed on eastern and southern European immigrants; but such restrictions were, in effect, indistinguishable from the restrictions placed on Japanese immigration.

[3] This usage contrasts with that of van den Berghe (1967a:9–10) who reserves the term "ethnic" for groups socially defined by cultural differences. In his definition, ethnicity is not necessarily inherited. I would contend that, while persons of mixed ancestry may be problematic and are often assigned arbitrarily by the societies in which they reside, inheritance is implied in the common application of the word.

[4] Sojourners often use their political resources and low price of labor to enter business for themselves (a process which will be fully analyzed in another paper). This does not remove the split in the labor market, though it makes the conflict more complex.

[5] It is, of course, no accident that color and resources have been historically related. Poverty among non-white nations has in part resulted from European imperialism. Nevertheless, I would argue that the critical factor in the development of ethnic segmentation in a country is the meeting that occurs in the labor market of that country. The larger economic forces help determine the resources of entering parties, but it is not such forces to which workers respond. Rather they react to the immediate conflicts and threats in their daily lives.

[6] Such a split was not found in the early Cape Colony, where business was one ethnicity— white, and labor another—non-white. Actually in neither case was the ethnic composition simple or homogeneous; but the important fact is that, among the laborers, who included so-called Hottentots, and slaves from Madagascar, Mozambique, and the East Indies (cf. van den Berghe, 1967b:14), no element was significantly more expensive. The early Cape is thus structurally similar, in terms of the variables I consider important, to countries like Brazil and

Mexico. And it is also noted for its "softened" tone of race relations as reflected in such practices as intermarriage.

[7] Ethnically based labor aristocracies are much less sensitive about cheap labor in any form than are systems that do not arrive at this resolution because they are protected from it. Thus, Sutherland and Cressey (1970:561–2) report that both the deep south and South Africa continue to use various forms of prison contract labor, in contrast to the northern U.S. where the contract system was attacked by rising labor organizations as early as 1880.

REFERENCES

Bailey, Thomas A. 1934. Theodore Roosevelt and the Japanese-American Crises. Stanford: Stanford University Press.

Becker, Gary. 1957. The Economics of Discrimination. Chicago: University of Chicago Press.

Berg, E. J. 1966. "Backward-sloping labor supply functions in dual economies—the Africa case." Pp. 114–136 in Immanuel Wallerstein (ed.), Social Change: The Colonial Situation. New York: Wiley.

Blalock, H. M., Jr. 1967. Toward a Theory of Minority-Group Relations. New York: Wiley.

Blauner, Robert. 1969. "Internal colonialism and ghetto revolt." Social Problems 16 (Spring): 393–408.

Cox, Oliver C. 1948. Caste, Class and Race. New York: Modern Reader.

Daniels, Roger. 1966. The Politics of Prejudice. Gloucester, Massachusetts: Peter Smith.

Daniels, Roger, and Harry H. L. Kitano. 1970. American Racism. Englewood Cliffs: Prentice-Hall.

Davis, Allison W., B. B. Gardner, and M. R. Gardner. 1941. Deep South. Chicago: University of Chicago Press.

Despres, Leo A. 1969. "Differential adaptations and micro-cultural evolution in Guyana." Southwestern Journal of Anthropology 25 (Spring):14–44.

Doxey, G. V. 1961. The Industrial Colour Bar in South Africa. Cape Town: Oxford University Press.

Ferguson-Davie, C. J. 1952. The Early History of Indians in Natal. Johannesburg: South African Institute of Race Relations.

Gillion, K. L. 1962. Fiji's Indian Migrants. Melbourne: Oxford University Press.

Harris, Marvin. 1964. Patterns of Race in the Americas. New York: Walker.

Heneman, H. G., and Dale Yoder. 1965. Labor Economics. Cincinnati: Southwestern.

Higham, John. 1965. Strangers in the Land. New York: Athenium.

Hutchison, Emilie J. 1968. Women's Wages. New York: Ams Press.

Ichihashi, Yamato. 1932. Japanese in the United States. Stanford: Stanford University Press.

Iwata, Masakazu. 1962. "The Japanese immigrants in California agriculture." Agricultural History 36 (January):25–37.

King, Cameron H., Jr. 1908. "Asiatic exclusion." International Socialist Review 8 (May): 661–669.

Lenin, V. I. 1964. "Imperialism and the split in socialism." Pp. 105–120 in Collected Works, Volume 23, August 1916–March 1917. Moscow: Progress.

Lieberson, Stanley. 1961. "A societal theory of race and ethnic relations." American Sociological Review 26 (December):902–910.

Lind, Andrew W. 1968. An Island Community. New York: Greenwood.

Loewen, James W. 1971. The Mississippi Chinese. Cambridge: Harvard University Press.

Mason, Philip. 1970. Patterns of Dominance. London: Oxford University Press.

McWilliams, Carey. 1945. Prejudice: Japanese-Americans. Boston: Little, Brown.

Millis, H. A. 1915. The Japanese Problem in the United States. New York: Macmillan.

Moles, I. N. 1968. "The Indian coolie labour issue." Pp. 40–48 in A. T. Yarwood (ed.), Attitudes to Non-European Immigration. Melbourne: Cassell Australia.

Noel, Donald L. 1968. "A theory of the origin of ethnic stratification." Social Problems 16 (Fall):157–172.

Reich, Michael. 1971. "The economics of racism." Pp. 107–113 in David M. Gordon (ed.), Problems in Political Economy. Lexington, Massachusetts: Heath.

Schermerhorn, R. A. 1970. Comparative Ethnic Relations. New York: Random House.

Shibutani, Tamotsu, and Kian M. Kwan. 1965. Ethnic Stratification. New York: Macmillan.

Siu, Paul C. P. 1952. "The sojourner." American Journal of Sociology 58 (July):34–44.

Sutherland, Edwin H., and Donald R. Cressey. 1970. Criminology. Philadelphia: Lippincott.

van den Berghe, Pierre L. 1966. "Paternalistic versus competitive race relations: an ideal-type approach." Pp. 53–69 in Bernard E. Segal (ed.), Racial and Ethnic Relations. New York: Crowell.

_____. 1967a. Race and Racism. New York: Wiley.

_____. 1967b. South Africa: A Study in Conflict. Berkeley: University of California Press.

Van der Horst, Sheila T. 1965. "The effects of industrialization on race relations in South Africa." Pp. 97–140 in Guy Hunter (ed.), Industrialization and Race Relations. London: Oxford University Press.

Willard, Myra. 1967. History of the White Australia Policy to 1920. London: Melbourne University Press.

Williams, Eric. 1944. Capitalism and Slavery. Chapel Hill: University of North Carolina Press.

Wittke, Carl. 1953. "Immigration policy prior to World War I." Pp. 1–10 in Benjamin M. Ziegler (ed.), Immigration: An American Dilemma. Boston: Heath.

Yarwood, A. T. 1964. Asian Immigration to Australia. London: Cambridge University Press.

Yarwood, A. T. (ed.). 1968. Attitudes to Non-European Immigration. Melbourne: Cassell Australia.

11

THE DECLINING
SIGNIFICANCE OF RACE

BLACKS AND CHANGING
AMERICAN INSTITUTIONS

William Julius Wilson

◆◆◆

Race relations in America have undergone fundamental changes in recent years, so much so that now the life chances of individual blacks
have more to do with their economic class position than with their day-to-
day encounters with whites. In earlier years the systematic efforts of whites
to suppress blacks were obvious to even the most insensitive observer.
Blacks were denied access to valued and scarce resources through various in-
genious schemes of racial exploitation, discrimination, and segregation,
schemes that were reinforced by elaborate ideologies of racism. But the situation has changed. However determinative such practices were for the
previous efforts of the black population to achieve racial equality, and however significant they were in the creation of poverty-stricken ghettoes and a
vast underclass of black proletarians—that massive population at the very

William Julius Wilson, *The Declining Significance of Race: Blacks and Changing American Institutions,* pp.
1–9, 12–23, 183–185. Copyright 1978 by the University of Chicago Press.

bottom of the social class ladder plagued by poor education and low-paying, unstable jobs—they do not provide a meaningful explanation of the life chances of black Americans today. The traditional patterns of interaction between blacks and whites, particularly in the labor market, have been fundamentally altered.

In the antebellum period, and in the latter half of the nineteenth century through the first half of the twentieth century, the continuous and explicit efforts of whites to construct racial barriers profoundly affected the lives of black Americans. Racial oppression was deliberate, overt, and is easily documented, ranging from slavery to segregation, from the endeavors of the white economic elite to exploit black labor to the actions of the white masses to eliminate or neutralize black competition, particularly economic competition.[1] As the nation has entered the latter half of the twentieth century, however, many of the traditional barriers have crumbled under the weight of the political, social, and economic changes of the civil rights era. A new set of obstacles has emerged from basic structural shifts in the economy. These obstacles are therefore impersonal but may prove to be even more formidable for certain segments of the black population. Specifically, whereas the previous barriers were usually designed to control and restrict the entire black population, the new barriers create hardships essentially for the black underclass; whereas the old barriers were based explicitly on racial motivations derived from intergroup contact, the new barriers have racial significance only in their consequences, not in their origins. In short, whereas the old barriers bore the pervasive features of racial oppression, the new barriers indicate an important and emerging form of class subordination.

It would be shortsighted to view the traditional forms of racial segregation and discrimination as having essentially disappeared in contemporary America; the presence of blacks is still firmly resisted in various institutions and social arrangements, for example, residential areas and private social clubs. However, in the economic sphere, class has become more important than race in determining black access to privilege and power. It is clearly evident in this connection that many talented and educated blacks are now entering positions of prestige and influence at a rate comparable to or, in some situations, exceeding that of whites with equivalent qualifications. It is equally clear that the black underclass is in a hopeless state of economic stagnation, falling further and further behind the rest of society. . . .

THREE STAGES OF AMERICAN RACE RELATIONS

My basic thesis is that American society has experienced three major stages of black-white contact and that each stage embodies a different form of racial stratification structured by the particular arrangement of both the economy and the polity. Stage one coincides with antebellum slavery and the early postbellum era and may be designated the period of *plantation economy and racial-caste oppression*. Stage two begins in the last quarter of the nineteenth century and ends at roughly the New Deal era and may be identified as the period of *industrial expansion, class conflict, and racial oppression*. Finally, stage three is associated with the modern, industrial, post–World War II era, which really began to crystallize during the 1960s and 1970s, and may be characterized as the period of *progressive transition from racial inequalities to class inequalities*. For the sake of brevity I shall identify the different periods respectively as the preindustrial, industrial, and modern industrial stages of American race relations.

Although this abbreviated designation of the periods of American race re-lations seems to relate racial change to fundamental economic changes rather directly, it bears repeating that the different stages of race relations are struc-tured by the unique arrangements and interactions of the economy and the polity. Although I stress the economic basis of structured racial inequality in the preindustrial and industrial periods of race relations, I also attempt to show how the polity more or less interacted with the economy either to re-inforce patterns of racial stratification or to mediate various forms of racial conflict. Moreover, for the modern industrial period, I try to show how race relations have been shaped as much by important economic changes as by important political changes. Indeed, it would not be possible to understand fully the subtle and manifest changes in race relations in the modern indus-trial period without recognizing the dual and often reciprocal influence of structural changes in the economy and political changes in the state. Thus, my central argument is that different systems of production and/or different arrangements of the polity have imposed different constraints on the way in which racial groups have interacted in the United States, constraints that have structured the relations between racial groups and that have produced dissimilar contexts not only for the manifestation of racial antagonisms but also for racial group access to rewards and privileges.

In contrast to the modern industrial period in which fundamental eco-nomic and political changes have made economic class affiliation more important than race in determining Negro prospects for occupational advancement, the preindustrial and industrial periods of black-white relations have one central feature in common, namely, overt efforts of whites to solidify economic racial domination (ranging from the manipulation of black labor to the neutralization or elimination of black economic competition) through various forms of juridical, political, and social discrimination. Since racial problems during these two periods were principally related to group struggles over economic resources, they readily lend themselves to the economic class theories of racial antagonisms that associate racial antipathy with class conflict. A brief consideration of these theories, followed by a discussion of their basic weaknesses, will help to raise a number of theoretical issues that will be useful for analyzing the dynamics of racial conflict in the preindustrial and industrial stages of American race relations. However, in a later section of this chapter I shall attempt to explain why these theories are not very relevant to the modern industrial stage of American race relations.

ECONOMIC CLASS THEORIES

Students of race relations have paid considerable attention to the economic basis of racial antagonism in recent years, particularly to the theme that racial problems in historical situations are related to the more general problems of economic class conflict. A common assumption of this theme is that racial conflict is merely a special manifestation of class conflict. Accordingly, ideologies of racism, racial prejudices, institutionalized discrimination, segregation, and other factors that reinforce or embody racial stratification are seen as simply part of a superstructure determined and shaped by the particular arrangement of the class structure.[2] However, given this basic assumption, which continues to be the most representative and widely used economic class argument,[3] proponents have advanced two major and somewhat divergent explanations of how class conflicts actually shape and determine racial relations—the orthodox Marxist theory of capitalist exploitation,[4] and the *split labor-market theory* of working-class antagonisms.[5]

The orthodox Marxist theory, which is the most popular variant of the Marxists' explanations of race,[6] postulates that because the ultimate goal of the capitalist class is to maximize profits, efforts will be made to suppress workers' demands for increased wages and to weaken their bargaining power by promoting divisions within their ranks. The divisions occur along racial lines to the extent that the capitalist class is able to isolate the lower-priced black labor force by not only supporting job, housing, and educational discrimination against blacks, but also by developing or encouraging racial prejudices and ideologies of racial subjugation such as racism. The net effect of such a policy is to insure a marginal working class of blacks and to establish a relatively more privileged position for the established white labor force. Since discrimination guarantees a situation where the average wage rate of the black labor force is less than the average wage rate of the established white labor force, the probability of labor solidarity against the capitalist class is diminished.

At the same time, orthodox Marxists argue, the members of the capitalist class benefit not only because they have created a reserved army of labor that is not united against them and the appropriation of surplus from the black labor force is greater than the exploitation rate of the white labor force,[7] but also because they can counteract ambitious claims of the white labor force for higher wages either by threatening to increase the average wage rate of black workers or by replacing segments of the white labor force with segments of the black labor force in special situations such as strikes. The weaker the national labor force, the more likely it is that it will be replaced by lower-paid black labor especially during organized strikes demanding wage increases and improved working conditions. In short, orthodox Marxists argue that racial antagonism is designed to be a "mask for privilege" that effectively conceals the efforts of the ruling class to exploit subordinate minority groups and divide the working class.

In interesting contrast to the orthodox Marxist approach, the split labor-market theory posits the view that rather than attempting to protect a segment of the laboring class, business "supports a liberal or *laissez faire* ideology that would permit all workers to compete freely in an open market. Such open competition would displace higher paid labor. Only under duress does business yield to a labor aristocracy [i.e., a privileged position for white workers]."[8]

The central hypothesis of the split labor-market theory is that racial antagonism first develops in a labor market split along racial lines. The term "antagonism" includes all aspects of intergroup conflict, from beliefs and ideologies (e.g., racism), to overt behavior (e.g., discrimination), to institutions (e.g., segregationist laws). A split labor market occurs when the price of labor for the same work differs for at least two groups, or would differ if they performed the same work. The price of labor "refers to labor's total cost to the employer, including not only wages, but the cost of recruitment, transportation, room and board, education, health care (if the employer must bear these), and the cost of labor unrest."[9]

There are three distinct classes in a split labor market: (1) business or employers; (2) higher-paid labor; and (3) cheaper labor. Conflict develops between these three classes because of different interests. The main goal of business or employers is to maintain as cheap a labor force as possible in order to compete effectively with other businesses and to maximize economic returns. Employers will often import laborers from other areas if local labor costs are too high or if there is a labor shortage. Whenever a labor shortage exists, higher-paid labor is in a good bargaining position. Accordingly, if business is able to attract cheaper labor to the market place, the interests of higher-paid labor are threatened. They may lose some of the privileges they enjoy, they may lose their bargaining power, and they may even lose their jobs. Moreover, the presence of cheaper labor in a particular job market may not only represent actual competition but potential competition as well. An "insignificant trickle" could be seen as the beginning of a major immigration. If the labor market is split along ethnic lines, for example, if higher-paid labor is white and lower-paid labor is black, class antagonisms are transformed into racial antagonisms. Thus, "while much rhetoric of ethnic antagonism concentrates on ethnicity and race, it really in large measure (though probably not entirely) expresses this class conflict."[10]

In some cases members of the lower-paid laboring class, either from within the territorial boundaries of a given country or from another country, are drawn into or motivated to enter a labor market because they feel they can improve their standard of living. As Edna Bonacich points out, "the poorer the economy of the recruits, the less the inducement needed for them to enter the new labor market."[11] In other cases, individuals are forced into a new labor-market situation, such as the involuntary migration of blacks into a condition of slavery in the United States. In this connection, the greater the employer's control over lower-priced labor, the more threatening is lower-paid labor to higher-paid labor.

However, if more expensive labor is strong enough, that is, if it possesses the power resources to preserve its economic interests, it can prevent being replaced or undercut by cheaper labor. On the one hand it can exclude lower-paid labor from a given territory. "Exclusion movements clearly serve the interests of higher paid labor. Its standards are protected, while the capitalist class is deprived of cheaper labor."[12] On the other hand, if it is not possible for higher-paid labor to rely on exclusion (cheaper labor may be indigenous to the territory or may have been imported early in business-labor relations when higher-paid labor could not prevent the move) then it will institutionalize a system of ethnic stratification which could (1) monopolize skilled positions, thereby ensuring the effectiveness of strike action; (2) prevent cheaper labor from developing the skills necessary to compete with higher-paid labor (for example, by imposing barriers to equal access to education); and (3) deny cheaper labor the political resources that would enable them to undercut higher-paid labor through, say, governmental regulations. "In other words, the solution to the devastating potential of weak, cheap labor is, paradoxically, to weaken them further, until it is no longer in business' immediate interest to use them as replacement."[13] Thus, whereas orthodox Marxist arguments associate the development and institutionalization of racial stratification with the motivations and activities of the capitalist class, the split labor-market theory traces racial stratification directly to the powerful, higher-paid working class.

Implicit in both of these economic class theories is a power-conflict thesis associating the regulation of labor or wages with properties (ownership of land or capital, monopolization of skilled positions) that determine the scope and degree of a group's ability to influence behavior in the labor market. Furthermore, both theories clearly demonstrate the need to focus on the different ways and situations in which various segments of the dominant racial group perceive and respond to the subordinate racial group. However, as I examine the historical stages of race relations in the United States, I find that the patterns of black/white interaction do not consistently and sometimes do not conveniently conform to the propositions outlined in these explanations of racial antagonism. In some cases, the orthodox Marxian explanation seems more appropriate; in other instances, the split labor-market theory seems more appropriate; and in still others, neither theory can, in isolation, adequately explain black-white conflict.

If we restrict our attention for the moment to the struggle over economic resources, then the general pattern that seems to have characterized race relations in the United States during the preindustrial and industrial stages was that the economic elite segments of the white population have been principally responsible for those forms of racial inequality that entail the exploitation of labor (as in slavery), whereas whites in the lower strata have been largely responsible for those forms of imposed racial stratification that are designed to eliminate economic competition (as in job segregation). Moreover, in some situations, the capitalist class and white workers form an alliance to keep blacks suppressed. Accordingly, restrictive arguments to the effect that racial stratification was the work of the capitalist class or was due to the "victory" of higher-paid white labor obscure the dynamics of complex and variable patterns of black-white interaction.

However, if we ignore the more categorical assertions that attribute responsibility for racial stratification to a particular class and focus seriously on the analyses of interracial contact in the labor market, then I will be able to demonstrate that, depending on the historical situation, each of the economic class theories provides arguments that help to illuminate race relations during the preindustrial and industrial periods of black-white contact. By the same token, I hope to explain why these theories have little application to the third, and present, stage of modern industrial race relations. My basic argument is that the meaningful application of the arguments in each theory for any given historical period depends considerably on knowledge of the constraints imposed by the particular systems of production and by the particular laws and policies of the state during that period, constraints that shape the structural relations between racial and class groups and which thereby produce different patterns of intergroup interaction. . . .

The Influence of the System of Production

The term "system of production" not only refers to the technological basis of economic processes or, in Karl Marx's terms, the "forces of production," but it also implies the "social relations of production," that is, "the interaction (for example, through employment and property arrangement) into which men enter at a given level of the development of the forces of production."[14] As I previously indicated, different systems of production impose constraints on racial group interaction. In the remainder of this section I should like to provide a firmer analytical basis for this distinction as it applies specifically to the three stages of American race relations, incorporating in my discussion relevant theoretical points raised in the foregoing sections of this chapter.

It has repeatedly been the case that a non-manufacturing or plantation economy with a simple division of labor and a small aristocracy that dominates the economic and political life of a society has characteristically generated a paternalistic rather than a competitive form of race relations, and the antebellum South was no exception.[15] Paternalistic racial patterns reveal close symbiotic relationships marked by dominance and subservience, great social distance and little physical distance, and clearly symbolized rituals of racial etiquette. The southern white aristocracy created a split labor market along racial lines by enslaving blacks to perform tasks at a cheaper cost than free laborers of the dominant group. This preindustrial form of race relations was not based on the actions of dominant-group laborers, who, as we shall see, were relatively powerless to effect significant change in race relations during this period, but on the structure of the relations established by the aristocracy. Let me briefly amplify this point.

In the southern plantation economy, public power was overwhelmingly concentrated in the hands of the white aristocracy. This power was not only reflected in the control of economic resources and in the development of a juridical system that expressed the class interests of the aristocracy, but also in the way the aristocracy was able to impose its viewpoint on the larger society.[16] This is not to suggest that these aspects of public power have not been disproportionately controlled by the economic elite in modern industrialized Western societies; rather it indicates that the hegemony of the southern ruling elite was much greater in degree, not in kind, than in these societies. The southern elite's hegemony was embodied in an economy that required little horizontal or vertical mobility. Further, because of the absence of those gradations of labor power associated with complex divisions of labor, white workers in the antebellum and early postbellum South had little opportunity to challenge the control of the aristocracy. Because white laborers lacked power resources in the southern plantation economy, their influence on the form and quality of racial stratification was minimal throughout the antebellum and early postbellum periods. Racial stratification therefore primarily reflected the relationships established between blacks and the white aristocracy, relationships which were not characterized by competition for scarce resources but by the exploitation of black labor.[17] Social distance tended to be clearly symbolized by rituals of racial etiquette: gestures and behavior reflecting dominance and subservience. Consequently, any effort to impose a system of public segregation was superfluous. Furthermore, since the social gap between the aristocracy and black slaves was wide and stable, ideologies of racism played less of a role in the subordination of blacks than they subsequently did in the more competitive systems of race relations following the Civil War. In short, the relationship represented intergroup paternalism because it allowed for "close symbiosis and even intimacy, without any threat to status inequalities."[18] This was in sharp contrast to the more competitive forms of race relations that accompanied the development of industrial capitalism in the late nineteenth century and first few decades of the twentieth century (the industrial period of American race relations), wherein the complex division of labor and opportunities for greater mobility not only produced interaction, competition, and labor-market conflict between blacks and the white working class, but also provided the latter with superior resources (relative to those they possessed under the plantation economy) to exert greater influence on the form and content of racial stratification.

The importance of the system of production in understanding race relations is seen in a comparison of Brazil and the southern United States during the post-slavery periods. In the United States, the southern economy experienced a fairly rapid rate of expansion during the late nineteenth century, thereby creating various middle level skilled and unskilled positions that working-class whites attempted to monopolize for themselves. The efforts of white workers to eliminate black competition in the South generated an elaborate system of Jim Crow segregation that was reinforced by an ideology of biological racism. The white working class was aided not only by its numerical size, but also by its increasing accumulation of political resources that accompanied changes in its relation to the means of production.

As white workers gradually translated their increasing labor power into political power, blacks experienced greater restrictions in their efforts to achieve a satisfactory economic, political, and social life. In Brazil, on the other hand, the large Negro and mulatto population was not thrust into competition with the much smaller white population over access to higher-status positions because, as Marvin Harris notes, "there was little opportunity for any member of the lower class to move upward in the social hierarchy."[19] No economic class group or racial group had much to gain by instituting a rigid system of racial segregation or cultivating an ideology of racial inferiority. Racial distinctions were insignificant to the landed aristocracy, who constituted a numerically small upper class in what was basically a sharply differentiated two-class society originally shaped during slavery. The mulattoes, Negroes, and poor whites were all in the same impoverished lower-ranking position. "The general economic stagnation which has been characteristic of lowland Latin America since the abolition of slavery," observes Marvin Harris, "tends to reinforce the pattern of pacific relationships among the various racial groups in the lower ranking levels of the social hierarchy. Not only were the poor whites out-numbered by the mulattoes and Negroes, but there was little of a significant material nature to struggle over in view of the generally static condition of the economy."[20] Accordingly, in Brazil, segregation, discrimination, and racist ideologies failed to crystallize in the first several decades following the end of slavery. More recently, however, industrialization has pushed Brazil toward a competitive type of race relations, particularly the southern region (for example, São Paulo) which has experienced rapid industrialization and has blacks in economic competition with many lower-status white immigrants.[21]

Whereas the racial antagonism in the United States during the period of industrial race relations (such as the Jim Crow segregation movement in the South and the race riots in northern cities) tended to be either directly or indirectly related to labor-market conflicts, racial antagonism in the period of modern industrial relations tends to originate outside the economic order and to have little connection with labor-market strife. Basic changes in the system of production have produced a segmented labor structure in which blacks are either isolated in the relatively non-unionized, low-paying, basically undesirable jobs of the noncorporate sector, or occupy the higher-paying corporate and government industry positions in which job competition is either controlled by powerful unions or is restricted to the highly trained and educated, regardless of race. If there is a basis for labor-market conflict in the modern industrial period, it is most probably related to the affirmative action programs originating from the civil rights legislation of the 1960s. However, since affirmative action programs are designed to improve job opportunities for the talented and educated, their major impact has been in the higher-paying jobs of the expanding government sector and the corporate sector. The sharp increase of the more privileged blacks in these industries has been facilitated by the combination of affirmative action and rapid industry growth. Indeed despite the effectiveness of affirmative action programs the very expansion of these sectors of the economy has kept racial friction over higher-paying corporate and government jobs to a minimum.

Unlike the occupational success achieved by the more talented and educated blacks, those in the black underclass find themselves locked in the low-paying and dead-end jobs of the noncorporate industries, jobs which are not in high demand and which therefore do not generate racial competition or strife among the national black and white labor force. Many of these jobs go unfilled, and employers often have to turn to cheap labor from Mexico and Puerto Rico. As Nathan Glazer has pointed out, "Expectations have changed, and fewer blacks and whites today will accept a life at menial labor with no hope for advancement, as their fathers and older brothers did and as European immigrants did."[22]

Thus in the modern industrial era neither the corporate nor government sectors nor the noncorporate low-wage sector provide the basis for the kind of interracial competition and conflict that has traditionally plagued the labor market in the United States. This, then, is the basis for my earlier contention that the economic class theories which associate labor-market conflicts with racial antagonism have little application to the present period of modern industrial race relations.

THE POLITY AND AMERICAN RACE RELATIONS

If the patterned ways in which racial groups have interacted historically have been shaped in major measure by different systems of production, they have also been undeniably influenced by the changing policies and laws of the state. For analytical purposes, it would be a mistake to treat the influences of the polity and the economy as if they were separate and unrelated. The legal and political systems in the antebellum South were effectively used as instruments of the slaveholding elite to strengthen and legitimate the institution of slavery. But as industrialization altered the economic class structure in the postbellum South, the organizing power and political consciousness of the white lower class increased and its members were able to gain enough control of the political and juridical systems to legalize a new system of racial domination (Jim Crow segregation) that clearly reflected their class interests.

In effect, throughout the preindustrial period of race relations and the greater portion of the industrial period the role of the polity was to legitimate, reinforce, and regulate patterns of racial inequality. However, it would be unwarranted to assume that the relationship between the economic and political aspects of race necessarily implies that the latter is simply a derivative phenomenon based on the more fundamental processes of the former. The increasing intervention, since the mid-twentieth century, of state and federal government agencies in resolving or mediating racial conflicts has convincingly demonstrated the political system's autonomy in handling contemporary racial problems. Instead of merely formalizing existing racial alignments as in previous periods, the political system has, since the initial state and municipal legislation of the 1940s, increasingly created changes leading to the erosion of traditional racial alignments; in other words, in-

stead of reinforcing racial barriers created during the preindustrial and industrial periods, the political system in recent years has tended to promote racial
equality.

Thus, in the previous periods the polity was quite clearly an instrument of
the white population in suppressing blacks. The government's racial practices
varied, as I indicated above, depending on which segment of the white population was able to assert its class interests. However, in the past two decades the
interests of the black population have been significantly reflected in the racial
policies of the government, and this change is one of the clearest indications
that the racial balance of power has been significantly altered. Since the early
1940s the black population has steadily gained political resources and, with the
help of sympathetic white allies, has shown an increasing tendency to utilize
these resources in promoting or protecting its group interests.

By the mid-twentieth century the black vote had proved to be a major ve-
hicle for political pressure. The black vote not only influenced the outcome
of national elections but many congressional, state, and municipal elections
as well. Fear of the Negro vote produced enactment of public accommodation and fair employment practices laws in northern and western
municipalities and states prior to the passage of federal civil rights legislation
in 1964. This political resurgence for black Americans increased their sense
of power, raised their expectations, and provided the foundation for the proliferation of demands which shaped the black revolt during the 1960s. But
there were other factors that helped to buttress Negro demands and contributed to the developing sense of power and rising expectations, namely, a
growing, politically active black middle class following World War II and the
emergence of the newly independent African states.

The growth of the black middle class was concurrent with the growth of
the black urban population. It was in the urban areas, with their expanding
occupational opportunities, that a small but significant number of blacks
were able to upgrade their occupations, increase their income, and improve
their standard of living. The middle-class segment of an oppressed minority
is most likely to participate in a drive for social justice that is disciplined and
sustained. In the early phases of the civil rights movement, the black middle
class channeled its energies through organizations such as the National Association for the Advancement of Colored People, which emphasized
developing political resources and successful litigation through the courts.
These developments were paralleled by the attack against traditional racial
alignments in other parts of the world. The emerging newly independent

African states led the assault. In America, the so-called "leader of the free world," the manifestation of racial tension and violence has been a constant source of embarrassment to national government officials. This sensitivity to world opinion made the national government more vulnerable to pressures of black protest at the very time when blacks had the greatest propensity to protest.

The development of black political resources that made the government more sensitive to Negro demands, the motivation and morale of the growing black middle class that resulted in the political drive for racial equality, and the emergence of the newly independent African states that increased the federal government's vulnerability to civil rights pressures all combined to create a new sense of power among black Americans and to raise their expectations as they prepared to enter the explosive decade of the 1960s. The national government was also aware of this developing sense of power and responded to the pressures of black protest in the 1960s with an unprecedented series of legislative enactments to protect black civil rights.

The problem for blacks today, in terms of government practices, is no longer one of legalized racial inequality. Rather the problem for blacks, especially the black underclass, is that the government is not organized to deal with the new barriers imposed by structural changes in the economy. With the passage of equal employment legislation and the authorization of affirmative action programs the government has helped clear the path for more privileged blacks, who have the requisite education and training, to enter the mainstream of American occupations. However, such government programs do not confront the impersonal economic barriers confronting members of the black underclass, who have been effectively screened out of the corporate and government industries. And the very attempts of the government to eliminate traditional racial barriers through such programs as affirmative action have had the unintentional effect of contributing to the growing economic class divisions within the black community.

CLASS STRATIFICATION AND CHANGING BLACK EXPERIENCES

The problems of black Americans have always been compounded because of their low position in both the economic order (the average economic class position of blacks as a group) and the social order (the social prestige or honor accorded individual blacks because of their ascribed racial status). It is of course true that the low economic position of blacks has helped to shape the categorical social definitions attached to blacks as a racial group, but it is also true that the more blacks become segmented in terms of economic class position, the more their concerns about the social significance of race will vary.

In the preindustrial period of American race relations there was of course very little variation in the economic class position of blacks. The system of racial-caste oppression relegated virtually all blacks to the bottom of the economic class hierarchy. Moreover, the social definitions of racial differences were heavily influenced by the ideology of racism and the doctrine of paternalism, both of which clearly assigned a subordinate status for blacks vis-à-vis whites. Occasionally, a few individual free blacks would emerge and accumulate some wealth or property, but they were the overwhelming exception. Thus the uniformly low economic class position of blacks reinforced and, in the eyes of most whites, substantiated the social definitions that asserted Negroes were culturally and biogenetically inferior to whites. The uniformly low economic class position of blacks also removed the basis for any meaningful distinction between race issues and class issues within the black community.

The development of a black middle class accompanied the change from a preindustrial to an industrial system of production. Still, despite the fact that some blacks were able to upgrade their occupation and increase their education and income, there were severe limits on the areas in which blacks could in fact advance. Throughout most of the industrial period of race relations, the growth of the black middle class occurred because of the expansion of institutions created to serve the needs of a growing urbanized black population. The black doctor, lawyer, teacher, minister, businessman, mortician, excluded from the white community, was able to create a niche in the segregated black community. Although the income levels and life-styles of the black professionals were noticeably and sometimes conspicuously different from those of the black masses, the two groups had one basic thing in common, a racial status contemptuously regarded by most whites in society. If E. Franklin Frazier's analysis of the black bourgeosie is correct, the black professionals throughout the industrial period of American race relations tended to react to their low position in the social order by an ostentatious display of material possessions and a conspicuous effort to disassociate themselves from the black masses.[23]

Still, as long as the members of the black middle class were stigmatized by their racial status; as long as they were denied the social recognition accorded their white counterparts; more concretely, as long as they remained restricted in where they could live, work, socialize, and be educated, race would continue to be a far more salient and important issue in shaping their sense of group position than their economic class position. Indeed, it was the black middle class that provided the leadership and generated the momentum for the civil rights movement during the mid-twentieth century. The influence and interests of this class were clearly reflected in the way the race issues were defined and articulated. Thus, the concept of "freedom" quite clearly implied, in the early stages of the movement, the right to swim in certain swimming pools, to eat in certain restaurants, to attend certain movie theaters, and to have the same voting privileges as whites. These basic concerns were reflected in the 1964 Civil Rights Bill which helped to create the illusion that, when the needs of the black middle class were met, so were the needs of the entire black community.

However, although the civil rights movement initially failed to address the basic needs of the members of the black lower class, it did increase their awareness of racial oppression, heighten their expectations about improving race relations, and increase their impatience with existing racial arrangements. These feelings were dramatically manifested in a series of violent ghetto outbursts that rocked the nation throughout the late 1960s. These outbreaks constituted the most massive and sustained expression of lower-class black dissatisfaction in the nation's history. They also forced the political system to recognize the problems of human survival and de facto segregation in the nation's ghettoes—problems pertaining to unemployment and underemployment, inferior ghetto schools, and deteriorated housing.

However, in the period of modern industrial race relations, it would be difficult indeed to comprehend the plight of inner-city blacks by exclusively focusing on racial discrimination. For in a very real sense, the current problems of lower-class blacks are substantially related to fundamental structural changes in the economy. A history of discrimination and oppression created a huge black underclass, and the technological and economic revolutions have combined to insure it a permanent status.

As the black middle class rides on the wave of political and social changes, benefiting from the growth of employment opportunities in the growing corporate and government sectors of the economy, the black underclass falls behind the larger society in every conceivable respect. The economic and political systems in the United States have demonstrated remarkable flexibility in allowing talented blacks to fill positions of prestige and influence at the same time that these systems have shown persistent rigidity in handling the problems of lower-class blacks. As a result, for the first time in American history class issues can meaningfully compete with race issues in the way blacks develop or maintain a sense of group position.[24]

CONCLUSION

The foregoing sections of this chapter present an outline and a general analytical basis for the arguments that will be systematically explored [elsewhere].[25] I have tried to show that race relations in American society have been historically characterized by three major stages and that each stage is represented by a unique form of racial interaction which is shaped by the particular arrangement of the economy and the polity. My central argument is that different systems of production and/or different policies of the state have imposed different constraints on the way in which racial groups interact—constraints that have structured the relations between racial groups and produced dissimilar contexts not only for the manifestation of racial antagonisms but also for racial-group access to rewards and privileges. I emphasized in this connection that in the preindustrial and industrial periods of American race relations the systems of production primarily shaped the patterns of racial stratification and the role of the polity was to legitimate, reinforce, or regulate these patterns. In the modern industrial period, however, both the system of production and the polity assume major importance in creating new patterns of race relations and in altering the context of racial strife. Whereas the preindustrial and industrial stages were principally related to group struggles over economic resources as different segments of the white population overtly sought to create and solidify economic racial domination (ranging from the exploitation of black labor in the preindustrial period to the elimination of black competition for jobs in the industrial period) through various forms of political, juridical, and social discrimination; in the modern industrial period fundamental economic and political changes have made economic class position more important than race in determining black chances for occupational mobility. Finally, I have outlined the importance of racial norms or belief systems, especially as they relate to the general problem of race and class conflict in the preindustrial and industrial periods.

My argument that race relations in America have moved from economic racial oppression to a form of class subordination for the less-privileged blacks is not meant to suggest that racial conflicts have disappeared or have even been substantially reduced. On the contrary, the basis of such conflicts have shifted from the economic sector to the sociopolitical order and therefore do not play as great a role in determining the life chances of individual black Americans as in the previous periods of overt economic racial oppression.

NOTES

¹ See, William J. Wilson, *Power, Racism and Privilege: Race Relations in Theoretical and Sociohistorical Perspectives* (New York: The Free Press, 1973).

² In Marxist terminology, the "superstructure" refers to the arrangements of beliefs, norms, ideologies, and noneconomic institutions.

³ However, not all theorists who emphasize the importance of economic class in explanations of race relations simply relegate problems of race to the superstructure. The Marxist scholars Michael Burawoy and Eugene Genovese recognize the reciprocal influence between the economic class structure and aspects of the superstructure (belief systems, political systems, etc.), a position which I also share and which is developed more fully in subsequent sections of this chapter. See Eugene D. Genovese, *Roll, Jordan, Roll: The World the Slaves Made* (New York: Pantheon, 1974); idem, *In Red and Black: Marxian Explorations in Southern and Afro-American History* (New York: Vintage Press, 1971); and Michael Burawoy, "Race, Class, and Colonialism," *Social and Economic Studies* 23 (1974): 521–50.

⁴ Oliver C. Cox, *Caste, Class and Race: A Study in Social Dynamics* (Garden City, New York: Doubleday, 1948); Paul A. Baran and Paul M. Sweezy, *Monopoly Capital: An Essay on the American Economic and Social Order* (Harmondsworth: Penguin, 1966); Michael Reich, "The Economics of Racism," in *Problems in Political Economy*, ed. David M. Gordon (Lexington, Mass.: Heath, 1971); and M. Nikolinakos, "Notes on an Economic Theory of Racism," *Race: A Journal of Race and Group Relations* 14 (1973): 365–81.

⁵ Edna Bonacich, "A Theory of Ethnic Antagonism: The Split Labor Market," *American Sociological Review* 37 (October 1972): 547–59; idem, "Abolition, the Extension of Slavery and the Position of Free Blacks: A Study of Split Labor Markets in the United States," *American Journal of Sociology* 81 (1975): 601–28.

⁶ For examples of alternative and less orthodox Marxist explanations of race, see Eugene D. Genovese, *The Political Economy of Slavery: Studies in the Economy and Society of the Slave South* (New York: Pantheon, 1966); idem, *The World the Slaveholders Made: Two Essays in Interpretation* (New York: Pantheon, 1969); idem, *In Red and Black*; idem, *Roll, Jordan, Roll*; and Burawoy, "Race, Class, and Colonialism."

⁷ "Exploitation," in Marxian terminology, refers to the difference between the wages workers receive and the value of the goods they produce. The size of this difference, therefore, determines the degree of exploitation.

⁸ Bonacich, "A Theory of Ethnic Antagonism," p. 557.

⁹ Ibid., p. 549.

¹⁰ Ibid., p. 553.

¹¹ Ibid., p. 549.

¹² Ibid., p. 555.

¹³ Ibid., p. 556.

[14] Neil J. Smelser, *Karl Marx on Society and Social Change* (Chicago: University of Chicago Press, 1974), p. xiv. According to Smelser, Marx used the notions "forces of production" and "social relations of production" as constituting the "mode of production." However, in Marx's writings the mode of production is often discussed as equivalent only to the "forces of production." To avoid confusion, I have chosen the term "system of production" which denotes the interrelation of the forces of production and the mode of production.

[15] Pierre L. van den Berghe, *Race and Racism: A Comparative Perspective* (New York: John Wiley and Sons, 1967), p. 26.

[16] See, for example, Genovese, *Roll, Jordan, Roll.*

[17] An exception to this pattern occurred in the cities of the antebellum South, where non-slaveholding whites played a major role in the development of urban segregation. However, since an overwhelming majority of the population resided in rural areas, race relations in the antebellum southern cities were hardly representative of the region.

[18] van den Berghe, *Race and Racism,* p. 27.

[19] Marvin Harris, *Patterns of Race in the Americas* (New York: Walker, 1964), p. 96.

[20] Ibid., p. 96.

[21] van den Berghe, *Race and Racism,* p. 28.

[22] Nathan Glazer, "Blacks and Ethnic Groups: The Difference, and the Political Difference It Makes," in *Key Issues in the Afro-American Experience,* ed. Nathan I. Huggins, Martin Kilson, and Daniel M. Fox (New York: Harcourt Brace Jovanovich, 1971), 2: 209.

[23] E. Franklin Frazier, *Black Bourgeoisie* (New York: The Free Press, 1957). See also Nathan Hare, *Black Anglo-Saxons* (New York: Collier, 1965).

[24] The theoretical implications of this development for ethnic groups in general are discussed by Milton Gordon under the concept "ethclass." See Milton M. Gordon, *Assimilation in American Life* (New York: Oxford University Press, 1964).

[25] See William Julius Wilson, *The Declining Significance of Race: Blacks and Changing American Institutions* (Chicago and London: University of Chicago Press, 1978).

12

THE IMMIGRANT ENCLAVE

THEORY AND EMPIRICAL EXAMPLES

Alejandro Portes and Robert D. Manning

I. INTRODUCTION

The purpose of this chapter is to review existing theories about the process of immigrant adaptation to a new society and to recapitulate the empirical findings that have led to an emerging perspective on the topic. This emerging view revolves around the concepts of different modes of structural incorporation and of the immigrant enclave as one of them. These concepts are set in explicit opposition to two previous viewpoints on the adaptation process, generally identified as assimilation theory and the segmented labor markets approach.

The study of immigrant groups in the United States has produced a copious historical and sociological literature, written mostly from the assimilation perspective. Although the experiences of particular groups varied, the common theme of these writings is the unrelenting efforts of immigrant minorities to surmount obstacles impeding their entry into the "mainstream" of American society (Handlin, 1941, 1951; Wittke, 1952; Child, 1943; Vecoli, 1977).

From this perspective, the adaptation process of particular immigrant groups followed a sequential path from initial economic hardship and discrimination to eventual socioeconomic mobility arising from increasing knowledge of American culture and acceptance by the host society (Warner and Srole, 1945; Gordon, 1964; Sowell, 1981). The focus on a "core" culture, the emphasis on consensus-building, and the assumption of a basic patterned sequence of adaptation represent central elements of assimilation theory. From this perspective, the failure of individual immigrants or entire ethnic groups to move up through the social hierarchies is linked either to their reluctance to shed traditional values or to the resistance of the native majority to accept them because of racial, religious, or other shortcomings. Hence, successful adaptation depends, first of all, on the willingness of immigrants to relinquish a "backward" way of life and, second, on their acquisition of characteristics making them acceptable to the host society (Eisenstadt, 1970). Throughout, the emphasis is placed on the social psychological processes of motivation, learning, and interaction and on the cultural values and perceptions of the immigrants themselves and those who surround them.

The second general perspective takes issue with this psychosocial and culturalist orientation as well as with the assumption of a single basic assimilation path. This alternative view begins by noting that immigrants and their descendants do not necessarily "melt" into the mainstream and that many groups seem not to want to do so, preferring instead to preserve their distinct ethnic identities (Greeley, 1971; Glazer and Moynihan, 1970). A number of writers have focused on the resilience of these communities and described their functions as sources of mutual support and collective political power (Suttles, 1968; Alba and Chamlin, 1983; Parenti, 1967). Others have gone beyond descriptive accounts and attempted to establish the causes of the persistence of ethnicity. Without exception, these writers have identified the roots of the phenomenon in the economic sphere and, more specifically, in the labor-market roles that immigrants have been called on to play.

Within this general perspective, several specific theoretical approaches exist. The first focuses on the situation of the so-called unmeltable ethnics—blacks, Chicanos, and American Indians—and finds the source of their plight in a history of internal colonialism during which these groups have been confined to specific areas and made to work under uniquely unfavorable conditions. In a sense, the role of colonized minorities has been to bypass the free labor market, yielding in the process distinct benefits both to direct employers of their labor and, indirectly, to other members of the dominant racial group (Blauner, 1972; Geschwender, 1978). The continuation of colonialist practices to our day explains, according to this view, the spatial isolation and occupational disadvantages of these minorities (Barrera, 1980).

A second approach attempts to explain the persistence of ethnic politics and ethnic mobilization on the basis of the organization of subordinate groups to combat a "cultural division of labor." The latter confined members of specific minorities to a quasi-permanent situation of exploitation and social inferiority. Unlike the first view, this second approach does not envision the persistence of ethnicity as a consequence of continuing exploitation, but rather as a "reactive formation" on the part of the minority to reaffirm its identity and its interests (Hechter, 1977; Despres, 1975). For this reason, ethnic mobilizations are often most common among groups who have already abandoned the bottom of the social ladder and started to compete for positions of advantage with members of the majority (Nagel and Olzak, 1982).

A final variant focuses on the situation of contemporary immigrants to the United States. Drawing on the dual labor market literature, this approach views recent immigrants as the latest entrants into the lower tier of a segmented labor market where women and other minorities already predominate. Relative to the latter, immigrants possess the advantages of their lack of experience in the new country, their legal vulnerability, and their greater initial motivation. All of these traits translate into higher productivity and lower labor costs for the firms that employ them (Sassen-Koob, 1980). Jobs in the secondary labor market are poorly paid, require few skills, and offer limited mobility opportunities. Hence, confinement of immigrants to this sector insures that those who do not return home are relegated to a quasi-permanent status as disadvantaged and discriminated minorities (Piore, 1975, 1979).

What these various structural theories have in common is the view of resilient ethnic communities formed as the result of a consistently disadvantageous economic position and the consequent absence of a smooth path of assimilation. These situations, ranging from slave labor to permanent confinement to the secondary labor market, are not altered easily. They have given rise, in time, either to hopeless communities of "unmeltable" ethnics or to militant minorities, conscious of a common identity and willing to support a collective strategy of self-defense rather than rely on individual assimilation.

These structural theories have provided an effective critique of the excessively benign image of the adaptation process presented by earlier writings. However, while undermining the former, the new structural perspective may have erred in the opposite direction. The basic hypothesis advanced in this chapter is that several identifiable modes of labor-market incorporation exist and that not all of them relegate newcomers to a permanent situation of exploitation and inferiority. Thus, while agreeing with the basic thrust of structural theories, we propose several modifications that are necessary for an adequate understanding of the different types of immigrant flows and their distinct processes of adaptation.

II. Modes of Incorporation

In the four decades since the end of World War II, immigration to the United States has experienced a vigorous surge reaching levels comparable only to those at the beginning of the century (National Research Council, 1985, chapter 2). Even if one restricts attention to this movement, disregarding multiple other migrations elsewhere in the world, it is not the case that the inflow has been of a homogeneous character. Low-wage labor immigration itself has taken different forms, including temporary contract flows, undocumented entries, and legal immigration. More importantly, it is not the case that all immigrants have been directed to the secondary labor market. For example, since the promulgation of the Immigration Act of 1965, thousands of professionals, technicians, and craftsmen have come to the United States, availing themselves of the occupational preference categories of the law. This type of inflow, dubbed "brain drain" in the sending nations, encompasses today sizable contingents of immigrants from such countries as India, South Korea, the Philippines, and Taiwan, each an important contributor to U.S. annual immigration.

The characteristics of this type of migration have been described in detail elsewhere (Portes, 1976, 1981). Two such traits deserve mention, however. First, occupationally skilled immigrants—including doctors, nurses, engineers, technicians, and craftsmen—generally enter the "primary" labor market; they contribute to alleviate domestic shortages in specific occupations and gain access, after a period of time, to the mobility ladders available to native workers. Second, immigration of this type does not generally give rise to spatially concentrated communities; instead, immigrants are dispersed throughout many cities and regions, following different career paths.

Another sizable contingent of entrants whose occupational future is not easily characterized *a priori* are political refugees. Large groups of refugees, primarily from Communist-controlled countries, have come to the United States, first after the occupation of Eastern Europe by the Soviet Army, then after the advent of Fidel Castro to power in Cuba, and finally in the aftermath of the Vietnam War. Unlike purely "economic" immigrants, refugees have often received resettlement assistance from various governmental agencies (Zolberg, 1983; Keely, 1981). All the available evidence runs contrary to the notion of a uniform entry of political refugees into low-wage secondary occupations; on the contrary, there are indications of their employment in many different lines of work.

A third mode of incorporation has gained the attention of a number of scholars in recent years. It consists of small groups of immigrants who are inserted or insert themselves as commercial intermediaries in a particular country or region. These "middleman minorities" are distinct in nationality, culture, and sometimes race from both the superordinate and subordinate groups to which they relate (Bonacich, 1973; Light, 1972). They can be used by dominant elites as a buffer to deflect mass frustration and also as an instrument to conduct commercial activities in impoverished areas. Middlemen accept these risks in exchange for the opportunity to share in the commercial and financial benefits gained through such instruments as taxation, higher retail prices, and usury. Jews in feudal and early modern Europe represent the classic instance of a middleman minority. Other examples include Indian merchants in East Africa, and Chinese entrepreneurs in Southeast Asia and throughout the Pacific Basin (Bonacich and Modell, 1980, chapter 1). Contemporary examples in the United States include Jewish, Korean, and other Oriental merchants in inner-city ghetto areas and Cubans in Puerto Rico (Kim, 1981; Cobas, 1984).

Primary labor immigration and middleman entrepreneurship represent two modes of incorporation that differ from the image of an homogeneous flow into low-wage employment. Political refugees, in turn, have followed a variety of paths, including both of the above as well as insertion into an ethnic enclave economy. The latter represents a fourth distinct mode. Although frequently confused with middleman minorities, the emergence and structure of an immigrant enclave possess distinct characteristics. The latter have significant theoretical and practical implications, for they set apart groups adopting this entry mode from those following alternative paths. We turn now to several examples of immigrant enclaves to clarify their internal dynamics and causes of their emergence.

III. Immigrant Enclaves

Immigration to the United States before World War I was, overwhelmingly, an unskilled labor movement. Impoverished peasants from southern Italy, Poland, and the eastern reaches of the Austro-Hungarian Empire settled in dilapidated and crowded areas, often immediately adjacent to their points of debarcation, and took any menial jobs available. From these harsh beginnings, immigrants commenced a slow and often painful process of acculturation and economic mobility. Theirs was the saga captured by innumerable subsequent volumes written from both the assimilation and the structural perspectives.

Two sizable immigrant groups did not follow this pattern, however. Their most apparent characteristic was the economic success of the first generation, even in the absence of extensive acculturation. On the contrary, both groups struggled fiercely to preserve their cultural identity and internal solidarity. Their approach to adaptation thus directly contradicted subsequent assimilation predictions concerning the causal priority of acculturation to economic mobility. Economic success and "clannishness" also earned for each minority the hostility of the surrounding population. These two immigrant groups did not have a language, religion, or even race in common and they never overlapped in significant numbers in any part of the United States. Yet, arriving at opposite ends of the continent, Jews and Japanese pursued patterns of economic adaptation that were quite similar both in content and in their eventual consequences.

A. Jews in Manhattan

The first major wave of Jewish immigration to the United States consisted of approximately 50,000 newcomers of German origin, arriving between 1840 and 1870. These immigrants went primarily into commerce and achieved, in the course of a few decades, remarkable success. By 1900, the average income of German-Jewish immigrants surpassed that of the American population (Rischin, 1962). Many individuals who started as street peddlers and small merchants had become, by that time, heads of major industrial, retail, and financial enterprises.

The second wave of Jewish immigration exhibited quite different characteristics. Between 1870 and 1914, over two million Jews left the Pale of Settlement and other Russian-dominated regions, escaping Czarist persecution. Major pogroms occurred before and during this exodus (Dinnerstein,

1977). Thus, unlike most immigrants of the period, the migration of Russian and Eastern Europe Jews was politically motivated and their move was much more permanent. In contrast to German Jews, who were relatively well educated, the Yiddish-speaking newcomers came, for the most part, from modest origins and had only a rudimentary education. Although they viewed the new Russian wave with great apprehension, German Jews promptly realized that their future as an ethnic minority depended on the successful integration of the newcomers (Rischin, 1962). Charitable societies were established to provide food, shelter, and other necessities, and private schools were set up to teach immigrants English, civics, and the customs of the new country (Howe and Libo, 1979).

Aside from its size and rapidity of arrival, turn-of-the-century Jewish immigration had two other distinct characteristics. First was its strong propensity toward commerce and self-employment in general in preference to wage labor: as German Jews before them, many Russian immigrants moved directly into street peddling and other commercial activities of the most modest sort. Second was its concentration into a single, densely populated urban area—the lower East Side of Manhattan. Within this area, those who did not become storekeepers and peddlers from the start found employment in factories owned by German Jews, learning the necessary rudiments for future self-employment (Sowell, 1981, chapter 4).

The economic activities of this population created, in the course of two decades, a dense network of industrial, commercial, and financial enterprises. Close physical proximity facilitated exchanges of information and access to credit and raw materials. Characteristic of this emerging Jewish enclave is that production and marketing of goods was not restricted to the ethnic community, but went well beyond it into the general economy. Jews entered the printing, metal, and building trades; they became increasingly prominent in jewelry and cigar-making; above all, the garment industry became the primary domain of Jewish entrepreneurship, with hundreds of firms of all sizes engaged in the trade (Rischin, 1962; Howe and Libo, 1979).

The economic success of many of these ventures did not require and did not entail rapid acculturation. Immigrants learned English and those instrumental aspects of the new culture required for economic advancement. For the rest, they preferred to remain with their own and maintained, for the most part, close adherence to their original religion, language, and values (Wirth, 1956; Howe, 1976). Jewish enclave capitalism depended, for its emergence and advancement, precisely on those resources made available by a solidaristic ethnic community: protected access to labor and markets, informal sources of credit, and business information. It was through these resources that upstart immigrant enterprises could survive and eventually compete effectively with better-established firms in the general economy.

The emergence of a Jewish enclave in East Manhattan helped this group bypass the conventional assimilation path and achieve significant economic mobility in the course of the first generation, well ahead of complete acculturation. Subsequent generations also pursued this path, but the resources accumulated through early immigrant entrepreneurship were dedicated primarily to further the education of children and their entry into the professions. It was at this point that outside hostility became most patent, as one university after another established quotas to prevent the onrush of Jewish students. The last of these quotas did not come to an end until after World War II (Dinnerstein, 1977).

Despite these and other obstacles, the movement of Jews into higher education continued. Building on the economic success of the first generation, subsequent ones achieved levels of education, occupation, and income that significantly exceed the national average (Featherman, 1971; Sowell, 1981, chapter 4). The original enclave is now only a memory, but it provided in its time the necessary platform for furthering the rapid social and economic mobility of the minority. Jews did enter the mainstream of American society, but they did not do so starting uniformly at the bottom, as most immigrant groups had done; instead, they translated resources made available by early ethnic entrepreneurship into rapid access to positions of social prestige and economic advantage.

B. Japanese on the West Coast

The specific features of Japanese immigration differ significantly from the movement of European Jews, but their subsequent adaptation and mobility patterns are similar. Beginning in 1890 and ending with the enactment of the Gentlemen's Agreement of 1908, approximately 150,000 Japanese men immigrated to the West Coast. They were followed primarily by their spouses until the Immigration Act of 1924 banned any further Asiatic immigration. Although nearly 300,000 Japanese immigrants are documented in this period (Daniels, 1977), less than half of this total remained in the United States (Petersen, 1971). This is due, in contrast to the case of the Jews, to the sojourner character of Japanese immigrants: the intention of many was to accumulate sufficient capital for purchasing farm land or settling debts in Japan. Hence this population movement included commercial and other members of the Japanese middle class who, not incidentally, were explicitly sponsored by their national government.

The residential patterns of Japanese immigrants were not as concentrated as those of Jews in Manhattan, but they were geographically clustered. Almost two-thirds of the 111,010 Japanese reported in the U.S. Census of 1920 lived in California. Further, one-third of California's Japanese residents lived in Los Angeles County in 1940, while another one-third lived in six nearby counties (Daniels, 1977). However, it was not the residential segregation of Japanese immigrants but rather their occupational patterns that eventually mobilized the hostility of the local population.

Japanese immigrants were initially welcomed and recruited as a form of cheap agricultural labor. Their reputation as thrifty and diligent workers made them preferable to other labor sources. Nativist hostilities crystallized, however, when Japanese immigrants shifted from wage labor to independent ownership and small-scale farming. This action not only reduced the supply of laborers but it also increased competition for domestic growers in the fresh-produce market. In 1900, only about 40 Japanese farmers in the entire United States leased or owned a total of 5000 acres of farmland. By 1909, the number of Japanese farmers had risen to 6000 and their collective holdings exceeded 210,000 acres (Petersen, 1971). Faced with such "unfair" competition, California growers turned to the political means at their disposal. In 1913, the state legislature passed the first Alien Land Law, which restricted land ownership by foreigners. This legislation did not prove sufficient, however, and, in subsequent years, the ever-accommodating legislature passed a series of acts closing other legal loopholes to Japanese farming (Petersen, 1971).

These proscriptions, which barred most of the Japanese from the lands, accelerated their entry into urban enterprise. In 1909, Japanese entrepreneurs owned almost 3000 small shops in several Western cities. Forty percent of Japanese men in Los Angeles were self-employed. They operated businesses such as dry-cleaning establishments, fisheries, lunch counters, and produce stands that marketed the production of Japanese farms (Light, 1972).

The ability of the first-generation *Issei* to escape the status of stoop labor in agriculture was based on the social cohesion of their community. Rotating credit associations offered scarce venture capital, while mutual-aid organizations provided assistance in operating farms and urban businesses. Light (1972) reports that capitalizations as high as $100,000 were financed through ethnic credit networks. Economic success was again accompanied by limited instrumental acculturation and by careful preservation of national identity and values. It was the availability of investment capital, cooperative business associations, and marketing practices (forward and backward economic linkages) within the ethnic enclave that enabled Japanese entrepreneurs to expand beyond its boundaries and compete effectively in the general economy. This is illustrated by the production and marketing of fresh produce. In 1920, the value of Japanese crops was about 10% of the total for California, when the Japanese comprised less than 1% of the state's population; many retail outlets traded exclusively with a non-Japanese clientele (Light, 1972; Petersen, 1971).

During the early 1940s, the Japanese ethnic economy was seriously disrupted but not eliminated by the property confiscations and camp internments accompanying World War II. After the war, economic prosperity and other factors combined to reduce local hostility toward the Japanese. Older *Issei* and many of their children returned to small business, while other second-generation *Nisei,* like their Jewish predecessors, pursued higher education and entered the white-collar occupations *en masse.* This mobility path was completed by the third or *Sansei* generation, with 88% of their members attending college. Other third-generation Japanese have continued, however, the entrepreneurial tradition of their parents (Bonacich and Modell, 1980). Like Jews before them, Japanese Americans have made use of the resources made available by early immigrant entrepreneurship to enter the mainstream of society in positions of relative advantage. The mean educational and occupational attainment of the group's 600,000 members surpasses at present all other ethnic and native groups, while its average family income is exceeded among American ethnic groups only by the Jews (Sowell, 1981).[1] . . .

IV. CONCLUSION: A TYPOLOGY OF THE
PROCESS OF INCORPORATION

We can now attempt a summary description of the characteristics of immigrant enclaves and how they differ from other paths. The emergence of an ethnic enclave economy has three prerequisites: first, the presence of a substantial number of immigrants, with business experience acquired in the sending country; second, the availability of sources of capital; and third, the availability of sources of labor. The latter two conditions are not too difficult to meet. The requisite labor can usually be drawn from family members and, more commonly, from recent arrivals. Surprisingly perhaps, capital is not a major impediment either since the sums initially required are usually small. When immigrants did not bring them from abroad, they could be accumulated through individual savings or pooled resources in the community. It is the first condition that appears critical. The presence of a number of immigrants skilled in what Franklin Frazier (1949) called the art of "buying and selling" is common [not only to the Jewish and Japanese cases reviewed above but also to contemporary enclave economies among Koreans and Cubans]. Such an entrepreneurial-commercial class among early immigrant cohorts can usually overcome other obstacles; conversely, its absence within an immigrant community will confine the community to wage employment even if sufficient resources of capital and labor are available.

Enclave businesses typically start small and cater exclusively to an ethnic clientele. Their expansion and entry into the broader market requires, as seen above, an effective mobilization of community resources. The social mechanism at work here seems to be a strong sense of reciprocity supported by collective solidarity that transcends the purely contractual character of business transactions. For example, receipt of a loan from a rotating credit association entails the duty of continuing to make contributions so that others can have access to the same source of capital. Although, in principle, it would make sense for the individual to withdraw once his loan is received, such action would cut him off from the very sources of community support on which his future business success depends (Light, 1972).

Similarly, relations between enclave employers and employees generally transcend a contractual wage bond. It is understood by both parties that the wage paid is inferior to the value of labor contributed. This is willingly accepted by many immigrant workers because the wage is only *one* form of compensation. Use of their labor represents often the key advantage making poorly capitalized enclave firms competitive. In reciprocity, employers are expected to respond to emergency needs of their workers and to promote their advancement through such means as on-the-job training, advancement to supervisory positions, and aid when they move into self-employment. These opportunities represent the other part of the "wage" received by enclave workers. The informal mobility ladders thus created are, of course, absent in the secondary labor market where there is no primary bond between owners and workers or no common ethnic community to enforce the norm of reciprocity.

Paternalistic labor relations and strong community solidarity are also characteristic of middleman minorities. Although both modes of incorporation are similar and are thus frequently confused, there are three major structural differences between them. First, immigrant enclaves are not exclusively commercial. Unlike middleman minorities, whose economic role is to mediate commercial and financial transactions between elites and masses, enclave firms include in addition a sizable productive sector. The latter may comprise agriculture, light manufacturing, and construction enterprises; their production, marketed often by coethnic intermediaries, is directed toward the general economy and not exclusively to the immigrant community.

Second, relationships between enclave businesses and established native ones are problematic. Middleman groups tend to occupy positions complementary and subordinate to the local owning class; they fill economic niches either disdained or feared by the latter. Unlike them, enclave enterprises often enter in direct competition with existing domestic firms. There is no evidence, for example, that domestic elites deliberately established or supported the emergence of the Jewish, Japanese, Korean, or Cuban business communities as means to further their own economic interests. There is every indication, on the other hand, that this mode of incorporation was largely self-created by the immigrants, often in opposition to powerful domestic interests. Although it is true that enclave entrepreneurs have been frequently employed as subcontractors by outside firms in such activities as garment and construction (Bonacich, 1978), it is incorrect to characterize this role as the exclusive or dominant one among these enterprises.

Third, the enclave is concentrated and spatially identifiable. By the very nature of their activities, middleman minorities must often be dispersed among the mass of the population. Although the immigrants may live in certain limited areas, their businesses require proximity to their mass clientele and a measure of physical dispersion within it. It is true that middleman activities such as money-lending have been associated in several historical instances with certain streets and neighborhoods, but this is not a necessary or typical pattern. Street peddling and other forms of petty commerce require merchants to go into the areas where demand exists and avoid excessive concentration of the goods and services they offer. This is the typical pattern found today among middleman minorities in American cities (Cobas, 1984; Kim, 1981).

Enclave businesses, on the other hand, are spatially concentrated, especially in their early stages. This is so for three reasons: first, the need for proximity to the ethnic market which they initially serve; second, proximity to each other which facilitates exchange of information, access to credit, and other supportive activities; third, proximity to ethnic labor supplies on which they crucially depend. Unlike the Jewish, Korean, or Cuban cases, the Japanese enclave economy does partially depart from the pattern of high physical concentration. This can be attributed to the political persecution to which this group was subjected. Originally, Japanese concentration was a rural phenomenon based on small farms linked together by informal bonds and cooperative associations. Forced removal of this minority from the land compelled their entry into urban businesses and their partial dispersal into multiple activities.

Physical concentration of enclaves underlies their final characteristic. Once an enclave economy has fully developed, it is possible for a newcomer to live his life entirely within the confines of the community. Work, education, and access to health care, recreation, and a variety of other services can be found without leaving the bounds of the ethnic economy. This institutional completeness is what enables new immigrants to move ahead economically, despite very limited knowledge of the host culture and language. Supporting empirical evidence comes from studies showing low levels of English knowledge among enclave minorities and the absence of a net effect of knowledge of English on their average income levels (Light, 1980; Portes and Bach, 1985).

Table 12.1 summarizes this discussion by presenting the different modes of incorporation and their principal characteristics. Two caveats are necessary. First, this typology is not exhaustive, since other forms of adaptation have existed and will undoubtedly emerge in the future. Second, political refugees are not included, since this entry label does not necessarily entail a unique adaptation path. Instead, refugees can select or be channelled in many different directions, including self-employment, access to primary labor markets, or confinement to secondary sector occupations.

Having discussed the characteristics of enclaves and middleman minorities, a final word must be said about the third alternative to employment in the lower tier of a dual labor market. As a mode of incorporation, primary sector immigration also has distinct advantages, although they are of a different order from those pursued by "entrepreneurial" minorities. Dispersal throughout the receiving country and career mobility based on standard promotion criteria makes it imperative for immigrants in this mode to become fluent in the new language and culture (Stevens, Goodman, and Mick, 1978). Without a supporting ethnic community, the second generation also becomes thoroughly steeped in the ways of the host society. Primary

Variable	Primary sector immigration	Secondary sector immigration	Immigrant enclaves	Middleman minorities
Size of immigrant population	Small	Large	Large	Small
Spatial concentration, national	Dispersed	Dispersed	Concentrated	Concentrated
Spatial concentration, local	Dispersed	Concentrated	Concentrated	Dispersed
Original class composition	Homogeneous: skilled workers and professionals	Homogeneous: manual laborers	Heterogenous: entrepreneurs, professionals, and workers	Homogeneous: merchants and some professionals
Present occupational status distribution	High mean status/low variance	Low mean status/low variance	Mean status/high variance	Mean status/low variance
Mobility opportunities	High: formal promotion ladders	Low	High: informal ethnic ladders	Average: informal ethnic ladders
Institutional diversification of ethnic community	None	Low: weak social institutions	High: institutional completeness	Medium: strong social and economic institutions
Participation in ethnic organizations	Little or none	Low	High	High
Resilience of ethnic culture	Low	Average	High	High
Knowledge of host country language	High	Low	Low	High
Knowledge of host country institutions	High	Low	Average	High
Modal reaction of host community	Acceptance	Discrimination	Hostility	Mixed: elite acceptance/mass hostility

Table 12.1 Typology of Modes of Incorporation

sector immigration thus tends to lead to very rapid social and cultural integration. It represents the path that approximates most closely the predictions of assimilation theory with regard to (1) the necessity of acculturation for social and economic progress and (2) the subsequent rewards received by immigrants and their descendants for shedding their ethnic identities.

Clearly, however, this mode of incorporation is open only to a minority of immigrant groups. In addition, acculturation of professionals and other primary sector immigrants is qualitatively different from that undergone by others. Regardless of their differences, immigrants in other modes tend to learn the new language and culture with a heavy "local" content. Although acculturation may be slow, especially in the case of enclave groups, it carries with it elements unique to the surrounding community—its language inflections, particular traditions, and loyalties (Greeley, 1971; Suttles, 1968). On the contrary, acculturation of primary sector immigrants is of a more cosmopolitan sort. Because career requirements often entail physical mobility, the new language and culture are learned more rapidly and more generally, without strong attachments to a particular community. Thus, while minorities entering menial labor, enclave, or middleman enterprise in the United States have eventually become identified with a certain city or region, the same is not true for immigrant professionals, who tend to "disappear," in a cultural sense, soon after their arrival (Stevens *et al.*, 1978; Cardona and Cruz, 1980).

Awareness of patterned differences among immigrant groups in their forms of entry and labor market incorporation represents a significant advance, in our view, from earlier undifferentiated descriptions of the adaptation process. This typology is, however, a provisional effort. Just as detailed research on the condition of particular minorities modified or replaced earlier broad generalizations, the propositions advanced here will require revision. New groups arriving in the United States at present and a revived interest in immigration should provide the required incentive for empirical studies and theoretical advances in the future.

NOTES

[1] The original article from which this excerpt was drawn includes a further discussion of contemporary Korean and Cuban enclaves.—ED.

REFERENCES

Alba, Richard D., and Chamlin, Mitchell B. (1983). Ethnic identification among whites. *American Sociological Review* 48:240–247.

Barrera, Mario (1980). *Race and class in the Southwest: A theory of racial inequality.* Notre Dame, Indiana: Notre Dame University Press.

Blauner, Robert (1972). *Racial oppression in America.* New York: Harper and Row.

Bonacich, Edna (1973). A theory of middleman minorities. *American Sociological Review* 38 (October):583–594.

Bonacich, Edna (1978). U.S. capitalism and Korean immigrant small business. Riverside, California: Department of Sociology, University of California—Riverside, mimeographed.

Bonacich, Edna, and Modell, John (1980). *The economic basis of ethnic solidarity: Small business in the Japanese-American community.* Berkeley, California: University of California Press.

Cardona, Ramiro C., and Cruz, Carmen I. (1980). *El exodo de Colombianos.* Bogota: Ediciones Tercer Mundo.

Child, Irving L. (1943). *Italian or American? The second generation in conflict.* New Haven, Connecticut: Yale University Press.

Cobas, Jose (1984). Participation in the ethnic economy, ethnic solidarity and ambivalence toward the host society: The case of Cuban emigres in Puerto Rico. Presented at the American Sociological Association Meeting, San Antonio, Texas: August.

Daniels, Roger (1977). The Japanese-American experience: 1890–1940. In *Uncertain Americans* (L. Dinnerstein and F. C. Jaher, eds.), pp. 250–267. New York: Oxford University Press.

Despres, Leo (1975). Toward a theory of ethnic phenomena. In *Ethnicity and resource competition* (Leo Despres, ed.), pp. 209–212. The Hague: Mouton.

Dinnerstein, Leonard (1977). The East European Jewish migration. In *Uncertain Americans* (L. Dinnerstein and F. C. Jaher, eds.), pp. 216–231. New York: Oxford University Press.

Eisenstadt, S. N. (1970). The process of absorbing new immigrants in Israel. In *Integration and development in Israel* (S. N. Eisenstadt, RivKah Bar Yosef, and Chaim Adler, eds.), pp. 341–367. Jerusalem: Israel University Press.

Featherman, David L. (1971). The socioeconomic achievement of white religio-ethnic subgroups: Social and psychological explanations. *American Sociological Review* 36 (April): 207–222.

Frazier, E. Franklin (1949). *The Negro in the United States.* New York: Macmillan.

Geschwender, James A. (1978). *Racial stratification in America.* Dubuque, Iowa: William C. Brown.

Glazer, Nathan, and Moynihan, Daniel P. (1970). *Beyond the melting pot: The Negroes, Puerto Ricans, Jews, Italians and Irish of New York City.* Cambridge, Massachusetts: M.I.T. Press.

Gordon, Milton M. (1964). *Assimilation in American life: The role of race, religion, and national origins.* New York: Oxford University Press.

Greeley, Andrew (1971). *Why can't they be like us? America's white ethnic groups.* New York: Dutton.

Handlin, Oscar (1941). *Boston's immigrants: A study of acculturation.* Cambridge: Harvard University Press.

Handlin, Oscar (1951). *The uprooted: The epic story of the great migrations that made the American people.* Boston: Little, Brown.

Hechter, Michael (1977). *Internal colonialism, the Celtic fringe in British national development, 1536–1966.* Berkeley, California: University of California Press.

Howe, Irving (1976). *World of our fathers.* New York: Harcourt, Brace, Jovanovich.

Howe, Irving, and Libo, Kenneth (1979). *How we lived, a documentary history of immigrant Jews in America.* New York: Richard March.

Keely, Charles B. (1981). *Global refugee policy: The case for a development-oriented strategy.* New York: The Population Council.

Kim, Illsoo (1981). *New urban immigrants, the Korean community in New York.* Princeton, New Jersey: Princeton University Press.

Light, H. Ivan (1972). *Ethnic enterprise in America: Business and welfare among Chinese, Japanese, and Blacks.* Berkeley, California: University of California Press.

Light, H. Ivan (1980). Asian enterprise in America: Chinese, Japanese, and Koreans in small business. In *Self-help in urban America* (Scott Cummings, ed.), pp. 33–57. New York: Kennikat Press.

Nagel, Joane, and Olzak, Susan (1982). Ethnic mobilization in new and old states: An extension of the competition model. *Social Problems* 30:127–143.

National Research Council (1985). Immigration statistics: A story of neglect. Report of the Panel on Immigration Statistics. Washington, D.C.: National Academy of Sciences.

Parenti, Michael (1967). Ethnic politics and the persistence of ethnic identification. *American Political Science Review* 61:717–726.

Petersen, William (1971). *Japanese Americans, oppression and success.* New York: Random House.

Piore, Michael J. (1975). Notes for a theory of labor market stratification. In *Labor market segmentation* (Richard C. Edwards, Michael Reich, and David M. Gordon, eds.), pp. 125–171. Lexington, Massachusetts: Heath.

Piore, Michael J. (1979). *Birds of passage, migrant labor and industrial societies.* New York: Cambridge University Press.

Portes, Alejandro (1976). Determinants of the brain drain. *International Migration Review* 10 (Winter):489–508.

Portes, Alejandro (1981). Modes of structural incorporation and theories of labor immigration. In *Global Trends in Migration, Theory and Research on International Population Movements* (Mary M. Kritz, Charles B. Keely, and Silvano M. Tomasi, eds.), pp. 279–297. New York: Center for Migration Studies.

Portes, Alejandro, and Bach, Robert L. (1985). *Latin journey, Cuban and Mexican immigrants in the United States.* Berkeley, California: University of California Press.

Rischin, Moses (1962). *The promised city, New York Jews 1870–1914.* Cambridge, Massachusetts: Harvard University Press.

Sassen-Koob, Saskia (1980). Immigrant and minority workers in the organization of the labor process. *Journal of Ethnic Studies* (1/Spring): 1–34.

Sowell, Thomas (1981). *Ethnic America: A history.* New York: Basic Books.

Stevens, Rosemary, Goodman, Louis W., and Mick, Stephen (1978). *The alien doctors, foreign medical graduates in American hospitals.* New York: Wiley.

Suttles, Gerald D. (1968). *The social order of the slum, ethnicity and territory in the inner city.* Chicago: University of Chicago Press.

Vecoli, Rudolph (1977). The Italian Americans. In *Uncertain Americans* (L. Dinnerstein and F. C. Jaher, eds.), pp. 201–215. New York: Oxford University Press.

Warner, W. Lloyd, and Srole, Leo (1945). *The social systems of American ethnic groups.* New Haven: Yale University Press.

Wirth, Louis (1956). *The ghetto.* Chicago: University of Chicago Press.

Wittke, Carl (1952). *Refugees of revolution: The German Forty-eighters in America.* Philadelphia: University of Pennsylvania Press.

Zolberg, Aristide (1983). Contemporary transnational migrations in historical perspective: Patterns and dilemmas. In *U.S. immigration and refugee policy* (Mary M. Kritz, ed.), pp. 15–51. Lexington, Massachusetts: Heath.

13

THE UNHAPPY MARRIAGE OF
MARXISM AND FEMINISM

TOWARDS A MORE PROGRESSIVE UNION

Heidi Hartmann

◆◆◆

We can usefully define patriarchy as a set of social relations between men, which have a material base, and which, though hierarchical, establish or create interdependence and solidarity among men that enable them to dominate women. Though patriarchy is hierarchical and men of different classes, races, or ethnic groups have different places in the patriarchy, they also are united in their shared relationship of dominance over their women; they are dependent on each other to maintain that domination. Hierarchies "work" at least in part because they create vested interests in the status quo. Those at the higher levels can "buy off" those at the lower levels by offering them power over those still lower. In the hierarchy of patriarchy, all men, whatever their rank in the patriarchy, are bought off by being able to control at least some women. There is some evidence to suggest that when patriarchy was first institutionalized in state societies, the ascending rulers

Heidi Hartmann, "The Unhappy Marriage of Marxism and Feminism: Towards a More Progressive Union," in *Women and Revolution,* edited by Lydia Sargent, pp. 14–23, 25–27, 37–38, 40–41. Copyright by South End Press. Reprinted by permission of South End Press.

literally made men the heads of their families (enforcing their control over their wives and children) in exchange for the men's ceding some of their tribal resources to the new rulers.¹ Men are dependent on one another (despite their hierarchical ordering) to maintain their control over women.

The material base upon which patriarchy rests lies most fundamentally in men's control over women's labor power. Men maintain this control by excluding women from access to some essential productive resources (in capitalist societies, for example, jobs that pay living wages) and by restricting women's sexuality. Monogamous heterosexual marriage is one relatively recent and efficient form that seems to allow men to control both these areas. Controlling women's access to resources and their sexuality, in turn, allows men to control women's labor power, both for the purpose of serving men in many personal and sexual ways and for the purpose of rearing children. The services women render men, and which exonerate men from having to perform many unpleasant tasks (like cleaning toilets) occur outside as well as inside the family setting. Examples outside the family include the harassment of women workers and students by male bosses and professors as well as the common use of secretaries to run personal errands, make coffee, and provide "sexy" surroundings. Rearing children, whether or not the children's labor power is of immediate benefit to their fathers, is nevertheless a crucial task in perpetuating patriarchy as a system. Just as class society must be reproduced by schools, work places, consumption norms, etc., so must patriarchal social relations. In our society children are generally reared by women at home, women socially defined and recognized as inferior to men, while men appear in the domestic picture only rarely. Children raised in this way generally learn their places in the gender hierarchy well. Central to this process, however, are the areas outside the home where patriarchal behaviors are taught and the inferior position of women enforced and reinforced: churches, schools, sports, clubs, unions, armies, factories, offices, health centers, the media, etc.

The material base of patriarchy, then, does not rest solely on childrearing in the family, but on all the social structures that enable men to control women's labor. The aspects of social structures that perpetuate patriarchy are theoretically identifiable, hence separable from their other aspects. Gayle Rubin has increased our ability to identify the patriarchal element of these social structures enormously by identifying "sex/gender systems":

"sex/gender system" is the set of arrangements by which a society transforms biological sexuality into products of human activity, and in which these transformed sexual needs are satisfied.[2]

We are born female and male, biological sexes, but we are created woman and man, socially recognized genders. *How* we are so created is that second aspect of the *mode* of production of which Engels spoke, "the production of human beings themselves, the propagation of the species."[3]

How people propagate the species is socially determined. If, biologically, people are sexually polymorphous, and society were organized in such a way that all forms of sexual expression were equally permissible, reproduction would result only from some sexual encounters, the heterosexual ones. The strict division of labor by sex, a social invention common to all known societies, creates two very separate genders and a need for men and women to get together for economic reasons. It thus helps to direct their sexual needs toward heterosexual fulfillment, and helps to ensure biological reproduction. In more imaginative societies, biological reproduction might be ensured by other techniques, but the division of labor by sex appears to be the universal solution to date. Although it is theoretically possible that a sexual division of labor not imply inequality between the sexes, in most known societies, the socially acceptable division of labor by sex is one which accords lower status to women's work. The sexual division of labor is also the underpinning of sexual subcultures in which men and women experience life differently; it is the material base of male power which is exercised (in our society) not just in not doing housework and in securing superior employment, but psychologically as well.

How people meet their sexual needs, how they reproduce, how they inculcate social norms in new generations, how they learn gender, how it feels to be a man or a woman—all occur in the realm Rubin labels the sex/gender system. Rubin emphasizes the influence of kinship (which tells you with whom you can satisfy sexual needs) and the development of gender specific personalities via childrearing and the "oedipal machine." In addition, however, we can use the concept of the sex/gender system to examine all other social institutions for the roles they play in defining and reinforcing gender hierarchies. Rubin notes that theoretically a sex/gender system could be female dominant, male dominant, or egalitarian, but declines to label various known sex/gender systems or to periodize history accordingly. We choose to label our present sex/gender system patriarchy, because it appropriately captures the notion of hierarchy and male dominance which we see as central to the present system.

Economic production (what Marxists are used to referring to as *the* mode of production) and the production of people in the sex/gender sphere both determine "the social organization under which the people of a particular historical epoch and a particular country live," according to Engels. The whole of society, then, can be understood by looking at both these types of production and reproduction, people and things. There is no such thing as "pure capitalism," nor does "pure patriarchy" exist, for they must of necessity coexist. What exists is patriarchal capitalism, or patriarchal feudalism, or egalitarian hunting/ gathering societies, or matriarchal horticultural societies, or patriarchal horticultural societies, and so on. There appears to be no necessary connection between *changes* in the one aspect of production and changes in the other. A society could undergo transition from capitalism to socialism, for example, and remain patriarchal. Common sense, history, and our experience tell us, however, that these two aspects of production are so closely intertwined, that change in one ordinarily creates movement, tension, or contradiction in the other.

Racial hierarchies can also be understood in this context. Further elaboration may be possible along the lines of defining color/race systems, arenas of social life that take biological color and turn it into a social category, race. Racial hierarchies, like gender hierarchies, are aspects of our social organization, of how people are produced and reproduced. They are not fundamentally ideological; they constitute that second aspect of our mode of production, the production and reproduction of people. It might be most accurate then to refer to our societies not as, for example, simply capitalist, but as patriarchal capitalist white supremacist.

Capitalist development creates the places for a hierarchy of workers, but traditional Marxist categories cannot tell us who will fill which places. Gender and racial hierarchies determine who fills the empty places. *Patriarchy is not simply hierarchical organization,* but hierarchy in which *particular* people fill *particular* places. It is in studying patriarchy that we learn why it is women who are dominated and how. While we believe that most known societies have been patriarchal, we do not view patriarchy as a universal, unchanging phenomenon. Rather patriarchy, the set of interrelations among men that allow men to dominate women, has changed in form and intensity over time. It is crucial that the hierarchy among men, and their differential access to patriarchal benefits, be examined. Surely, class, race, nationality, and even marital status and sexual orientation, as well as the obvious age, come into play here. And women of different class, race, national, marital status, or sexual orientation groups are subjected to different degrees of patriarchal power. Women may themselves exercise class, race, or national power, or even patriarchal power (through their family connections) over men lower in the patriarchal hierarchy than their own male kin.

To recapitulate, we define patriarchy as a set of social relations which has a material base and in which there are hierarchical relations between men and solidarity among them which enable them in turn to dominate women. The material base of patriarchy is men's control over women's labor power. That control is maintained by excluding women from access to necessary economically productive resources and by restricting women's sexuality. Men exercise their control in receiving personal service work from women, in not having to do housework or rear children, in having access to women's bodies for sex, and in feeling powerful and being powerful. The crucial elements of patriarchy as we *currently* experience them are: heterosexual marriage (and consequent homophobia), female childrearing and housework, women's economic dependence on men (enforced by arrangements in the labor market), the state, and numerous institutions based on social relations among men— clubs, sports, unions, professions, universities, churches, corporations, and armies. All of these elements need to be examined if we are to understand patriarchal capitalism. . . .

INDUSTRIALIZATION AND THE DEVELOPMENT
OF FAMILY WAGES

Marxists made quite logical inferences from a selection of the social phenomena they witnessed in the nineteenth century. But Marxists ultimately underestimated the strength of the preexisting patriarchal social forces with which fledgling capital had to contend and the need for capital to adjust to these forces. The industrial revolution was drawing all people into the labor force, including women and children; in fact the first factories used child and female labor almost exclusively. That women and children could earn wages separately from men both undermined authority relations and kept wages low for everyone. Kautsky, writing in 1892, described the process this way:

[Then with] the wife and young children of the working-man . . . able
to take care of themselves, the wages of the male worker can safely be reduced to the level of his own personal needs without the risk of
stopping the fresh supply of labor power.

The labor of women and children, moreover, affords the additional
advantage that these are less capable of resistance than men [sic]; and
their introduction into the ranks of the workers increases tremendously
the quantity of labor that is offered for sale in the market.

Accordingly, the labor of women and children . . . also diminishes
[the] capacity [of the male worker] for resistance in that it overstocks
the market; owing to both these circumstances it lowers the wages of
the working-man.[4]

The terrible effects on working class family life of low wages and of forced
participation of all family members in the labor force were recognized by
Marxists. Kautsky wrote:

The capitalist system of production does not in most cases destroy the
single household of the workingman, but robs it of all but its unpleasant features. The activity of woman today in industrial pursuits . . .
means an increase of her former burden by a new one. *But one cannot
serve two masters.* The household of the working-man suffers whenever
his wife must help to earn the daily bread.[5]

Working men as well as Kautsky recognized the disadvantages of female
wage labor. Not only were women "cheap competition" but working women
were their very wives, who could not "serve two masters" well. Male workers
resisted the wholesale entrance of women and children into the labor force,
and sought to exclude them from union membership and the labor force as
well. In 1846 the *Ten-Hours' Advocate* stated:

It is needless for us to say, that all attempts to improve the morals and
physical condition of female factory workers will be abortive, unless
their hours are materially reduced. Indeed we may go so far as to say,
that married females would be much better occupied in performing the
domestic duties of the household, than following the never-tiring motion of machinery. We therefore hope the day is not distant, when the

husband will be able to provide for his wife and family, without sending the former to endure the drudgery of a cotton mill.[6]

In the United States in 1854 the National Typographical Union resolved not to "encourage by its act the employment of female compositors." Male unionists did not want to afford union protection to women workers; they tried to exclude them instead. In 1879 Adolph Strasser, president of the Cigarmakers International Union, said: "We cannot drive the females out of the trade, but we can restrict their daily quota of labor through factory laws."[7]

While the problem of cheap competition could have been solved by organizing the wage-earning women and youths, the problem of disrupted family life could not be. Men reserved union protection for men and argued for protective labor laws for women and children. Protective labor laws, while they may have ameliorated some of the worst abuses of female and child labor, also limited the participation of adult women in many "male" jobs. Men sought to keep high wage jobs for themselves and to raise male wages generally. They argued for wages sufficient for their wage labor alone to support their families. This "family wage" system gradually came to be the norm for stable working class families at the end of the nineteenth century and the beginning of the twentieth. Several observers have declared the non–wage-working wife to be part of the standard of living of male workers. Instead of fighting for equal wages for men and women, male workers sought the family wage, wanting to retain their wives' services at home. In the absence of patriarchy a unified working class might have confronted capitalism, but patriarchal social relations divided the working class, allowing one part (men) to be bought off at the expense of the other (women). Both the hierarchy between men and the solidarity among them were crucial in this process of resolution. Family wages may be understood as a resolution of the conflict over women's labor power which was occurring between patriarchal and capitalist interests at that time.

Family wages for most adult men imply men's acceptance, and collusion in, lower wages for others, young people, women, and socially defined inferior men as well (Irish, blacks, etc., the lowest groups in the patriarchal hierarchy who are denied many of the patriarchal benefits). Lower wages for women and children and inferior men are enforced by job segregation in the labor market, in turn maintained by unions and management as well as by auxiliary institutions like schools, training programs, and even families. Job segregation by sex, by insuring that women have the lower paid jobs, both assures women's economic dependence on men and reinforces notions of appropriate spheres for women and men. For most men, then, the development of family wages secured the material base of male domination in two ways. First, men have the better jobs in the labor market and earn higher wages than women. The lower pay women receive in the labor market both perpetuates men's material advantage over women and encourages women to choose wifery as a career. Second, then, women do housework, childcare, and perform other services at home which benefit men directly. Women's home responsibilities in turn reinforce their inferior labor market position.

The resolution that developed in the early twentieth century can be seen to benefit capitalist interests as well as patriarchal interests. Capitalists, it is often argued, recognized that in the extreme conditions which prevailed in the early nineteenth century industrialization, working class families could not adequately reproduce themselves. They realized that housewives produced and maintained healthier workers than wage-working wives and that educated children became better workers than noneducated ones. The bargain, paying family wages to men and keeping women home, suited the capitalists at the time as well as the male workers. Although the terms of the bargain have altered over time, it is still true that the family and women's work in the family serve capital by providing a labor force and serve men as the space in which they exercise their privilege. Women, working to serve men and their families, also serve capital as consumers.[8] The family is also the place where dominance and submission are learned, as Firestone, the Frankfurt School, and many others have explained.[9] Obedient children become obedient workers; girls and boys each learn their proper roles.

While the family wage shows that capitalism adjusts to patriarchy, the changing status of children shows that patriarchy adjusts to capital. Children, like women, came to be excluded from wage labor. As children's ability to earn money declined, their legal relationship to their parents changed. At the beginning of the industrial era in the United States, fulfilling children's need for their fathers was thought to be crucial, even primary, to their happy development; fathers had legal priority in cases of contested custody. As children's ability to contribute to the economic well-being of the family declined, mothers came increasingly to be viewed as crucial to the happy development of their children, and gained legal priority in cases of contested custody.[10] Here patriarchy adapted to the changing economic role of children: when children were productive, men claimed them; as children became unproductive, they were given to women. . . .

THE FAMILY AND THE FAMILY WAGE TODAY

We argued above that, with respect to capitalism and patriarchy, the adaptation, or mutual accommodation, took the form of the development of the family wage in the early twentieth century. The family wage cemented the partnership between patriarchy and capital. Despite women's increased labor force participation, particularly rapid since World War II, the family wage is still, we argue, the cornerstone of the present sexual division of labor—in which women are primarily responsible for housework and men primarily for wage work. Women's lower wages in the labor market (combined with the need for children to be reared by someone) assure the continued existence of the family as a necessary income pooling unit. The family, supported by the family wage, thus allows the control of women's labor by men both within and without the family.

Though women's increased wage work may cause stress for the family (similar to the stress Kautsky and Engels noted in the nineteenth century), it would be wrong to think that as a consequence, the concepts and the realities of the family and of the sexual division of labor will soon disappear. The sexual division of labor reappears in the labor market, where women work at women's jobs, often the very jobs they used to do only at home—food preparation and service, cleaning of all kinds, caring for people, and so on. As these jobs are low-status and low-paying patriarchal relations remain intact, though their material base shifts somewhat from the family to the wage differential, from family-based to industrially based patriarchy.[11]

Industrially based patriarchal relations are enforced in a variety of ways. Union contracts which specify lower wages, lesser benefits, and fewer advancement opportunities for women are not just atavistic hangovers—a case of sexist attitudes or male supremacist ideology—they maintain the material base of the patriarchal system. While some would go so far as to argue that patriarchy is already absent from the family (see, for example, Stewart Ewen, *Captains of Consciousness*),[12] we would not. Although the terms of the compromise between capital and patriarchy are changing as additional tasks formerly located in the family are capitalized, and the location of the deployment of women's labor power shifts, it is nevertheless true, as we have argued above, that the wage differential caused by extreme job segregation in the labor market reinforces the family, and, with it, the domestic division of labor, by encouraging women to marry. The "ideal" of the family wage—that a man can earn enough to support an entire family—may be giving way to a new ideal that both men and women contribute through wage earning to the cash income of the family. The wage differential, then, will become increasingly necessary in perpetuating patriarchy, the male control of women's labor power. The wage differential will aid in *defining* women's work as secondary to men's at the same time it necessitates women's actual continued economic dependence on men. The sexual division of labor in the labor market and elsewhere should be understood as a manifestation of patriarchy which serves to perpetuate it.

Many people have argued that though the partnership between capital and patriarchy exists now, it may *in the long run* prove intolerable to capitalism; capital may eventually destroy both familial relations and patriarchy. The argument proceeds logically that capitalist social relations (of which the family is not an example) tend to become universalized, that women will become increasingly able to earn money and will increasingly refuse to submit to subordination in the family, and that since the family is oppressive particularly to women and children, it will collapse as soon as people can support themselves outside it.

We do not think that the patriarchal relations embodied in the family can be destroyed so easily by capital, and we see little evidence that the family system is presently disintegrating. Although the increasing labor force participation of women has made divorce more feasible, the incentives to divorce are not overwhelming for women. Women's wages allow very few women to support themselves and their children independently and adequately. The evidence for the decay of the traditional family is weak at best. The divorce rate has not so much increased, as it has evened out among classes; moreover, the remarriage rate is also very high. Up until the 1970 census, the first-marriage age was continuing its historic decline. Since 1970 people seem to have been delaying marriage and childbearing, but most recently, the birth rate has begun to increase again. It is true that larger proportions of the population are now living outside traditional families. Young people, especially, are leaving their parents' homes and establishing their own households before they marry and start traditional families. Older people, especially women, are finding themselves alone in their own households, after their children are grown and they experience separation or death of a spouse. Nevertheless, trends indicate that the new generations of young people will form nuclear families at some time in their adult lives in higher proportions than ever before. The cohorts, or groups of people, born since 1930 have much higher rates of eventual marriage and childrearing than previous cohorts. The duration of marriage and childrearing may be shortening, but its incidence is still spreading.[13]

The argument that capital destroys the family also overlooks the social forces which make family life appealing. Despite critiques of nuclear families as psychologically destructive, in a competitive society the family still meets real needs for many people. This is true not only of long-term monogamy, but even more so for raising children. Single parents bear both financial and psychic burdens. For working class women, in particular, these burdens make the "independence" of labor force participation illusory. Single parent families have recently been seen by policy analysts as transitional family formations which become two-parent families upon remarriage.[14]

It could be that the effects of women's increasing labor force participation are found in a declining sexual division of labor within the family, rather than in more frequent divorce, but evidence for this is also lacking. Statistics on who does housework, even in families with wage-earning wives, show little change in recent years; women still do most of it.[15] The double day is a reality for wage-working women. This is hardly surprising since the sexual division of labor outside the family, in the labor market, keeps women financially dependent on men—even when they earn a wage themselves. The future of patriarchy does not, however, rest solely on the future of familial relations. For patriarchy, like capital, can be surprisingly flexible and adaptable.

Notes

[1] See Viana Muller, "The Formation of the State and the Oppression of Women: Some Theoretical Considerations and a Case Study in England and Wales," *Review of Radical Political Economics*, Vol. 9, no. 3 (Fall 1977), pp. 7–21.

[2] Gayle Rubin, "The Traffic in Women," in *Toward an Anthropology of Women*, ed. Rayna Rapp Reiter (New York: Monthly Review Press, 1975), p. 159.

[3] Frederick Engels, "Preface to the First Edition," *The Origin of the Family, Private Property and the State,* edited, with an introduction by Eleanor Burke Leacock (New York: International Publishers, 1972). The first aspect of the mode of production is, according to Engels, "the production of the means of existence, of food, clothing, and shelter and the tools necessary for that production."— ED.

[4] Karl Kautsky, *The Class Struggle* (New York: Norton, 1971), pp. 25–26.

[5] We might add, "outside the household." Kautsky, *Class Struggle*, p. 26, our emphasis.

[6] Cited in Neil Smelser, *Social Change and the Industrial Revolution* (Chicago: University of Chicago Press, 1959), p. 301.

[7] These examples are from Heidi I. Hartmann, "Capitalism, Patriarchy, and Job Segregation by Sex," *Signs: Journal of Women in Culture and Society,* Vol. 1, no. 3, pt. 2 (Spring 1976), pp. 162–163.

[8] See Batya Weinbaum and Amy Bridges, "The Other Side of the Paycheck: Monopoly Capital and the Structure of Consumption," *Monthly Review,* Vol. 28, no. 3 (July-August 1976), pp. 88–103, for a discussion of women's consumption work.

[9] Shulamith Firestone, *The Dialectic of Sex* (New York: Bantam Books, 1971). For the view of the Frankfurt School, see Max Horkheimer, "Authority and the Family," in *Critical Theory* (New York: Herder & Herder, 1972) and Frankfurt Institute of Social Research, "The Family," in *Aspects of Sociology* (Boston: Beacon, 1972).

[10] Carol Brown, "Patriarchal Capitalism and the Female-Headed Family," *Social Scientist* (India); no. 40–41 (November-December 1975), pp. 28–39.

[11] Carol Brown, in "Patriarchal Capitalism," argues, for example, that we are moving from "family based" to "industrially-based" patriarchy within capitalism.

[12] Stewart Ewen, *Captains of Consciousness* (New York: Random House, 1976).

[13] For the proportion of people in nuclear families, see Peter Uhlenberg, "Cohort Variations in Family Life Cycle Experiences of U.S. Females," *Journal of Marriage and the Family,* Vol. 36, no. 5 (May 1974), pp. 284–292. For remarriage rates see Paul C. Glick and Arthur J. Norton, "Perspectives on the Recent Upturn in Divorce and Remarriage," *Demography,* Vol. 10 (1974), pp. 301–314. For divorce and income levels see Arthur J. Norton and Paul C. Glick, "Marital Instability: Past, Present, and Future," *Journal of Social Issues,* Vol. 32, no. 1 (1976), pp. 5–20. Also see Mary Jo Bane, *Here to Stay: American Families in the Twentieth Century* (New York: Basic Books, 1976).

[14] Heather L. Ross and Isabel B. Sawhill, *Time of Transition: The Growth of Families Headed by Women* (Washington, D.C.: The Urban Institute, 1975).

[15] See Kathryn E. Walker and Margaret E. Woods, *Time Use: A Measure of Household Production of Family Goods and Services* (Washington, D.C.: American Home Economics Association, 1976); and Heidi I. Hartmann, "The Family as the Locus of Gender, Class, and Political Struggle: The Example of Housework," *Signs: Journal of Women in Culture and Society,* Vol. 6, no. 3 (Spring 1981), pp. 366–394.

14

LABOR MARKETS
AS QUEUES

A STRUCTURAL APPROACH TO CHANGING
OCCUPATIONAL SEX COMPOSITION

Barbara F. Reskin

◆◆◆

The historic persistence of sex segregation (Gross 1968; Beller 1984)
made women's dramatic gains during the 1970s in such diverse male
occupations as pharmacy, bank management, bartending, and typesetting
noteworthy. Why did women disproportionately enter these and a few other
male occupations when they made only modest progress in most and lost
ground in a few? To answer this question, Patricia Roos and I conducted a
two-part study: multivariate analyses of the changing sex composition in all
detailed census occupations and in-depth case studies of 14 occupations in
which women's representation increased at least twice as much as it had in
the labor force as a whole (see Table 14.1). This chapter draws on those case
studies: bank managers (Bird 1990), bartenders (Detman 1990), systems

Barbara F. Reskin, "Labor Markets as Queues: A Structural Approach to Changing Occupational Sex
Composition," in *Micro-macro Linkages in Sociology,* edited by Joan Huber, pp. 170–186, 188–192.
Copyright 1991 by Sage Publications, Inc.

Occupation	1970 %	1980 %	1988 %	1970–1988 Increase %
Financial managers	19.4	31.4	42.4	23.0
Accountants/auditors	24.6	38.1	49.6	25.0
Operation/systems analysts	11.1	27.7	39.6	28.5
Pharmacists	12.1	24.0	31.9	19.8
Public relations specialists	26.6	48.8	59.1	32.5
Editors and reporters	41.6	49.3	n.a.	n.a.
Insurance sales	12.9	25.4	29.7	16.8
Real estate sales	31.2	45.2	48.5	17.3
Insurance adjusters/examiners	29.6	60.2	72.2	42.6
Bartenders	21.2	44.3	49.6	28.4
Bakers	25.4	40.7	47.8	22.4
Bus Drivers	28.3	45.8	48.5	20.2
Typesetters/compositors	16.8	55.7	73.9	57.1
Labor force	38.0	42.6	45.0	7.0

Table 14.1 Percent Females in Feminizing Occupations, 1970, 1980, 1988

analysts (Donato 1990a), public relations specialists (Donato 1990b), pharmacists (Phipps 1990a), insurance adjusters/examiners (Phipps 1990b), typesetters/compositors (Roos 1990), insurance salespersons (Thomas 1990), real estate salespersons (Thomas and Reskin 1990), bakers (Steiger and Reskin 1990), book editors (Reskin and Roos 1990), print and broadcast reporters, and accountants.[1] Although the case studies revealed that widely different factors precipitated these occupations' feminization, the process of change can be encompassed in a single perspective—queuing. This chapter begins by outlining the queuing approach. It then shows how the determinants of occupational feminization conformed to queuing processes. Finally, it argues that the queue model as I have developed it offers a structural approach to understanding change in job composition.

Queuing: an Overview

Simply stated, a queuing perspective views labor markets as composed of labor queues and job queues that reflect, respectively, employers' ranking of possible workers and workers' ranking of jobs.[2] The idea of the *labor* queue originated in Lester Thurow's (1969) work on race differences in unemployment and was elaborated by Hodge (1973) and Lieberson (1980). Rotella's (1977) analysis of the feminization of clerical work, Lieberson's (1980) study of racial and ethnic inequality, and Strober's (1984) theory of sex segregation implicitly invoked *job* as well as *labor* queues. The queuing perspective presented here views occupational composition as resulting from the simultaneous operation of job and labor queues (also see Reskin and Roos 1990). Employers hire workers from as high in the labor queue as possible, and workers accept the best jobs available to them, so the most desirable jobs go to the most preferred workers, less attractive jobs go to workers lower in the labor queue, and the most lowly workers end up jobless or in jobs others have rejected.

Three structural properties characterize both job and labor queues: (a) the ordering of their elements, (b) whether or not their elements overlap, and (c) their shape. By *elements,* I mean the constituent units—groups of potential workers or jobs. Thus the *ordering of elements* simply indicates in what order workers rank possible jobs and employers rank prospective workers. I pass over how workers order jobs in the labor queue as something both sociologists and workers understand. In ordering the labor queue, employers

Panel A. Hypothetical labor queues ordered by race for predominately white and predominately black labor markets, respectively

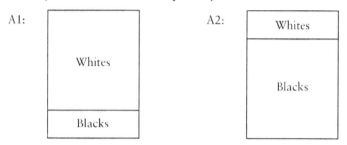

Panel B. Hypothetical job queues ordered by nonmanual-manual work for predominately nonmanual and predominately manual occupational structures, respectively

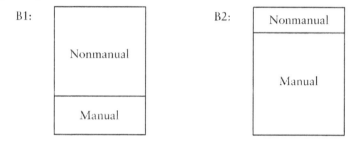

Figure 14.1 Illustration of Variation in the Shape of Labor and Job Queues

consider potential productivity and cost.[3] However, the indirect effect of workers' sex on employers' estimations of the former and its direct influence on how employers rank workers result in labor queues that encompass and often act as *gender queues.*

The absolute and relative numbers of elements in a queue determine its *shape.* Thus the number of prospective workers in each subgroup in a labor market sets the shape of the labor queue, and the number of jobs at each level in the job queue fixes its shape. Panels A and B of Figure 14.1 show how the shape of labor and job queues can vary while their order remains constant. This variation influences each group's probable access to occupations of varying desirability. (Put differently, it shows how a queue's shape influences each occupation's chance of recruiting workers from particular groups.) For example, in a society with relatively few workers in the preferred group (A2) and few desirable jobs (B2), preferred groups will monopolize

Panel A. Racial group membership is an overiding consideration to rankers. Employers hire applicants as qualified as possible, but hire unqualified whites before hiring highly qualified blacks.

Blacks Low	Blacks Moderate	Blacks High	Whites Low	Whites Moderate	Whites High

Level of Qualification

Panel B. Racial group membership is a minor consideration to rankers. Employers hire the most qualified applicants, but within levels of qualification, give white applicants an edge over equally qualified blacks.

Blacks Low	Whites Low	Blacks Moderate	Whites Moderate	Blacks High	Whites High

Level of Qualification

Panel C. Racial group membership is an intermediate consideration to rankers. Employers will prefer a more qualified white over a less qualified black, but will hire very qualified blacks over unqualified whites.

Blacks Low	Blacks Moderate	Whites Low	Blacks High	Whites Moderate	Whites High

Level of Qualification

Figure 14.2   Illustration of Variation in the Intensity of Raters' Preferences with Respect to Race

better or worse jobs than persons from their group normally command. In consequence, when good jobs sharply outnumber highly ranked workers as in panels A2 and B1, employers must fill the better jobs with workers from lower in the labor queue than they usually hire. In contrast, when the *job queue* is bottom heavy, only the highest-ranked workers get desirable jobs, and workers moderately high in the labor queue are forced to settle for less. As Lieberson (1980, p. 297) has shown, both the *absolute* and the *relative* sizes of each group in the labor queue affect lower-ranked workers' chances of getting desirable jobs. The larger a subordinate group relative to the size of the preferred group, the more costly it is for employers to deny its members good jobs (Hodge 1973).

Whether or not *elements overlap* denotes the strength of rankers' prefer-ences for one element over another. Among some employers, group membership is the overriding consideration in ordering the labor queue, and rankers favor persons from the group they prefer, regardless of qualifi-cations. For other labor queues, employers are indifferent to group membership except to break ties between otherwise equally qualified prospects. Figure 14.2 illustrates variation in the intensity of raters' prefer-ences with respect to workers' race in three hypothetical labor queues. The space between the races in panel A depicts the ranking for employers who invariably hire the lowest-ranked white worker over the best black worker; the overlapping groups in panel B depict the situation in which raters' aversion to blacks is slight. Panel C illustrates an intermediate situation in which employers prefer white workers over equally qualified blacks but will set aside racial biases to hire very talented blacks over mediocre whites. Where preferences are weak, substantial job-level integration exists. In con-trast, when preferences are overriding, all members of the favored group precede all members of the disfavored group in the labor queue, and the la-bor market is totally segmented.

Workers' job preferences also vary in intensity. Some workers may categor-ically prefer any job in a high-ranked occupation to working in a lower occupation (expressed, for example, in rejecting manual jobs in favor of non-manual work). Alternatively, they may be more attuned to specific job characteristics than their overall rank, occasionally eschewing jobs in occupa-tions usually reserved for the preferred group and appropriating more desirable jobs within lower-ranked occupations that usually go to less pre-ferred groups. Strong preferences mean that workers invariably prefer one type of job (e.g., professional or nonmanual work) over another.

Changes in any of these structural features of queues—employers' rank-ings of workers or workers' ranking of jobs, the intensity of either groups' preferences, and the relative distributions of workers or jobs—can transform occupations' composition.

QUEUING MODELS AS STRUCTURAL APPROACHES
TO OCCUPATIONAL COMPOSITION

Queuing emphasizes how employers rank groups of potential workers as well as how workers rank jobs. Because rankings simply boil down to preferences, is *queuing* not simply a fancy way to say that workers' and employers' preferences affect their labor market decisions? What does the queuing perspective add to the neoclassical economic approach to occupational segregation?

The neoclassical economic approach assumes (a) that workers' labor market decisions represent attempts to maximize their lifetime earnings, (b) that differences in the sexes' distributions across jobs stem primarily from women's family responsibilities, (c) that employers act to maximize revenues, and (d) that, in the short run, discriminatory "tastes" sometimes divert employers from their economic best interests, but, in the long run, competitive disadvantages that accrue from indulging economically irrational tastes lead discrimination to decline over time (Becker 1957). Thus traditional economic analysis treats sex segregation as the *aggregate* outcome of the mostly rational choices of *individual* workers and employers.

A queuing approach to changing occupational sex composition differs in several ways. First, queuing emphasizes the *collective* nature of sex segregation that results from *socially structured rankings* by *groups in conflict*. In contrast to the neoclassical perspective, queuing highlights the roles played by power and conflict between groups with contradictory interests in shaping occupations' composition. As I show below, the queuing perspective elucidates the role of group power in determining occupational access.

Second, it takes seriously the effects of noneconomic factors on workers' rankings of occupations and employers' rankings of prospective workers. It reminds us that working conditions, autonomy, social standing, career opportunities, and sex composition influence how workers appraise jobs and that employers' prejudices, stereotypes, and desire to preserve their own and other men's advantages influence how they rank workers.

Third, the queuing perspective assumes that the sexes rank most occupations similarly, so it predicts women's influx into accessible male occupations in view of their superior rewards. In explaining occupational feminization, it directs our attention to changes in employers' need for women and to declining barriers to women's access to traditionally male jobs. In other words, the queuing perspective redirects us from characteristics of female workers to structural properties of labor markets that in turn are shaped by the preferences of employers and male workers.

POWER AND COALITIONS IN ORDERING THE LABOR QUEUE

In examining how conflict affects occupations' composition, we must bear in mind three points: First, three groups with competing interests have a stake in which sex predominates in an occupation—employers (who are over-whelmingly male), male workers, and female workers. Second, the greater social and economic power of employers and of men give them a substantial advantage in the struggle over what sex heads the queue for desirable occupations. Third, the outcome of the struggle over what sex dominates an occupation—occupations' sex compositions—represents a de facto coalition between competing groups.

Employers.   Given their orientation toward minimizing costs and maximizing labor docility, employers should prefer female workers for all jobs. That so few have done so reminds us that other considerations affect male employers' labor decisions. Foremost among these is the personal stake of both male employers and male workers in excluding women from male-labeled jobs to preserve sex differentiation and hence male privilege in all spheres. Because sex differentiation both legitimates and facilitates unequal treatment, physically segregating the sexes at work and assigning them different tasks preserves male dominance by legitimating unequal wages, insulating men from female competition, supporting men's dominance in other public realms and the home, and shoring up myths of essential sex differences and male superiority (Reskin 1988). As Cockburn (1988, p. 41) put it, "Behind occupational segregation is gender differentiation, and behind that is male power."

Other considerations inclining employers to preserve good jobs for men include (a) the ability of male workers—and sometimes customers—to penalize employers for hiring women for "men's" jobs (Bergmann and Darity 1981; Strober 1988); (b) organizational inertia that makes following standard practices the course of least resistance; (c) custom—in other words, jobs' sex labels—combined with the uncertainties attendant on radically altering employment practices (Cohn 1985; Strom 1987; Figart and Bergmann 1989, p. 36); (d) gender solidarity with male workers;[4] and (e) forestalling later threats to their own jobs. As long as employers can operate profitably, preserving male jobs can be a fairly cheap amenity, especially if their competitors also practice male preference (Stolzenberg 1982; Strober 1988). Thus, in reserving male-dominated jobs for men, employers at once appease male workers, who could make hiring women costly; simplify organizational decisions; and shore up the gender hierarchy from which they benefit.

Male Workers.   Male workers' disadvantaged economic position vis-à-vis employers and their advantaged sex status divide their interests. They stand to gain in the long run from acting collectively with *all* workers, but, in the short run, men are vulnerable to job and wage competition from women who must settle for lower wages. Equal job opportunities for women can also cost men domestic benefits they derive from sex inequality in the workplace and can threaten the gender hierarchy from which working men benefit (Hartmann 1976; Reskin 1988). Thus, for the most part, male workers do better in the short run by monopolizing male jobs than by welcoming female coworkers with whom they could collectively fight for better pay. Only when large numbers of women already have their foot in the door, or when labor shortages or outside agencies have imposed integration, are male workers freed to pursue their class interests collectively with female workers (Hirsch 1986; Milkman 1987; Cobble forthcoming). Under such conditions, male unions have tried to organize women and advocated equal pay.

Coalitions Between Employers and Male Workers. Male workers' monopoly of most occupations stems from the de facto coalition between male employers and male workers. Although I use the term *coalition* figuratively, employers' power to hire workers and assign them jobs means that ordinarily male workers can resist women's entry only with their male bosses' active contrivance (Baker 1964; Hartmann 1976; Cockburn 1988). The result of this coalition between male workers and employers is also seen in feminizing occupations in women's confinement to the least desirable jobs, thereby providing male workers a refuge from integration in still-male jobs (Cockburn 1988). For example, when outside pressure forced a large publishing firm to promote women to jobs as editorial assistants, it created a new, higher rank into which it promoted male former editorial assistants (Osterman 1979).

Despite the forces that preserve sex segregation, it broke down in the occupations we studied when male employers or male workers withdrew from their coalition. Employers never violated a coalition by directly substituting women for men, but they set aside customary practices, their own sex biases, and concern with the reactions of male workers when their firms' survival depended on cutting labor costs or averting unionization. In the occupations we studied, increased competition and the concomitant need to cut costs as well as vulnerability to work disruptions by unions precipitated this action. For example, industrywide demand for increased profits during the high-inflation 1970s prompted insurance companies to cut costs by standardizing the work of insurance adjusters and examiners. Heightened competition for customers following deregulation forced banks to provide more customer services while trying to increase productivity and keep the lid on wages. In typesetting and composing, the International Typographical Union's frequent recourse to strikes spurred newspaper publishers to develop a printing technology that the union could not control, and then they hired women for the newly clericalized typesetting and composing jobs. It is important, however, that, in occupations that became less attractive to men for reasons not tied to employers' actions (book editing, real estate sales, retail pharmacy, and bartending), employers did not counter by improving male jobs. Employers' economic interests prevailed, and they replaced men with cheaper women.

In sum, the case studies suggested that employers put women ahead of men in labor queues *only* when labor costs became a pressing concern or when action by women or government regulators raised the cost of male preference.[5] Faced with economic exigencies, employers' willingness to donate profits to support white male privilege went by the wayside, and they struck a bargain with women workers.

Coalitions Between Male Employers and Female Workers. Why women should enter into de facto coalitions with male employers is no mystery. Disadvantaged relative to both male workers and male employers, women stand to gain from cooperating with either group. Employers are more likely to accept a coalition with women when their numbers are large. Cobble's (forthcoming) comparison of women's efforts early in this century to preserve the right to serve drinks with their efforts to tend bar illustrates the importance of numbers. Women waitresses' moderate representation within union locals gave them the clout to block proposed restrictions against their serving alcoholic drinks. In contrast, women's small numbers doomed their efforts to tend bar until they could invoke the Civil Rights Act. In the 1970s, women capitalized on their numbers in the book publishing, newspaper, broadcasting, and banking industries to challenge their exclusion from male jobs or their confinement in low-status posts. Large numbers mean that women can better spot their concentration in the least desirable jobs and more effectively protest it. Thus women's increased share in labor queues for male occupations contributed to their gains both by increasing the odds that employers would

get down to women in the hiring queue and by making them more powerful adversaries.

Resistance by Male Workers.   Male workers' stake in monopolizing the
best jobs encourages them to oppose employers' efforts to integrate
women. To this end, they may try to reduce women's productivity by
denying them training and information or withhold their own labor
(Doeringer and Piore 1971; Bergmann and Darity 1981).[6] Whether men
win the battle depends on their power base. For example, early in the Industrial Revolution, before strong unions existed, employers could easily
feminize jobs (Kessler-Harris 1982, p. 266; Cohn 1985; Milkman 1987;
Cockburn 1988). However, once unions were well established, they could
preserve their domains. They did so in bartending, baking, and typesetting and composing as well as many other occupations throughout most
of the century.

Obviously, men did not ultimately prevent women's entry in the occupations we studied. In most of those occupations, by abandoning jobs,
male workers gave employers the go-ahead to hire women. Sometimes
men do not see women as a threat. For instance, although men fought
women's integration into clerical jobs in the British railroads (Cohn
1985), they did not resist women's movement in similar jobs in the
United States because integration occurred slowly, and Pullman reserved
the best jobs for men (Hirsch 1986, p. 33). In rapidly growing occupations, men did not resist women's entry because growth ensured that good
jobs were plentiful, and within-occupation segregation assured men's access to the best jobs.

Thus the case studies of accounting and systems analysis revealed no
systematic efforts to exclude women. Male incumbents in high-turnover
occupations like book editing, bartending, and residential real estate sales
had no stake in what happened in the long run. High turnover also means
workers were too poorly organized to resist integration. Finally, in reor-
ganizing work, employers had an effective tool in phasing out men. By
changing the work process to incorporate female-labeled tasks, employers
could disguise the fact that they were filling what had been men's jobs
with women (Davies 1975, p. 282; Rotella 1977, pp. 162, 165) and recast
them as women's work. For instance, after transforming the work of adjusters, industry trade journals construed the ideal insurance adjuster as a
woman.[7]

However, men did effectively resist women's employment in the most desirable specialties within desegregating occupations, such as production baking, commercial real estate, and industrial pharmacy—partly by informal pressures that discouraged women's entry. I suspect, however, that women's continued exclusion depended more on employer discrimination in job assignment and promotion practices than on male workers' actions.

CONCLUSIONS

In summary, the queuing model proposed here holds that (a) employers rank prospective workers in terms of their potential productivity as well as their personal characteristics, but that they are also influenced by current employees and others who can impose costs for hiring or failing to hire women; (b) shortages—whether from job growth or from a job's inability to attract enough customary workers—prompt employers to hire workers from lower in the labor queue; (c) male workers affect women's access to jobs through their ability to preempt jobs, their power to enforce their monopoly over desirable jobs, and their ability, in abandoning jobs, to bestow them on workers lower in the labor queue; and (d) women's search for better jobs leads them to individually and collectively challenge their exclusion from men's jobs and to move into male lines of work that become open. The case study data support these predictions. I caution readers that our selection of case studies of occupations in which women's gains were exceptionally large limits the generalizability of these findings. However, most occupations included specialties or work settings that had feminized at varying rates, so the case studies provide variation on the dependent variable. Nonetheless, the bases for women's movement into occupations not marked by rapid feminization may have differed. Patricia Roos and I addressed this question in statistical analyses of all 503 detailed occupations (Reskin and Roos 1985).

The case studies support two empirical generalizations both of which are consistent with the operation of queuing processes. First, in most of the occupations we studied, after they had become less attractive to men, employers hired disproportionate numbers of women. Second, within these nominally desegregating occupations, women tended to be relegated to female enclaves, while men retained the most desirable jobs.[8] These findings confirm Bielby and Baron's (1986) contention that greater balance in the sex composition of *occupations* does not necessarily imply decreased segregation of *jobs* and also establish the fallacy of inferring declines in sex segregation from occupational-level data. Yet social analysts cannot ignore such data, because policymakers and the media use them to assess change, and, as W. I. Thomas said, situations men define as real are real in their consequences. Exaggerated conclusions about women's progress in male occupations support claims that governmental agencies no longer need to intervene in the workplace to ensure equal treatment. Thus it is incumbent on researchers to determine whether or not the trends that superficial comparisons imply are genuine.

NOTES

I am grateful to Ross Boylan, Lowell L. Hargens, Heidi Hartmann, and Patricia A. Roos for their comments on earlier drafts of this chapter and to James N. Baron and Ronnie Steinberg for helpful discussions of the issues it addresses. The larger study that gave rise to the ideas in this chapter is a collaborative project with Patricia A. Roos. The case studies on which this chapter is based appears in our book, *Job Queues, Gender Queues: Explaining Women's Inroads into Male Occupations* (1990).

[1] I conducted the last two unpublished studies. Unless otherwise noted, assertions about these occupations are based on the case studies whose full citations are in the references. For a description of the case study method, see Reskin and Roos (1990).

[2] This analysis takes for granted the existence of multiple labor markets, each composed of a labor queue of potential workers and a job queue of available jobs.

[3] Incumbent workers can affect the ordering of the labor queue, for example, through seniority rules that restrict employers' hiring prerogatives.

[4] This should be especially common among bosses who share a similar background with male workers, previously held the jobs in question, and currently work with or remain friendly with their former coworkers. Two examples are blue-collar supervisors or sales managers.

[5] Unless it is backed by threats from regulatory agencies, pressure from women rarely suffices to persuade employers to assign women to male jobs, partly because it elicits opposition from male workers.

[6] Employers can rarely forestall resistance by feminizing entire work teams. Seniority rules may prevent their replacing men, they may doubt whether enough qualified women are available, and they may be unable to train women because male unions control training or because training is too long and expensive.

[7] Kessler-Harris (1986) and Strober and Arnold (1987) also recounted how banks exploited sex stereotypes to justify hiring women for banking jobs as well as to exclude them from the same jobs.

[8] For further evidence on this point, see Chapter 3 in Reskin and Roos (1990).

REFERENCES

Baker, Ross. 1964. "Entry of Women into Federal Job World—At a Price." *Smithsonian* 8:82–91.

Becker, Gary. 1957. *The Economics of Discrimination.* Chicago: University of Chicago Press.

Beller, Andrea. 1984. "Trends in Occupational Segregation by Sex, 1960–1981." Pp. 11–26 in *Sex Segregation in the Workplace: Trends, Explanations, Remedies,* edited by B. Reskin. Washington, DC: National Academy Press.

Bergmann, Barbara R., and William Darity. 1981. "Social Relations, Productivity, and Employer Discrimination." *Monthly Labor Review* 104:47–49.

Bielby, William T., and James N. Baron. 1986. "Men and Women at Work: Sex Segregation and Statistical Discrimination." *American Journal of Sociology* 91:759–99.

Bird, Chloe. 1990. "High Finance, Small Change: Women's Increased Representation in Bank Management." Pp. 145–66 in B. F. Reskin and P. A. Roos, *Job Queues, Gender Queues: Explaining Women's Inroads into Male Occupations,* Philadelphia: Temple University Press.

Cobble, Dorothy Sue. Forthcoming. "'Drawing the Line': The Construction of a Gendered Workforce in the Food Service Industry." In *Work Engendered,* edited by Ava Baron. Ithaca: Cornell University Press.

Cockburn, Cynthia. 1988. "The Gendering of Jobs: Workplace Relations and the Reproduction of Sex Segregation." Pp. 29–42 in *Gender Segregation at Work,* edited by S. Walby. Milton Keynes, England; New York: Open University Press.

Cohn, Samuel. 1985. *The Process of Occupational Sex-Typing: The Feminization of Clerical Labor in Great Britain.* Philadelphia: Temple University Press.

Davies, Margery W. 1975. "Women's Place Is at the Typewriter: The Feminization of the Clerical Labor Force." Pp. 279–96 in *Labor Market Segmentation,* edited by R. Edwards, M. Reich, and D. Gordon. Lexington, MA: D. C. Heath.

Detman, Linda. 1990. "Women Behind Bars: The Feminization of Bartending." Pp. 241–56 in B. F. Reskin and P. A. Roos, *Job Queues, Gender Queues: Explaining Women's Inroads into Male Occupations.* Philadelphia: Temple University Press.

Doeringer, Peter B., and Michael J. Piore. 1971. *Internal Labor Markets and Manpower Analysis.* Lexington, MA: D. C. Heath.

Donato, Katharine M. 1990a. "Programming for Change? The Growing Demand for Women Systems Analysts." Pp. 167–82 in B. F. Reskin and P. A. Roos, *Job Queues, Gender Queues: Explaining Women's Inroads into Male Occupations.* Philadelphia: Temple University Press.

———. 1990b. "Keepers of the Corporate Image: Women in Public Relations." Pp. 129–44 in B. F. Reskin and P. A. Roos, *Job Queues, Gender Queues: Explaining Women's Inroads into Male Occupations.* Philadelphia: Temple University Press.

Figart, Deborah M., and Barbara Bergmann. 1989. "Facilitating Women's Occupational Integration." Paper prepared for the U.S. Department of Labor, Commission on Workforce Quality and Labor Market Efficiency, American University.

Gross, Edward. 1968. "*Plus ça Change.* . . . The Sexual Segregation of Occupations over Time." *Social Problems* 16:198–208.

Hartmann, Heidi I. 1976. "Capitalism, Patriarchy, and Segregation by Sex." *Signs* 1: 137–70.

Hirsch, Susan E. 1986. "Rethinking the Sexual Division of Labor: Pullman Repair Shops, 1900–1969." *Radical History Review* 3:26–48.

Hodge, Robert W. 1973. "Toward a Theory of Racial Differences in Employment." *Social Forces* 52:16–31.

Kessler-Harris, Alice. 1982. *Out to Work.* New York: Oxford University Press.

———. 1986. "Women's History Goes to Trial: EEOC vs. Sears, Roebuck and Co." *Signs* 1:767–79.

Lieberson, Stanley. 1980. *A Piece of the Pie.* Berkeley: University of California Press.

Milkman, Ruth. 1987. *Gender at Work.* Urbana: University of Illinois Press.

Osterman, Paul. 1979. "Sex Discrimination in Professional Employment: A Case Study." *Industrial and Labor Relations Review* 32: 451–64.

Phipps, Polly A. 1990a. "Occupational and Industrial Change: Prescription for Feminization." Pp. 111–28 in B. F. Reskin and P. A. Roos, *Job Queues, Gender Queues: Explaining Women's Inroads into Male Occupations.* Philadelphia: Temple University Press.

———. 1990b. "Occupational Resegregation: A Case Study of Insurance Adjusters and Examiners." Pp. 224–40 in B. F. Reskin and P. A. Roos, *Job Queues, Gender Queues: Explaining Women's Inroads into Male Occupations.* Philadelphia: Temple University Press.

Reskin, Barbara F. 1988. "Bringing the Men Back In: Sex Differentiation and the Devaluation of Women's Work." *Gender & Society* 2:58–81.

Reskin, Barbara F., and Patricia A. Roos. 1985. "Collaborative Research on the Determinants of Changes in Occupations' Sex Composition Between 1970 and 1980." National Science Foundation Grant no. 85-NSF-SES–85–12452. Manuscript.

———. 1990. *Job Queues, Gender Queues: Explaining Women's Inroads into Male Occupations.* Philadelphia: Temple University Press.

Roos, Patricia A. 1990. "Hot Metal to Electronic Composition: Gender, Technology, and Social Change." Pp. 275–98 in B. F. Reskin and P. A. Roos, *Job Queues, Gender Queues: Explaining Women's Inroads into Male Occupations.* Philadelphia: Temple University Press.

Rotella, Elyce. 1977. *From Home to Office: U.S. Women at Work, 1870–1930.* Ann Arbor: UMI Research Press.

Steiger, Thomas, and Barbara F. Reskin. 1990. "Baking and Baking off: Deskilling and the Changing Sex Make Up of Bakers." Pp. 257–74 in B. F. Reskin and P. A. Roos, *Job Queues, Gender Queues: Explaining Women's Inroads into Male Occupations.* Philadelphia: Temple University Press.

Stolzenberg, Ross. 1982. "Industrial Profits and the Propensity to Employ Women Workers." Paper presented at the Workshop on Job Segregation by Sex, Committee on Women's Employment and Related Social Issues, National Research Council, Washington, DC.

Strober, Myra. 1984. "Toward a General Theory of Occupational Sex Segregation." Pp. 144–56 in *Sex Segregation in the Workplace: Trends, Explanations, Remedies,* edited by B. Reskin. Washington, DC: National Academy Press.

———. 1988. "The Processes of Occupational Segregation: Relative Attractiveness and Patriarchy." Paper presented at the meetings of the American Educational Research Association, New Orleans.

Strober, Myra, and Carolyn Arnold. 1987. "The Dynamics of Occupational Segregation Among Bank Tellers." Pp. 107–48 in *Gender in the Workplace,* edited by C. Brown and J. Pechman. Washington, DC: Brookings Institution.

Strom, Sharon Hartman. 1987. "'Machines Instead of Clerks': Technology and the Feminization of Bookkeeping, 1910–1950." Pp. 63–97 in *Computer Chips and Paper Clips.* Vol. 2, edited by H. Hartmann. Washington, DC: National Academy Press.

Thomas, Barbara J. 1990. "Women's Gains in Insurance Sales: Increased Supply, Uncertain Demand." Pp. 183–204 in B. F. Reskin and P. A. Roos, *Job Queues, Gender Queues: Explaining Women's Inroads into Male Occupations*. Philadelphia: Temple University Press.

Thomas, Barbara J., and Barbara F. Reskin. 1990. "A Woman's Place Is Selling Homes: Women's Movement into Real Estate Sales." Pp. 205–24 in B. F. Reskin and P. A. Roos, *Job Queues, Gender Queues: Explaining Women's Inroads into Male Occupations*. Philadelphia: Temple University Press.

Thurow, Lester. 1969. *Poverty and Discrimination*. Washington, DC: Brookings Institution.

_____. 1972. "Education and Economic Equality." *The Public Interest* 28:66–81.

15

SPONSORED AND CONTEST
MOBILITY AND THE
SCHOOL SYSTEM

Ralph H. Turner

◆◆◆

This paper suggests a framework for relating certain differences between American and English systems of education to the prevailing norms of upward mobility in each country. Others have noted the tendency of educational systems to support prevailing schemes of stratification, but this discussion concerns specifically the manner in which the *accepted mode of upward mobility* shapes the school system directly and indirectly through its effects on the values which implement social control.

Two ideal-typical normative patterns of upward mobility are described and their ramifications in the general patterns of stratification and social control are suggested. In addition to showing relationships among a number of differences between American and English schooling, the ideal-types have

Ralph H. Turner, "Sponsored and Contest Mobility and the School System," *American Sociological Review* 25 (December 1960), pp. 855–856, 859–862, 865–866.

broader implications than those developed in this paper: they suggest a major dimension of stratification which might be profitably incorporated into a variety of studies in social class; and they readily can be applied in further comparisons between other countries.

THE NATURE OF ORGANIZING NORMS

Many investigators have concerned themselves with rates of upward mobility in specific countries or internationally,[1] and with the manner in which school systems facilitate or impede such mobility.[2] But preoccupation with the *extent* of mobility has precluded equal attention to the predominant *modes* of mobility. The central assumption underlying this paper is that within a formally open class system that provides for mass education the organizing folk norm which defines the accepted mode of upward mobility is a crucial factor in shaping the school system, and may be even more crucial than the extent of upward mobility. In England and the United States there appear to be different organizing folk norms, here termed *sponsored mobility* and *contest mobility,* respectively. *Contest* mobility is a system in which elite[3] status is the prize in an open contest and is taken by the aspirants' own efforts. While the "contest" is governed by some rules of fair play, the contestants have wide latitude in the strategies they may employ. Since the "prize" of successful upward mobility is not in the hands of an established elite to give out, the latter cannot determine who shall attain it and who shall not. Under *sponsored* mobility elite recruits are chosen by the established elite or their agents, and elite status is *given* on the basis of some criterion of supposed merit and cannot be *taken* by any amount of effort or strategy. Upward mobility is like entry into a private club where each candidate must be "sponsored" by one or more of the members. Ultimately the members grant or deny upward mobility on the basis of whether they judge the candidate to have those qualities they wish to see in fellow members. . . .

SOCIAL CONTROL AND THE TWO NORMS

Every society must cope with the problem of maintaining loyalty to its social system and does so in part through norms and values, only some of which vary by class position. Norms and values especially prevalent within a given class must direct behavior into channels that support the total system, while those that transcend strata must support the general class differential. The way in which upward mobility takes place determines in part the kinds of norms and values that serve the indicated purposes of social control in each class and throughout the society.

The most conspicuous control problem is that of ensuring loyalty in the disadvantaged classes toward a system in which their members receive less than a proportional share of society's goods. In a system of contest mobility this is accomplished by a combination of futuristic orientation, the norm of ambition, and a general sense of fellowship with the elite. Each individual is encouraged to think of himself as competing for an elite position so that loyalty to the system and conventional attitudes are cultivated in the process of preparation for this possibility. It is essential that this futuristic orientation be kept alive by delaying a sense of final irreparable failure to reach elite status until attitudes are well established. By thinking of himself in the successful future the elite aspirant forms considerable identification with elitists, and evidence that they are merely ordinary human beings like himself helps to reinforce this identification as well as to keep alive the conviction that he himself may someday succeed in like manner. To forestall rebellion among the disadvantaged majority, then, a contest system must avoid absolute points of selection for mobility and immobility and must delay clear recognition of the realities of the situation until the individual is too committed to the system to change radically. A futuristic orientation cannot, of course, be inculcated successfully in all members of lower strata, but sufficient internalization of a norm of ambition tends to leave the unambitious as individual deviants and to forestall the latters' formation of a genuine subcultural group able to offer collective threat to the established system. Where this kind of control system operates rather effectively it is notable that organized or gang deviancy is more likely to take the form of an attack upon the conventional or moral order rather than upon the class system itself. Thus the United States has its "beatniks"[4] who repudiate ambition and most worldly values and its delinquent and criminal gangs who try to evade the limitations imposed by conventional means,[5] but very few active revolutionaries.

These social controls are inappropriate in a system of sponsorship since the elite recruits are chosen from above. The principal threat to the system would lie in the existence of a strong group the members of whom sought to *take* elite positions themselves. Control under this system is maintained by training the "masses" to regard themselves as relatively incompetent to manage society, by restricting access to the skills and manners of the elite, and by cultivating belief in the superior competence of the elite. The earlier that selection of the elite recruits is made the sooner others can be taught to accept their inferiority and to make "realistic" rather than fantasy plans. Early selection prevents raising the hopes of large numbers of people who might otherwise become the discontented leaders of a class challenging the sovereignty of the established elite. If it is assumed that the difference in competence between masses and elite is seldom so great as to support the usual differences in the advantages accruing to each,[6] then the differences must be artificially augmented by discouraging acquisition of elite skills by the masses. Thus a sense of mystery about the elite is a common device for supporting in the masses the illusion of a much greater hiatus of competence than in fact exists.

While elitists are unlikely to reject a system that benefits them, they must still be restrained from taking such advantage of their favorable situation as to jeopardize the entire elite. Under the sponsorship system the elite recruits—who are selected early, freed from the strain of competitive struggle, and kept under close supervision—may be thoroughly indoctrinated in elite culture. A norm of paternalism toward inferiors may be inculcated, a heightened sensitivity to the good opinion of fellow elitists and elite recruits may be cultivated, and the appreciation of the more complex forms of aesthetic, literary, intellectual, and sporting activities may be taught. Norms of courtesy and altruism easily can be maintained under sponsorship since elite recruits are not required to compete for their standing and since the elite may deny high standing to those who strive for position by "unseemly" methods. The system of sponsorship provides an almost perfect setting for the development of an elite culture characterized by a sense of responsibility for "inferiors" and for preservation of the "finer things" of life.

Elite control in the contest system is more difficult since there is no controlled induction and apprenticeship. The principal regulation seems to lie in the insecurity of elite position. In a sense there is no "final arrival" because each person may be displaced by newcomers throughout his life. The limited control of high standing from above prevents the clear delimitation of levels in the class system, so that success itself becomes relative: each success, rather than an accomplishment, serves to qualify the participant for competition at the next higher level.[7] The restraints upon the behavior of a person of high standing, therefore, are principally those applicable to a contestant who must not risk the "ganging up" of other contestants, and who must pay some attention to the masses who are frequently in a position to impose penalties upon him. But any special norm of paternalism is hard to establish since there is no dependable procedure for examining the means by which one achieves elite credentials. While mass esteem is an effective brake upon over-exploitation of position, it rewards scrupulously ethical and altruistic behavior much less than evidence of fellow-feeling with the masses themselves.

Under both systems, unscrupulous or disreputable persons may become or remain members of the elite, but for different reasons. In contest mobility, popular tolerance of a little craftiness in the successful newcomer, together with the fact that he does not have to undergo the close scrutiny of the old elite, leaves considerable leeway for unscrupulous success. In sponsored mobility, the unpromising recruit reflects unfavorably on the judgments of his sponsors and threatens the myth of elite omniscience; consequently he may be tolerated and others may "cover up" for his deficiencies in order to protect the unified front of the elite to the outer world.

Certain of the general values and norms of any society reflect emulation of elite values by the masses. Under sponsored mobility, a good deal of the protective attitudes toward and interest in classical subjects percolates to the masses. Under contest mobility, however, there is not the same degree of homogeneity of moral, aesthetic, and intellectual values to be emulated, so that the conspicuous attribute of the elite is its high level of material consumption—emulation itself follows this course. There is neither effective incentive nor punishment for the elitist who fails to interest himself in promoting the arts or literary excellence, or who continues to maintain the vulgar manners and mode of speech of his class origin. The elite has relatively less power and the masses relatively more power to punish or reward a man for his adoption or disregard of any special elite culture. The great importance of accent and of grammatical excellence in the attainment of high status in England as contrasted with the twangs and drawls and grammatical ineptitude among American elites is the most striking example of this difference. In a contest system, the class order does not function to support the *quality* of aesthetic, literary, and intellectual activities; only those well versed in such matters are qualified to distinguish authentic products from cheap imitations. Unless those who claim superiority in these areas are forced to submit their credentials to the elite for evaluation, poor quality is often honored equally with high quality and class prestige does not serve to maintain an effective norm of high quality.

This is not to imply that there are no groups in a "contest" society devoted to the protection and fostering of high standards in art, music, literature, and intellectual pursuits, but that such standards lack the support of the class system which is frequently found when sponsored mobility prevails. In California, the selection by official welcoming committees of a torch singer to entertain a visiting king and queen and "can-can" dancers to entertain Mr. Khrushchev illustrates how American elites can assume that high prestige and popular taste go together.

FORMAL EDUCATION

Returning to the conception of an organizing ideal norm, we assume that to the extent to which one such norm of upward mobility is prevalent in a society there are constant strains to shape the educational system into conformity with that norm. These strains operate in two fashions: directly, by blinding people to alternatives and coloring their judgments of successful and unsuccessful solutions to recurring educational problems; indirectly, through the functional interrelationships between school systems and the class structure, systems of social control, and other features of the social structure which are neglected in this paper.

The most obvious application of the distinction between sponsored and contest mobility norms affords a partial explanation for the different policies of student selection in the English and American secondary schools. Although American high school students follow different courses of study and a few attend specialized schools, a major educational preoccupation has been to avoid any sharp social separation between the superior and inferior students and to keep the channels of movement between courses of study as open as possible. Recent criticisms of the way in which superior students may be thereby held back in their development usually are nevertheless qualified by the insistence that these students must not be withdrawn from the mainstream of student life.[8] Such segregation offends the sense of fairness implicit in the contest norm and also arouses the fear that the elite and future elite will lose their sense of fellowship with the masses. Perhaps the most important point, however, is that schooling is presented as an opportunity, and making use of it depends primarily on the student's own initiative and enterprise.

The English system has undergone a succession of liberalizing changes during this century, but all of them have retained the attempt to sort out early in the educational program the promising from the unpromising so that the former may be segregated and given a special form of training to fit them for higher standing in their adult years. Under the Education Act of

1944, a minority of students has been selected each year by means of a battery of examinations popularly known as "eleven plus," supplemented in varying degrees by grade school records and personal interviews, for admission to grammar schools.[9] The remaining students attend secondary modern or technical schools in which the opportunities to prepare for college or to train for the more prestigeful occupations are minimal. The grammar schools supply what by comparative standards is a high quality of college preparatory education. Of course, such a scheme embodies the logic of sponsorship, with early selection of those destined for middle-class and higher-status occupations, and specialized training to prepare each group for its destined class position. This plan facilitates considerable mobility, and recent research reveals surprisingly little bias against children from manual laboring-class families in the selection for grammar school, when related to measured intelligence.[10] It is altogether possible that adequate comparative study would show a closer correlation of school success with measured intelligence and a lesser correlation between school success and family background in England than in the United States. While selection of superior students for mobility opportunity is probably more efficient under such a system, the obstacles for persons not so selected of "making the grade" on the basis of their own initiative or enterprise are probably correspondingly greater. . . .

EFFECTS OF MOBILITY ON PERSONALITY

Brief note may be made of the importance of the distinction between sponsored and contest mobility with relation to the supposed effects of upward mobility on personality development. Not a great deal is yet known about the "mobile personality" nor about the specific features of importance to the personality in the mobility experience.[11] However, today three aspects of this experience are most frequently stressed: first, the stress or tension involved in striving for status higher than that of others under more difficult conditions than they; second, the complication of interpersonal relations introduced by the necessity to abandon lower-level friends in favor of uncertain acceptance into higher-level circles; third, the problem of working out an adequate personal scheme of values in the face of movement between classes marked by somewhat variant or even contradictory value systems.[12] The impact of each of these three mobility problems, it is suggested, differ depending upon whether the pattern is that of the contest or of sponsorship.

Under the sponsorship system, recruits are selected early, segregated from their class peers, grouped with other recruits and with youth from the class to which they are moving, and trained specifically for membership in this class. Since the selection is made early, the mobility experience should be relatively free from the strain that comes with a series of elimination tests and long-extended uncertainty of success. The segregation and the integrated group life of the "public" school or grammar school should help to clarify the mobile person's social ties. (One investigator failed to discover clique formation along lines of social class in a sociometric study of a number of grammar schools.)[13] The problem of a system of values may be largely met when the elite recruit is taken from his parents and peers to be placed in a boarding school, though it may be less well clarified for the grammar school boy who returns each evening to his working-class family. Undoubtedly this latter limitation has something to do with the observed failure of working-class boys to continue through the last years of grammar school and into the universities.[14] In general, then, the factors stressed as affecting personality formation among the upwardly mobile probably are rather specific to the contest system, or to incompletely functioning sponsorship system.

NOTES

This is an expanded version of a paper presented at the Fourth World Congress of Sociology, 1959, and abstracted in the *Transactions* of the Congress. Special indebtedness should be expressed to Jean Floud and Hilde Himmelweit for helping to acquaint the author with the English school system.

[1] A comprehensive summary of such studies appears in Seymour M. Lipset and Reinhard Bendix, *Social Mobility in Industrial Society*, Berkeley and Los Angeles: University of California Press, 1959.

[2] *Cf.* C. A. Anderson, "The Social Status of University Students in Relation to Type of Economy: An International Comparison," *Transactions of the Third World Congress of Sociology*, London, 1956, Vol. V, pp. 51–63; J. E. Floud, *Social Class and Educational Opportunity*, London: Heinemann, 1956; W. L. Warner, R. J. Havighurst, and M. B. Loeb, *Who Shall Be Educated?* New York: Harper, 1944.

[3] Reference is made throughout the paper to "elite" and "masses." The generalizations, however, are intended to apply throughout the stratification continuum to relations between members of a given class and the class or classes above it. Statements about mobility are intended in general to apply to mobility from manual to middle-class levels, lower-middle to upper-middle class, and so on, as well as into the strictly elite groups. The simplified expressions avoid the repeated use of cumbersome and involved statements which might otherwise be required.

[4] See, e.g., Lawrence Lipton, *The Holy Barbarians*, New York: Messner, 1959.

[5] *Cf.* Albert K. Cohen, *Delinquent Boys: The Culture of the Gang,* Glencoe, Ill.: Free Press, 1955.

[6] D. V. Glass, editor, *Social Mobility in Britain,* Glencoe, Ill.: Free Press, 1954, pp. 144–145, reports studies showing only small variations in intelligence between occupational levels.

[7] Geoffrey Gorer, *The American People,* New York: Norton, 1948, pp. 172–187.

[8] See, e.g., *Los Angeles Times,* May 4, 1959, Part I, p. 24.

[9] The nature and operation of the "eleven plus" system are fully reviewed in a report by a committee of the British Psychological Society and in a report of extensive research into the adequacy of selection methods. See P. E. Vernon, editor, *Secondary School Selection: A British Psychological Inquiry,* London: Methuen, 1957; and Alfred Yates and D. A. Pidgeon, *Admission to Grammar Schools,* London: Newnes Educational Publishing Co., 1957.

[10] J. E. Floud, A. H. Halsey, and F. M. Martin, *Social Class and Educational Opportunity,* London: Heinemann, 1956.

[11] *Cf.* Lipset and Bendix, *op. cit.,* pp. 250 ff.

[12] See, e.g., August B. Hollingshead and Frederick C. Redlich, *Social Class and Mental Illness,* New York: Wiley, 1958; W. Lloyd Warner and James C. Abegglen, *Big Business Leaders in America,* New York: Harper, 1955; Warner *et al., Who Shall Be Educated?, op. cit.;* Peter M. Blau, "Social Mobility and Interpersonal Relations," *American Sociological Review,* 21 (June, 1956), pp. 290–300.

[13] A. N. Oppenheim, "Social Status and Clique Formation among Grammar School Boys," *British Journal of Sociology,* 6 (September, 1955), pp. 228–245. Oppenheim's findings may be compared with A. B. Hollingshead, *Elmtown's Youth,* New York: Wiley, 1949, pp. 204–242. See also Joseph A. Kahl, *The American Class Structure,* New York: Rinehart, 1957, pp. 129–138.

[14] Floud *et al., op. cit.,* pp. 115 ff.

16

THE PROCESS OF
STRATIFICATION

Peter M. Blau and Otis Dudley Duncan,
with the Collaboration of Andrea Tyree

♦♦♦

Stratification systems may be characterized in various ways. Surely one of the most important has to do with the processes by which individuals become located, or locate themselves, in positions in the hierarchy comprising the system. At one extreme we can imagine that the circumstances of a person's birth—including the person's sex and the perfectly predictable sequence of age levels through which he is destined to pass—suffice to assign him unequivocally to a ranked status in a hierarchical system. At the opposite extreme his prospective adult status would be wholly problematic and contingent at the time of birth. Such status would become entirely determinate

Peter M. Blau and Otis Dudley Duncan, *The American Occupational Structure,* pp. 163–177, 199–201, 203. Copyright 1967 by Peter M. Blau and Otis Dudley Duncan.

only as adulthood was reached, and solely as a consequence of his own actions taken freely—that is, in the absence of any constraint deriving from the circumstances of his birth or rearing. Such a pure achievement system is, of course, hypothetical, in much the same way that motion without friction is a purely hypothetical possibility in the physical world. Whenever the stratification system of any moderately large and complex society is described, it is seen to involve both ascriptive and achievement principles.

In a liberal democratic society we think of the more basic principle as being that of achievement. Some ascriptive features of the system may be regarded as vestiges of an earlier epoch, to be extirpated as rapidly as possible. Public policy may emphasize measures designed to enhance or to equalize opportunity—hopefully, to overcome ascriptive obstacles to the full exercise of the achievement principle.

The question of how far a society may realistically aspire to go in this direction is hotly debated, not only in the ideological arena but in the academic forum as well. Our contribution, if any, to the debate will consist largely in submitting measurements and estimates of the strength of ascriptive forces and of the scope of opportunities in a large contemporary society. The problem of the relative importance of the two principles in a given system is ultimately a quantitative one. We have pushed our ingenuity to its limit in seeking to contrive relevant quantifications.

The governing conceptual scheme in the analysis is quite a commonplace one. We think of the individual's life cycle as a sequence in time that can be described, however partially and crudely, by a set of classificatory or quantitative measurements taken at successive stages. Ideally we should like to have under observation a cohort of births, following the individuals who make up the cohort as they pass through life. As a practical matter we resorted to retrospective questions put to a representative sample of several adjacent cohorts so as to ascertain those facts about their life histories that we assumed were both relevant to our problem and accessible by this means of observation.

Given this scheme, the questions we are continually raising in one form or another are: how and to what degree do the circumstances of birth condition subsequent status? and, how does status attained (whether by ascription or achievement) at one stage of the life cycle affect the prospects for a subsequent stage? The questions are neither idle nor idiosyncratic ones. Current policy discussion and action come to a focus in a vaguely explicated notion of the "inheritance of poverty." Thus a spokesman for the Social Security Administration writes:

> It would be one thing if poverty hit at random and no one group were singled out. It is another thing to realize that some seem destined to poverty almost from birth—by their color or by the economic status or occupation of their parents.[1]

Another officially sanctioned concept is that of the "dropout," the person who fails to graduate from high school. Here the emphasis is not so much on circumstances operative at birth but on the presumed effect of early achievement on subsequent opportunities. Thus the "dropout" is seen as facing "a lifetime of uncertain employment,"[2] probable assignment to jobs of inferior status, reduced earning power, and vulnerability to various forms of social pathology.

In this study we do not have measurements on all the factors implicit in a full-blown conception of the "cycle of poverty" nor all those variables conceivably responding unfavorably to the achievement of "dropout" status. . . . This limitation, however, is not merely an analytical convenience. We think of the selected quantitative variables as being sufficient to describe the major outlines of status changes in the life cycle of a cohort. Thus a study of the relationships among these variables leads to a formulation of a basic model of the process of stratification.

A BASIC MODEL

To begin with, we examine only five variables. For expository convenience, when it is necessary to resort to symbols, we shall designate them by arbitrary letters but try to remind the reader from time to time of what the letters stand for. These variables are:

> V: Father's educational attainment
> X: Father's occupational status
> U: Respondent's educational attainment
> W: Status of respondent's first job
> Y: Status of respondent's occupation in 1962

Each of the three occupational statuses is scaled by the [socioeconomic] index described [elsewhere],[3] ranging from 0 to 96. The two education variables are scored on the following arbitrary scale of values ("rungs" on the "educational ladder") corresponding to specified numbers of years of formal schooling completed:

0: No school
1: Elementary, one to four years
2: Elementary, five to seven years
3: Elementary, eight years
4: High school, one to three years
5: High school, four years
6: College, one to three years
7: College, four years
8: College, five years or more (i.e., one or more years of postgraduate study)

Actually, this scoring system hardly differs from a simple linear transformation, or "coding," of the exact number of years of school completed. In retrospect, for reasons given [elsewhere],[4] we feel that the score implies too great a distance between intervals at the lower end of the scale; but the resultant distortion is minor in view of the very small proportions scored 0 or 1.

A basic assumption in our interpretation of regression statistics—though not in their calculation as such—has to do with the causal or temporal ordering of these variables. In terms of the father's career we should naturally assume precedence of V (education) with respect to X (occupation when his son was 16 years old). We are not concerned with the father's career, however, but only with his statuses that comprised a configuration of background circumstances or origin conditions for the cohorts of sons who were respondents in the Occupational Changes in a Generation (OCG) study. Hence we generally make no assumption as to the priority of V with respect to X; in effect, we assume the measurements on these variables to be contemporaneous from the son's viewpoint. The respondent's education, U, is supposed to follow in time—and thus to be susceptible to causal influence from—the two measures of father's status. Because we ascertained X as of respondent's age 16, it is true that some respondents may have completed school before the age to which X pertains. Such cases were doubtlessly a small minority and in only a minor proportion of them could the father (or other family head) have changed status radically in the two or three years before the respondent reached 16.

The next step in the sequence is more problematic. We assume that W (first job status) follows U (education). The assumption conforms to the wording of the questionnaire, which stipulated "the first full-time job you had after you left school." In the years since the OCG study was designed we have been made aware of a fact that should have been considered more carefully in the design. Many students leave school more or less definitively, only to return, perhaps to a different school, some years later, whereupon they often finish a degree program.[5] The OCG questionnaire contained information relevant to this problem, namely the item on age at first job. Through an oversight no tabulations of this item were made for the present study. Tables prepared for another study[6] using the OCG data, however, suggest that approximately one-eighth of the respondents report a combination of age at first job and education that would be very improbable unless (a) they violated instructions by reporting a part-time or school-vacation job as the first job, or (b) they did, in fact, interrupt their schooling to enter regular employment. (These "inconsistent" responses include men giving 19 as their age at first job and college graduation or more as their education; 17 or 18 with some college or more; 14, 15, or 16 with high-school graduation or more; and under 14 with some high school or more.) When the two variables are studied in combination with occupation of first job, a very clear effect is evident. Men with a given amount of education beginning their first jobs early held lower occupational statuses than those beginning at a normal or advanced age for the specified amount of education.

Despite the strong probability that the U-W sequence is reversed for an appreciable minority of respondents, we have hardly any alternative to the assumption made here. If the bulk of the men who interrupted schooling to take their first jobs were among those ultimately securing relatively advanced education, then our variable W is downwardly biased, no doubt, as a measure of their occupational status immediately after they finally left school for good. In this sense, the correlations between U and W and between W and Y are probably attenuated. Thus, if we had really measured "job after completing education" instead of "first job," the former would in all likelihood have loomed somewhat larger as a variable intervening between education and 1962 occupational status. We do not wish to argue that our respondents erred in their reports on first job. We are inclined to conclude that their reports were realistic enough, and that it was our assumption about the meaning of the responses that proved to be fallible.

The fundamental difficulty here is conceptual. If we insist on *any* uniform sequence of the events involved in accomplishing the transition to independent adult status, we do violence to reality. Completion of schooling, departure from the parental home, entry into the labor market, and contracting of a first marriage are crucial steps in this transition, which all normally occur within a few short years. Yet they occur at no fixed ages nor in any fixed order. As soon as we aggregate individual data for analytical purposes we are forced into the use of simplifying assumptions. Our assumption here is, in effect, that "first job" has a uniform significance for all men in terms of its temporal relationship to educational preparation and subsequent work experience. If this assumption is not strictly correct, we doubt that it could be improved by substituting any other *single* measure of initial occupational status. (In designing the OCG questionnaire, the alternative of "job at the time of first marriage" was entertained briefly but dropped for the reason, among others, that unmarried men would be excluded thereby.)

One other problem with the U-W transition should be mentioned. Among the younger men in the study, 20 to 24 years old, are many who have yet to finish their schooling or to take up their first jobs or both—not to mention the men in this age group missed by the survey on account of their military service.[7] Unfortunately, an early decision on tabulation plans resulted in the inclusion of the 20 to 24 group with the older men in aggregate tables for men 20 to 64 years old. We have ascertained that this results in only minor distortions by comparing a variety of data for men 20 to 64 and for those 25 to 64 years of age. Once over the U-W hurdle, we see no serious objection to our assumption that both U and W precede Y, except in regard to some fraction of the very young men just mentioned.

In summary, then, we take the somewhat idealized assumption of temporal order to represent an order of priority in a causal or processual sequence, which may be stated diagrammatically as follows:

$$(V, X) - (U) - (W) - (Y).$$

In proposing this sequence we do not overlook the possibility of what Carlsson calls "delayed effects,"[8] meaning that an early variable may affect a later one not only via intervening variables but also directly (or perhaps through variables not measured in the study).

In translating this conceptual framework into quantitative estimates the first task is to establish the pattern of associations between the variables in the sequence. This is accomplished with the correlation coefficient. Table 16.1 supplies the correlation matrix on which much of the subsequent analysis is based. In discussing causal interpretations of these correlations, we shall have to be clear about the distinction between two points of view. On the one hand, the simple correlation—given our assumption as to direction of causation—measures the gross magnitude of the effect of the antecedent upon the consequent variable. Thus, if $r_{YW} = .541$, we can say that an increment of one standard deviation in first job status produces (whether directly or indirectly) an increment of just over half of one standard deviation in 1962 occupational status. From another point of view we are more concerned with net effects. If both first job and 1962 status have a common antecedent cause—say, father's occupation—we may want to state what part of the effect of W on Y consists in a transmission of the prior influence of X. Or, thinking of X as the initial cause, we may focus on the extent to which its influence on Y is transmitted by way of its prior influence on W.

We may, then, devote a few remarks to the pattern of gross effects before presenting the apparatus that yields estimates of net direct and indirect effects. Since we do not require a causal ordering of father's education with respect to his occupation, we may be content simply to note that $r_{XV} = .516$ is somewhat lower than the corresponding correlation, $r_{YU} = .596$, observed for the respondents themselves. The difference suggests a heightening of the effect of education on occupational status between the fathers' and the sons' generations. Before stressing this interpretation, however, we must remember that the measurements of V and X do not pertain to some actual cohort of men, here designated "fathers." Each "father" is represented in the data in proportion to the number of his sons who were 20 to 64 years old in March 1962.

The first recorded status of the son himself is education (U). We note that r_{UV} is just slightly greater than r_{UX}. Apparently both measures on the father represent factors that may influence the son's education.

Variable		Variable			
	Y	W	U	X	V
Y: 1962 occ. status		.541	.596	.406	.322
W: First-job status		--	.538	.417	.332
U: Education			--	.438	.453
X: Father's occ. status				--	.516
V: Father's education					--

Table 16.1 Simple Correlations for Five Status Variable

In terms of gross effects there is a clear ordering of influences on first job. Thus $r_{WU} > r_{WX} > r_{WV}$. Education is most strongly correlated with first job, followed by father's occupation, and then by father's education.

Occupational status in 1962 (Y) apparently is influenced more strongly by education than by first job; but our earlier discussion of the first-job measure suggests we should not overemphasize the difference between r_{YW} and r_{YU}. Each, however, is substantially greater than r_{YX}, which in turn is rather more impressive than r_{YV}.

Figure 16.1 is a graphic representation of the system of relationships among the five variables that we propose as our basic model. The numbers entered on the diagram, with the exception of r_{XV}, are path coefficients, the estimation of which will be explained shortly. First we must become familiar with the conventions followed in constructing this kind of diagram. The link between V and X is shown as a curved line with an arrowhead at both ends. This is to distinguish it from the other lines, which are taken to be paths of influence. In the case of V and X we may suspect an influence running from the former to the latter. But if the diagram is logical for the respondent's generation, we should have to assume that for the fathers, likewise, education and occupation are correlated not only because one affects the other but also because common causes lie behind both, which we have not measured. The bidirectional arrow merely serves to sum up all sources of correlation between V and X and to indicate that the explanation thereof is not part of the problem at hand.

The straight lines running from one measured variable to another represent *direct* (or net) influences. The symbol for the path coefficient, such as p_{YW}, carries a double subscript. The first subscript is the variable at the head of the path, or the effect; the second is the causal variable. (This resembles the convention for regression coefficients, where the first subscript refers to the "dependent" variable, the second to the "independent" variable.)

Finally, we see lines with no source indicated carrying arrows to each of the effect variables. These represent the residual paths, standing for all other influences on the variable in question, including causes not recognized or measured,

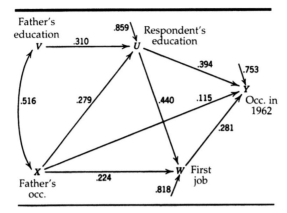

Figure 16.1   Path Coefficients in Basic Model of the Process of Stratification

errors of measurement, and departures of the true relationships from additivity and linearity, properties that are assumed throughout the analysis.

An important feature of this kind of causal scheme is that variables recognized as effects of certain antecedent factors may, in turn, serve as causes for subsequent variables. For example, U is caused by V and X, but it in turn influences W and Y. The algebraic representation of the scheme is a system of equations, rather than the single equation more often employed in multiple regression analysis. This feature permits a flexible conceptualization of the *modus operandi* of the causal network. Note that Y is shown here as being influenced directly by W, U, and X, but not by V (an assumption that will be justified shortly). But this does not imply that V has no influence on Y. V affects U, which does affect Y both directly and indirectly (via W). Moreover, V is correlated with X, and thus shares in the gross effect of X on Y, which is partly direct and partly indirect. Hence the gross effect of V on Y, previously described in terms of the correlation r_{YV}, is here interpreted as being entirely indirect, in consequence of V's effect on intervening variables and its correlation with another cause of Y.

PATH COEFFICIENTS

Whether a path diagram, or the causal scheme it represents, is adequate depends on both theoretical and empirical considerations. At a minimum, before constructing the diagram we must know, or be willing to assume, a causal ordering of the observed variables (hence the lengthy discussion of this matter earlier in this chapter). This information is external or *a priori* with respect to the data, which merely describe associations or correlations. Moreover, the causal scheme must be complete, in the sense that all causes are accounted for. Here, as in most problems involving analysis of observational data, we achieve a formal completeness of the scheme by representing unmeasured causes as a residual factor, presumed to be uncorrelated with the remaining factors lying behind the variable in question. If any factor is known or presumed to operate in some other way it must be represented in the diagram in accordance with its causal role, even though it is not measured. Sometimes it is possible to deduce interesting implications from the inclusion of such a variable and to secure useful estimates of certain paths in the absence of measurements on it, but this is not always so. A partial exception to the rule that all causes must be explicitly represented in the diagram is the unmeasured variable that can be assumed to operate strictly as an intervening variable. Its inclusion would enrich our understanding of a causal system without invalidating the causal scheme that omits it. Sociologists have only recently begun to appreciate how stringent are the logical requirements that must be met if discussion of causal processes is to go beyond mere impressionism and vague verbal formulations.[9] We are a long way from being able to make causal inferences with confidence, and schemes of the kind presented here had best be regarded as crude first approximations to adequate causal models.

On the empirical side, a minimum test of the adequacy of a causal diagram is whether it satisfactorily accounts for the observed correlations among the measured variables. In making such a test we employ the fundamental theorem in path analysis, which shows how to obtain the correlation between any two variables in the system, given the path coefficients and correlations entered on the diagram.[10] Without stating this theorem in general form we may illustrate its application here. For example,

$$r_{YX} = p_{YX} + p_{YU}r_{UX} + p_{YW}r_{WX}$$

and

$$r_{WX} = p_{WX} + p_{WU}r_{UX}.$$

We make use of each path leading to a given variable (such as Y in the first example) and the correlations of each of its causes with all other variables in the system. The latter correlations, in turn, may be analyzed; for example, r_{WX}, which appeared as such in the first equation, is broken down into two parts in the second. A complete expansion along these lines is required to trace out all the indirect connections between variables; thus,

$$r_{YX} = p_{YX} + p_{YU}p_{UX} + p_{YU}p_{UV}r_{VX} + p_{YW}p_{WX}$$

$$+ p_{YW}p_{WU}p_{UX} + p_{YW}p_{WU}p_{UV}r_{VX}$$

Now, if the path coefficients are properly estimated, and if there is no inconsistency in the diagram, the correlations calculated by a formula like the foregoing must equal the observed correlations. Let us compare the values computed from such a formula with the corresponding observed correlations:

$$r_{WV} = p_{WX}r_{XV} + p_{WU}r_{UV}$$

$$= (.224)(.516) + (.440)(.453)$$

$$= .116 + .199 = .315$$

which compares with the observed value of .332; and

$$r_{YV} = p_{YU}r_{UV} + p_{YX}r_{XV} + p_{YW}r_{WV}$$

$$= (.394)(.453) + (.115)(.516) + (.281)(.315)$$

$$= .326$$

(using here the calculated rather than the observed value of r_{WV}), which resembles the actual value, .322. Other such comparisons—for r_{YX}, for example—reveal, at most, trivial discrepancies (no larger than .001).

We arrive, by this roundabout journey, at the problem of getting numerical values for the path coefficients in the first place. This involves using equations of the foregoing type inversely. We have illustrated how to obtain correlations if the path coefficients are known, but in the typical empirical problem we know the correlations (or at least some of them) and have to estimate the paths. For a diagram of the type of Figure 16.1 the solution involves equations of the same form as those of linear multiple regression, except that we work with a recursive system of regression equations[11] rather than a single regression equation.

Table 16.2 records the results of the regression calculations. It can be seen that some alternative combinations of independent variables were studied. It turned out that the net regressions of both W and Y on V were so small as to be negligible. Hence V could be disregarded as a direct influence on these variables without loss of information. The net regression of Y on X was likewise small but, as it appears, not entirely negligible. Curiously, this net regression is of the same order of magnitude as the proportion of occupational inheritance in this population—about 10 percent, as discussed [elsewhere].[12] We might speculate that the direct effect of the father's occupation on the occupational status of a mature man consists of this modest amount of strict occupational inheritance. The remainder of the effect of X on Y is indirect, inasmuch as X has previously influenced U and W, the son's education and the occupational level at which he got his start. For reasons noted [elsewhere][13] we do not assume that the full impact of the tendency to take up the father's occupation is registered in the choice of first job.

With the formal properties of the model in mind we may turn to some general problems confronting this kind of interpretation of our results. One of the first impressions gained from Figure 16.1 is that the largest path coefficients in the diagram are those for residual factors, that is, variables not measured. The residual path is merely a convenient representation of the extent to which measured causes in the system fail to account for the variation in the effect variables. (The residual is obtained from the coefficient of determination; if $R^2_{Y(WUX)}$ is the squared multiple correlation of Y on the three independent variables, then the residual for Y is $\sqrt{1 - R^2_{Y(WUX)}}$.) Sociologists are often disappointed in the size of the residual, assuming that this is a measure of their success in "explaining" the phenomenon under study. They seldom reflect on what it would mean to live in a society where nearly perfect explanation of the dependent variable could be secured by studying causal variables like father's occupation or respondent's education. In such a society it would indeed be true that some are "destined to poverty almost from birth . . . by the economic status or occupation of their parents" (in the words of the reference cited in endnote 1). Others, of course, would be "destined" to affluence or to modest circumstances. By no effort of their own could they materially alter the course of destiny, nor could any stroke of fortune, good or ill, lead to an outcome not already in the cards.

Dependent Variables[a]	Independent Variables[a]				Coefficient of Determination (R^2)
	W	U	X	V	
U[b]	--	--	.279	.310	.26
W	--	.433	.214	.026	.33
W[b]	--	.440	.224	--	.33
Y	.282	.397	.120	-.014	.43
Y[b]	.281	.394	.115	--	.43
Y	.311	.428	--	--	.42

[a]V: Father's education
X: Father's occ. status
U: Respondent's education
W: First-job status
Y: 1962 occ. status
[b]Beta coefficients in these sets taken as estimates of path coefficients for Figure 16.1

Table 16.2 Partial Regression Coefficients in Standard Form (Beta Coefficients) and Coefficients of Determination, for Specified Combinations of Variables

Thinking of the residual as an index of the adequacy of an explanation gives rise to a serious misconception. It is thought that a high multiple correlation is presumptive evidence that an explanation is correct or nearly so, whereas a low percentage of determination means that a causal interpretation is almost certainly wrong. The fact is that the size of the residual (or, if one prefers, the proportion of variation "explained") is *no* guide whatever to the validity of a causal interpretation. The best-known cases of "spurious correlation"—a correlation leading to an egregiously wrong interpretation—are those in which the coefficient of determination is quite high.

The relevant question about the residual is not really its size at all, but whether the unobserved factors it stands for are properly represented as being uncorrelated with the measured antecedent variables. We shall entertain [elsewhere][14] some conjectures about unmeasured variables that clearly are not uncorrelated with the causes depicted in Figure 16.1. It turns out that these require us to acknowledge certain possible modifications of the diagram, whereas other features of it remain more or less intact. A delicate question in this regard is that of the burden of proof. It is all too easy to make a formidable list of unmeasured variables that someone has alleged to be crucial to the process under study. But the mere existence of such variables is already acknowledged by the very presence of the residual. It would seem to be part of the task of the critic to *show,* if only hypothetically, but *specifically,* how the modification of the causal scheme to include a new variable would disrupt or alter the relationships in the original diagram. His argument to this effect could then be examined for plausibility and his evidence, if any, studied in terms of the empirical possibilities it suggests.

Our supposition is that the scheme in Figure 16.1 is most easily subject to modification by introducing additional measures of the same kind as those used here. If indexes relating to socioeconomic background other than V and X are inserted we will almost certainly estimate differently the direct effects of these particular variables. If occupational statuses of the respondent intervening between W and Y were known we should have to modify more or less radically the right-hand portion of the diagram. Yet we should argue that such modifications may amount to an enrichment or extension of the basic model rather than an invalidation of it. The same may be said of other variables that function as intervening causes. In theory, it should be possible to specify these in some detail, and a major part of the research worker's task is properly defined as an attempt at such specification. In the course of such work, to be sure, there is always the possibility of a discovery that would require a fundamental reformulation, making the present model obsolete. Discarding the model would be a cost gladly paid for the prize of such a discovery.

Postponing the confrontation with an altered model, the one at hand is not lacking in interest. An instructive exercise is to compare the magnitudes of gross and net relationships. Here we make use of the fact that the correlation coefficient and the path coefficient have the same dimensionality. The correlation $r_{YX} = .405$ (Table 16.1) means that a unit change (one standard deviation) in X produces a change of 0.4 unit in Y, in gross terms. The path coefficient, $P_{YX} = .115$ (Figure 16.1), tells us that about one-fourth of this gross effect is a result of the direct influence of X on Y. (We speculated above on the role of occupational inheritance in this connection.) The remainder $(.405 - .115 = .29)$ is indirect, via U and W. The sum of all indirect effects, therefore, is given by the difference between the simple correlation and the path coefficient connecting two variables. We note that the indirect effects on Y are generally substantial, relative to the direct. Even the variable temporally closest (we assume) to Y has "indirect effects"—actually, common antecedent causes—nearly as large as the direct. Thus $r_{YW} = .541$ and $p_{YW} = .281$, so that the aggregate of "indirect effects" is .26, which in this case are common determinants of Y and W that spuriously inflate the correlation between them.

To ascertain the indirect effects along a given chain of causation we must multiply the path coefficients along the chain. The procedure is to locate on the diagram the dependent variable of interest, and then trace back along the paths linking it to its immediate and remote causes. In such a tracing we may reverse direction once but only once, following the rule "first back, then forward." Any bidirectional correlation may be traced in either direction. If the diagram contains more than one such correlation, however, only one may be used in a given compound path. In tracing the indirect connections no variable may be intersected more than once in one compound path. Having traced all such possible compound paths, we obtain the entirety of indirect effects as their sum.

Let us consider the example of effects of education on first job, U on W. The gross or total effect is $r_{WU} = .538$. The direct path is $p_{WU} = .440$. There are two indirect connections or compound paths: from W back to X then forward to U; and from W back to X, then back to V, and then forward to U. Hence we have:

$$r_{WU} = \underbrace{p_{WU}}_{} + \underbrace{p_{WX}p_{UX} + p_{WX}r_{XV}p_{UV}}_{}$$

$$(gross) \quad (direct) \qquad (indirect)$$

or, numerically,

$$.538 = .440 + (.224)(.279) + (.224)(.516)(.310)$$

$$= .440 + .062 + .036$$

$$= .440 + .098.$$

In this case all the indirect effect of U on W derives from the fact that both U and W have X (plus V) as a common cause. In other instances, when more than one common cause is involved and these causes are themselves interrelated, the complexity is too great to permit a succinct verbal summary.

A final stipulation about the scheme had best be stated, though it is implicit in all the previous discussion. The form of the model itself, but most particularly the numerical estimates accompanying it, are submitted as valid only for the population under study. No claim is made that an equally cogent account of the process of stratification in another society could be rendered in terms of this scheme. For other populations, or even for subpopulations within the United States, the magnitudes would almost certainly be different, although we have some basis for supposing them to have been fairly constant over the last few decades in this country. The technique of path analysis is not a method for discovering causal laws but a procedure for giving a quantitative interpretation to the manifestations of a known or assumed causal system as it operates in a particular population. When the same interpretive structure is appropriate for two or more populations there is something to be learned by comparing their respective path coefficients and correlation patterns. We have not yet reached the stage at which such comparative study of stratification systems is feasible. . . .

The Concept of a Vicious Circle

Although the concept of a "cycle of poverty" has a quasi-official sanction in U. S. public policy discussion, it is difficult to locate a systematic explication of the concept. As clear a formulation as any that may be found in academic writing is perhaps the following:[15]

> Occupational and social status are to an important extent self-perpetuating. They are associated with many factors which make it difficult for individuals to modify their status. Position in the social structure is usually associated with a certain level of income, education, family structure, community reputation, and so forth. These become part of a vicious circle in which each factor acts on the other in such a way as to preserve the social structure in its present form, as well as the individual family's position in that structure. . . . The cumulation of disadvantages (or of advantages) affects the individual's entry into the labor market as well as his later opportunities for social mobility.

The suspicion arises that the authors in preparing this summary statement were partly captured by their own rhetoric. Only a few pages earlier they had observed that the "widespread variation of educational attainment within classes suggests that one's family background plays an enabling and motivating rather than a determining role."[16] But is an "enabling and motivating role" logically adequate to the function of maintaining a "vicious circle"? In focusing closely on the precise wording of the earlier quotation we are not interested in splitting hairs or in generating a polemic. It merely serves as a convenient point of departure for raising the questions of what is specifically meant by "vicious circle," what are the operational criteria for this concept, and what are the limits of its usefulness.

To begin with, there is the question of fact—or, rather, of how the quantitative facts are to be evaluated. How "difficult" is it, in actuality, "for individuals to modify their status" (presumably reference is to the status of the family of orientation)? We have found that the father-son correlation for occupational status is of the order of .4. (Assuming attenuation by errors of measurement, this should perhaps be revised slightly upward.) Approaching the measurement problem in an entirely different way, we find that the amount of intergenerational mobility between census major occupation groups is no less than seven-eighths as much as would occur if there were no statistical association between the two statuses whatsoever, or five-sixths as much as the difference between the "minimum" mobility involved in the intergenerational shift in occupation distributions and the amount required for "perfect" mobility.[17] Evidently a very considerable amount of "status modification" or occupational mobility does occur. (There is nothing in the data exhibited by Lipset and Bendix to indicate the contrary.) If the existing amount of modification of status is insufficient in terms of some functional or normative criterion implicitly employed, the precise criterion should be made explicit: *How much mobility must occur to contradict the diagnosis of a "vicious circle"?*

Next, take the postulate that occupational status (of origin) is "associated with many factors" and that "each factor acts on the other" so as "to preserve . . . the individual family's position." Here the exposition virtually cries out for an explicit *quantitative* causal model; if not one of the type set forth in the first section of this chapter, then some other model that also takes into account the way in which several variables combine their effects. Taking our own earlier model, for want of a better alternative, as representative of the situation, what do we learn about the "associated factors"? Family "position" is, indeed, "associated with . . . education," and education in turn makes a sizable difference in early and subsequent occupational achievement. Yet of the total or gross effect of education (U) on Y, occupational status in 1962 (r_{YU} = .596), only a minor part consists in a transmission of the prior influence of "family position," at least as this is indicated by measured variables V (father's education) and X (father's occupation). . . . A relevant calculation concerns the compound paths through V and X linking Y to U. Using data for men 20 to 64 years old with nonfarm background, we find:

$$p_{YX}p_{UX} = .025$$

$$p_{YX}r_{XV}p_{UV} = .014$$

$$p_{YX}p_{WX}p_{UX} = .014$$

$$p_{YW}p_{WX}r_{XV}p_{UV} = .008$$

$$\overline{\qquad\qquad\qquad}$$

$$Sum = .061$$

This is the *entire* part of the effect of education that has to do with "perpetuating" the "family's position." By contrast, the direct effect is $p_{YU} = .407$ and the effect via W (exclusive of prior influence of father's education and occupation on respondent's first job) is $p_{YW}p_{WU} = .128$, for a total of .535. Far from serving in the main as a factor perpetuating initial status, education operates *primarily* to induce variation in occupational status that is independent of initial status. The simple reason is that the large residual factor for U is an indirect cause of Y. But by definition it is quite uncorrelated with X and V. This is not to gainsay the equally cogent point that the degree of "perpetuation" (as measured by r_{YX}) that does occur is mediated in large part by education. . . .

Our model also indicates where the "vicious circle" interpretation is vulnerable. In the passage on the vicious circle quoted there seems to be an assumption that because of the substantial intercorrelations between a number of background factors, each of which has a significant relationship to subsequent achievement, the total effect of origin on achievement is materially enhanced. Here, in other words, the concept of "cumulation" appears to refer to the intercorrelations of a collection of independent variables. But the effect of such intercorrelations is quite opposite to what the writers appear to suppose. They are not alone in arguing from a fallacious assumption that was caustically analyzed by Karl Pearson half a century ago.[18] The crucial point is that if the several determinants are indeed substantially intercorrelated with each other, then their combined effect will consist largely in redundancy, not in "cumulation." This circumstance does not relieve us from the necessity of trying to understand better *how* the effects come about (a point also illustrated in a less fortunate way in Pearson's work). It does imply that a refined estimate of how much effect results from a combination of "associated factors" will not differ greatly from a fairly crude estimate based on the two or three most important ones.

NOTES

[1] Mollie Orshansky, "Children of the Poor," *Social Security Bulletin*, 26(July 1963).

[2] Forrest A. Bogan, "Employment of High School Graduates and Dropouts in 1964," *Special Labor Force Report*, No. 54 (U. S. Bureau of Labor Statistics, June 1965), p. 643.

[3] Peter M. Blau and Otis Dudley Duncan, *The American Occupational Structure*, New York: The Free Press, 1967, ch. 4.

[4] *Ibid.*

[5] Bruce K. Eckland, "College Dropouts Who Came Back," *Harvard Educational Review*, 34(1964), 402–420.

[6] Beverly Duncan, *Family Factors and School Dropout: 1920–1960*, U. S. Office of Education, Cooperative Research Project No. 2258, Ann Arbor: Univ. of Michigan, 1965.

[7] Blau and Duncan, *op. cit.*, Appendix C.

[8] Gösta Carlsson, *Social Mobility and Class Structure*, Lund: CWK Gleerup, 1958, p. 124.

[9] H. M. Blalock, Jr., *Causal Inferences in Nonexperimental Research*, Chapel Hill: Univ. of North Carolina Press, 1964.

[10] Sewall Wright, "Path Coefficients and Path Regressions," *Biometrics*, 16(1960), 189–202; Otis Dudley Duncan, "Path Analysis," *American Journal of Sociology*, 72(1966), 1–16.

[11] Blalock, *op. cit.*, pp. 54 ff.

[12] Blau and Duncan, *op. cit.*, ch. 4.

[13] *Ibid.*, ch. 3.

[14] *Ibid.*, ch. 5.

[15] Seymour M. Lipset and Reinhard Bendix, *Social Mobility in Industrial Society*, Berkeley: Univ. of California Press, 1959, pp. 198–199.

[16] *Ibid.*, p. 190.

[17] U. S. Bureau of the Census, "Lifetime Occupational Mobility of Adult Males: March 1962," *Current Population Reports*, Series P–23, No. 11 (May 12, 1964), Table B.

[18] Karl Pearson, "On Certain Errors with Regard to Multiple Correlation Occasionally Made by Those Who Have Not Adequately Studied This Subject," *Biometrika*, 10(1914), 181–187.

17

THE EDUCATIONAL AND EARLY OCCUPATIONAL ATTAINMENT PROCESS

William H. Sewell, Archibald O. Haller, and Alejandro Portes

♦♦♦

Blau and Duncan (1967:165–172) have recently presented a path model of the occupational attainment process of the American adult male population. This basic model begins with two variables describing the early stratification position of each person; these are his father's educational and occupational attainment statuses. It then moves to two behavioral variables; these are the educational level the individual has completed and the prestige level of his first job. The dependent variable is the person's occupational prestige position in 1962. That the model is not without power is attested by the fact that it accounts for about 26 percent of the variance in educational attainment, 33 percent of the variance in first job, and 42 percent of the

William H. Sewell, Archibald O. Haller, and Alejandro Portes, "The Educational and Early Occupational Attainment Process," *American Sociological Review* 34 (February 1969), pp. 82–92.

variance in 1962 level of occupational attainment. Various additions to the basic model are presented in the volume, but none is clearly shown to make much of an improvement in it. These include nativity, migration, farm origin, subgroup position, marriage, and assortative mating. Without detracting from the excellence of the Blau and Duncan analysis, we may make several observations.

1) Because the dependent behaviors are occupational prestige attainments—attainment levels in a stratification system—it is appropriate to single out variables indicating father's stratification position as the most relevant social structural inputs. It is unfortunate that practical considerations prevented the inclusion of psychological inputs in their model, especially considering the repeated references to one such—mental ability—in the literature on differential occupational attainment (Lipset and Bendix, 1959:203–226; Sewell and Armer, 1966). More recently, this gap has been partially filled (Duncan, 1968).

2) Also omitted are social psychological factors which mediate the influence of the input variables on attainment. This, too, is unfortunate in view not only of the speculative theory but also the concrete research in social psychology, which suggests the importance of such intervening variables as reference groups (Merton, 1957:281–386), significant others (Gerth and Mills, 1953:84–91), self-concept (Super, 1957:80–100), behavior expectations (Gross et al., 1958), levels of educational and occupational aspiration (Haller and Miller, 1963; Kuvlesky and Ohlendorf, 1967; Ohlendorf et al., 1967), and experiences of success or failure in school (Parsons, 1959; Brookover et al., 1965).

It remains to be seen whether the addition of such psychological and social psychological variables is worthwhile, although there are reasons for believing that at least some of them may be. First, an explanation of a behavior system requires a plausible causal argument, not just a set of path coefficients among temporally ordered variables. As indicated in Duncan's (1969) recent work, the introduction of social psychological mediating variables offers this possibility, but it does not guarantee it. As it stands, the Blau-Duncan model fails to indicate why any connection at all would be expected between the input variables, father's education and occupation, and the three subsequent factors: respondent's education, respondent's first job, and respondent's 1962 occupation. Granting differences among social psychological positions, they all agree that one's cognitions and motivations (including, among others, knowledge, self-concept, and aspirations) are developed in structured situations (including the expectations of others), and that one's actions (attainments in this case) are a result of the cognitive and motivational orientations one brings to the action situation, as well as the factors in the new situation itself. Second, if valid, a social psychological model will suggest new points at which the causal system may be entered in order to change the attainment behaviors of persons, an issue not addressed by the Blau and Duncan volume. Variables such as the expectations of significant others offer other possibilities for manipulating the outcomes, including educational attainments. Third, in addition to the above advantages, a social psychological model of educational and occupational attainment might add to the explanation of variance in the dependent variables.

THE PROBLEM

The present report extends the attempts of the writers (Sewell and Armer, 1966; Sewell and Orenstein, 1965; Sewell and Shah, 1967; Sewell, 1964; Haller and Sewell, 1967; Portes et al., 1968; Haller, 1966; Haller and Miller, 1963; Miller and Haller, 1964; Sewell et al., 1957) to apply social psychological concepts to the explanation of variation in levels of educational and occupational attainment. We assume (1) that certain social structural and psychological factors—initial stratification position and mental ability, specifically—affect both the sets of significant others' influences bearing on the youth, and the youth's own observations of his ability; (2) that the influence of significant others, and possibly his estimates of his ability, affect the youth's levels of educational and occupational aspiration; (3) that the levels of aspiration affect subsequent levels of educational attainment; (4) that education in turn affects levels of occupational attainment. In the present analysis we assume that all effects are linear; also, that the social psychological variables perform only mediating functions.

More specifically, we present theory and data regarding what we believe to be a logically consistent social psychological model. This provides a plausible causal argument to link stratification and mental ability inputs through a set of social psychological and behavioral mechanisms to educational and occupational attainments. One compelling feature of the model is that some of the inputs may be manipulated through experimental or other purposive interventions. This means that parts of it can be experimentally tested in future

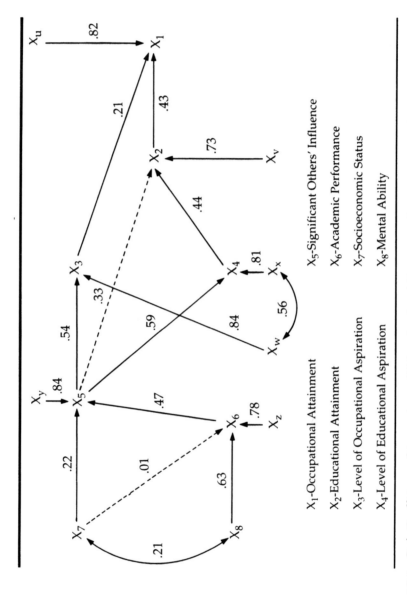

Diagram 17.1   Path Coefficients of Antecedents of Educational and Occupational Attainment Levels

X_1-Occupational Attainment

X_2-Educational Attainment

X_3-Level of Occupational Aspiration

X_4-Level of Educational Aspiration

X_5-Significant Others' Influence

X_6-Academic Performance

X_7-Socioeconomic Status

X_8-Mental Ability

research and that practical policy agents can reasonably hope to use it in order to change educational and occupational attainments.

A Social Psychological Model

The model treats causal relationships among eight variables. X_1 is the occupational prestige level attained by the adult person, or *occupational attainment* (OccAtt); X_2 is the educational level he had previously attained, or *educational attainment* (EdAtt); X_3 is the occupational prestige level to which he aspired as a youth, or *level of occupational aspiration* (LOA); X_4 is his *level of educational aspiration* as a youth (LEA); X_5 is the influence for educational achievement exerted upon him by significant others while still in high school, or *significant others' influence* (SOI); X_6 is the quality of his *academic performance* in high school (AP); X_7 is the level of his family in the stratification system, or *socioeconomic status* (SES); and X_8 is his *mental ability* as measured while he was in high school (MA). Path models (Blau and Duncan, 1967:165–172; Wright, 1934; Wright, 1960; Heise, 1969) require a knowledge of the causal order among the variables. Beyond the causal arguments presented below, additional credibility is suggested by the existence of a plausible temporal order among variables. X_7 (SES) and X_8 (MA) precede everything else. X_5 (SOI) and X_6 (AP) precede both aspirations and attainments, and it can be assumed that for the most part X_6 precedes X_5. Youthful aspirations obviously precede later educational and occupational attainments. Pre-adult educational attainments precede adult occupational attainments.

By no means do all of the possible causal linkages seem defensible. The most likely ones are indicated in Diagram 17.1. In it straight solid lines stand for causal lines that are to be theoretically expected, dotted lines stand for possible but theoretically debatable causal lines, and curved lines represent unanalyzed correlations among variables which cannot be assigned causal priority in present data.

Commencing from the left of the diagram, we assume, as has often been found before (Sewell and Shah, 1967; Sewell et al., 1957), that a low positive correlation, r_{78}, exists between the youth's measured mental ability (MA) and his parents' socioeconomic status (SES). This is the case: $r_{78} = .21$. We anticipate the existence of substantial effect of MA on academic performance (AP). We theorize that significant others' influence (SOI) is controlled by AP, and by socioeconomic status, as well as by exogenous factors, that they exert profound effects on aspiration, and that the latter in turn influences later attainments. A more detailed examination of the theory follows.

Working with partial conceptions of SOI (and using different terminology), Bordua (1960) and Sewell and Shah (1968) have shown that parents' expectations for the youths' attainments are important influences on later aspirations and attainment. Similarly, Cramer (1967), Alexander and Campbell (1964), Campbell and Alexander (1965), Haller and Butterworth (1960), and Duncan et al. (1968) have investigated peer influences on aspirations and attainments. Each of these sets of actors, plus some others, may be seen as a special case of reference group influence. Building on such thinking, we have concluded that the key variable here is significant others' influence. Significant others are the specific persons from whom the individual obtains his level of aspiration, either because they serve as models or because they communicate to him their expectations for his behavior (Woelfel, 1967). The term "significant others" is more appropriate than that of "reference group" because it eliminates the implication that collectivities such as one's friends, or work groups, or parents are necessarily the influential agents for all individuals. Experimental research, beginning with Sherif's work (1935), has shown the importance of other persons in defining one's own situation. One obtains his social behavior tendencies largely through the influence of others. Herriott (1963) has carried this line of thinking into the present area of research. He has shown that one's conception of the educational behavior others think appropriate to him is highly correlated with his level of educational aspiration. Thus, significant others' influence is a central variable in a social psychological explanation of educational and occupational attainment. It is obviously important to discover the causal paths determining SOI, as well as those by which it exerts its effects on attainment. We hypothesize a substantial direct path (p_{57}) from socioeconomic status (SES) to SOI. We also hypothesize a substantial effect of mental ability on SOI. This is because we expect that the significant others with whom the youth interacts base their expectations for his educational and occupational attainments in part on his demonstrated abilities. In turn, this implies that the path from mental ability (MA) to SOI is indirect by way of academic performance (AP). Thus, we hypothesize the existence of a pronounced path from MA to AP (p_{68}) and another from AP to SOI (p_{56}). So far we assume that one's grades in school are based on the quality of his performance. A strong undercurrent in the literature seems to have held, however, that the youth's family's SES has a direct influence on his grades (Havighurst and Neugarten,

1957:236–237). To our knowledge, this has not been adequately demonstrated, and in large high schools, often far removed from the youth's home and neighborhood, this may well be debatable. Nevertheless, since it is at least possible that school grades (the evidences of performance) are partly determined by teachers' desires to please prestigious parents or to reward "middle-class" behavior, we have drawn a dotted path (p_{67}) from SES to AP, allowing for the possibility of such an influence.

We hypothesize that the major effects of significant others' influence (SOI) on attainment are mediated by its effects on levels of aspiration. Thus, we have indicated a path (p_{35}) from SOI to level of occupational aspiration (LOA) and another (p_{45}) from SOI to level of educational aspiration (LEA). It is not inconsistent with this to suspect the possibility that SOI might have a direct influence on later educational attainment (EdAtt); we have thus included a dotted or debatable path (p_{25}) from SOI to EdAtt. Because we are here referring to SOI during late high school, it must necessarily refer largely to college education. There is, therefore, no reason to include such a path from SOI to occupational attainment.

Levels of educational aspiration (LEA) and occupational aspiration (LOA) are known to be highly correlated, since education is widely, and to some extent validly, considered to be a necessary condition for high occupational attainment (Haller and Miller, 1963:30, 39–42, 96). But LOA and LEA are not identical. (In these data, $r_{34.5} = r_{WX} = .56$.) We expect that LEA will have a pronounced effect on EdAtt (p_{24}), and that its entire effect on level of occupational attainment will be expressed through EdAtt. On the other hand, we do not hypothesize any effect of LOA on EdAtt which is not already contained in its correlation with LEA. Hence, there is no hypothetical path for LOA to EdAtt. A direct effect of LOA on OccAtt (p_{13}) is hypothesized, however.

There are 26 possible paths, given the sequence laid out above. As one can see by counting the paths (straight lines) in Diagram 17.1, we hypothesize noteworthy effects for only eight of these—ten if the dotted lines are counted. If this were a rigorous theoretical model, path coefficients would be calculated only for these eight (or ten) supposed causal connections. We believe that because of the fact that it is not rigorous, and at this stage of our knowledge probably cannot be, it would be well to calculate all of the possible 26 path coefficients, using the calculated values as rough indicators of the influences operating in the system. If the theoretic reasoning is a fair description of the reality to which it is addressed, the path coefficients for the eight (or ten) predicted causal lines should be considerably greater than those for the remainder where no causal prediction was made. Also, it is entirely possible that some unhypothesized causal lines might turn out to be of importance. This, too, argues for calculating the whole set of 26. These data are presented in tabular form in Table 17.3.

METHOD

In 1957 all high school seniors in Wisconsin responded to an extensive questionnaire concerning their educational and occupational aspirations and a number of potentially related topics. In 1964 one of the authors (Sewell) directed a follow-up in which data on later educational and occupational attainments were collected from an approximately one-third random sample of the respondents in the original survey.

This study is concerned with those 929 subjects for whom data are available at both times, in 1957 and 1964, and who (a) are males and (b) whose fathers were farmers in 1957. Zero-order correlations are computed on all 929 cases, using a computer program which accepts missing data. All higher order coefficients are based on 739 cases for whom data on each variable were complete. (The matrices of zero-order correlations between all eight variables for those two sets of cases are practically identical.)

Variables

Level of occupational attainment (X_1—OccAtt) was measured by Duncan's (1961) socioeconomic index of occupational status.

Level of educational attainment (X_2—EdAtt) was operationalized with data obtained in 1964 by dividing the sample into those who have had at least some college education and those who have not had any at all.[1]

Level of occupational aspiration (X_3—LOA) was determined by assigning Duncan's (1961) socioeconomic index scores to the occupation indicated by the respondent as the one he desired to fill in the future.

Level of educational aspiration (X_4—LEA) is a dichotomous variable corresponding to the respondent's statement in 1957 of whether or not he planned to attend college after graduating from high school.

Index of significant others' influence (X_5—SOI) is a simple summated score (range: zero to three) of three variables: (a) The youth's report of his parents' encouragement for college, dichotomized according to whether or not the respondent perceived direct parental encouragement for going to college. (b) The youth's report of his teachers' encouragement for college, dichotomized in a similar manner, according to whether or not direct teacher encouragement for college was perceived by the respondent. (c) Friends' college plans, dichotomized according to the respondent's statement that most of his close friends planned or did not plan to go to college. These variables, all emphasizing education, were combined because they reflect the same conceptual dimension, and that dimension is theoretically more relevant than any of its component parts. That the three components do in fact measure the same dimension is attested by the positive correlations among them and a subsequent factor analysis. These correlations and the correlation of each with the summated variable, significant others' influence, are shown in Table 17.1. It may be relevant to point out the composition of this significant others' index in the light of Kelley's distinction (1952). Clearly, the perceptions of direct parental and teacher pressures toward college conform to the classic case of normative reference groups. The educational plans of close friends, on the other hand, may be thought of as having mixed functions. First, close peer groups may exercise pressure toward conformity, and second, friends' plans also serve for the individual's cognitive comparison of himself with "people like himself." Therefore, though the main character of the dimension indicated by this index is clearly normative, it can be thought of as containing some elements of an evaluative function as well.

Quality of academic performance (X_6—AP) is measured by a reflected arc sine transformation of each student's rank in his high school class.

Socioeconomic status (X_7—SES) is measured by a factor-weighted combination of the education of the respondent's father and mother, his perception of the economic status of the family, his perception of possible parental support should he choose to go to college and the approximate amount of such support, and the occupation of his father.[2]

Measured mental ability (X_8—MA) is indexed by Henmon-Nelson test scores (1942). The data were taken when the youths were in the junior year of high school. The scores, originally recorded as percentile-ranks, were treated with an arc sine transformation to approximate a normal distribution.[3]

	Teachers' Influence	Friends' Influence	Index of Significant Others' Influence
Parental Influence	.37	.26	.74
Teachers' Influence	--	.32	.72
Friends' Influence	--	--	.68
Significant Others' Influence	--	--	--

Table 17.1   Zero-Order Correlations Between Indicators of Significant Others' Influence Regarding College

RESULTS

The zero-order correlation coefficients among eight variables are presented in Table 17.2. A complete path diagram would involve too many lines to be intelligible, because path coefficients presented in Diagram 17.1 were calculated for all 26 possible lines implied in the causal order specified above. With the exception of the theoretically dubious direct path from SES to AP, which turned out to be $p_{67} = .01$, each of the path coefficients for causal lines hypothesized in Diagram 17.1 is larger than those not hypothesized. Both sets of standardized beta (or path) coefficients are presented in Table 17.3.

This table shows that the reasoning presented in the above section, offering a social psychological explanation for educational and occupational attainment, cannot be too far off the mark. We had hypothesized that SOI (significant others' influence) was of central importance. In fact, it has notable direct effects on three subsequent variables, each of which bears ultimately on prestige level of occupational attainment. Both theory and data agree that SOI has direct effects on levels of educational and occupational aspiration, as well as educational (i.e., college) attainment. In turn, each aspiration variable appears to have the predicted substantial effects on its respective attainment variable. Looking at its antecedents, we note theory and data again agree that SOI is affected directly by SES and indirectly by measured mental ability through the latter's effect on the youth's academic performance. The latter variable is crucial because it provides (or is correlated with) palpable evidence that significant others can observe and, thus to a degree, align their expectations for the youth with his demonstrated ability.

None of the unpredicted paths is very strong, but we must recognize that there may be more operating in such a system than we were able to antici-

	X1 Occupational Attainment (Prestige Scores: Duncan)	X2 Educational Attainment (Years College)	X3 Level of Occupational Aspiration	X4 Level of Educational Aspiration	X5 Significant Others' Influence	X6 Academic Performance (Grade Point)	X7 Socio-economic Status	X8 Measured Mental Ability
X1-Occ. Att.	--	.52	.43	.38	.41	.37	.14	.33
X2-Ed. Att.	--	--	.53	.61	.57	.48	.23	.40
X3-LOA	--	--	--	.70	.53	.43	.15	.41
X4-LEA	--	--	--	--	.59	.46	.26	.40
X5-SOI	--	--	--	--	--	.49	.29	.41
X6-AP	--	--	--	--	--	--	.16	.62
X7-SES	--	--	--	--	--	--	--	.21
X8-MA	--	--	--	--	--	--	--	--

Table 17.2 Zero-Order Correlations

Independent Variables

Dependent Variables	X_2 EdAtt	X_1 LOA	X_4 LEA	X_5 SOI	X_6 AP	X_7 SES	X_8 MA
X_6 AP	--	--	--	--	--	*(.01)*	*.62*
X_5 SOI	--	--	--	--	*.39*	.21	.13
X_4 LEA	--	--	--	*.45*	.18	.07	.08
X_3 LOA	--	--	--	*.42*	.12	-.02	.16
X_2 EdAtt	--	.07	*.34*	*(.23)*	.17	.05	.03
X_1 OccAtt	*.38*	*.19*	-.10	.11	.06	.00	.04

Figures in italics are coefficients for paths hypothesized in Diagram 17.1.
Figures in parentheses refer to theoretically debatable causal lines.

Table 17.3 Standardized Beta Coefficients for Hypothesized and Non-Hypothesized Causal Paths

pate from previous thinking. There is a pair of perhaps consequential direct paths from academic performance to educational aspiration (p_{46} = .18) and to educational attainment (p_{26} = .17). There are several possibilities. The data might imply the existence of a mediating factor, such as one's self conception of his ability, a factor which could influence both educational aspirations and attainment. They also suggest that not all of the effect of ability on educational aspiration and attainments is mediated by SOI. Finally, one's ability may exert a continuing effect on his educational attainments quite apart from the mediation of either significant others or aspirations—and therefore apart from one's conception of his ability. Arguments such as these, however, should not be pressed too far because the figures are small. Another unexpected but noteworthy path links mental ability directly to level of occupational aspiration. We offer no speculation regarding it.

So far we have seen that a consistent and plausible social psychological position is at least moderately well borne out by the analysis of lines of apparent influence of its variables when they are arranged in causal order. How well does the total set of independent variables work in accounting for variance in the attainment variables? In brief, $R^2_{1.2345678}$ = .34 and $R^2_{2.345678}$ = .50. Thus, the variables account for 34 percent of the variance in level of occupational attainment and 50 percent of the variance in level of educational attainment. Obviously, variables X_3 through X_8 are much more effective in accounting for educational attainment than in accounting for occupational attainment. Indeed, educational attainment alone accounts for 27 percent of the variance in occupational attainment (from Table 17.3, r^2_{12} = .52^2 = .27). What we have here, then, is a plausible causal system functioning primarily to explain variation in educational attainment. This, in turn, has considerable effect on occupational attainment. The same set of variables adds a small but useful amount to the explanation of occupational attainment variance beyond that contributed by its explanation of educational attainment.[4]

DISCUSSION AND CONCLUSIONS

Using father's occupational prestige, the person's educational attainment, and his first job level, Blau and Duncan (1967:165–172) were able to account for 33 percent of the variance in occupational attainment of a nationwide sample of American men. Neither our sample nor our variables are identical with theirs; so it is impossible to assess the total contribution of this study to the state of knowledge as reflected in their work. Educational attainment is strategic in both studies and in this regard the studies are fairly comparable. The present model adds a great deal to the explanation of the social psychological factors affecting that variable. The prospects seem good, too, that if the present model were to be applied to a sample coming from a wider range of the American stratification system with greater age variation, it might prove to be more powerful than it appears with our sample of young farm-reared men. In general, the present take-off on the Blau-Duncan approach to occupational attainment levels seems worthy of further testing and elaboration.

Several comments are appropriate regarding the social psychological position and data presented here. (1) Clearly, the variable we have called significant others' influence is an important factor. The present evidence appears to show that once formed its effects are far-reaching. Also, besides being a powerful explanatory factor, significant others' influence should be amenable to manipulation. It thus suggests itself as a point at which external agents might intervene to change educational and occupational attainment levels. This means that at least part of the system is theoretically amenable to experimental testing. The parts of the present model which are hypothetically dependent upon this variable might be more securely tested if such experiments can be worked out. Also, practical change agents might be able to change levels of attainment, either by inserting themselves or others as new significant others or by changing the expectations existing significant others have for the individual. There may well be a substantial pay-off from more refined work with this variable.

(2) The results seem to indicate, too, that aspirations (a special class of attitudes) are in fact performing mediational functions in transmitting anterior factors into subsequent behaviors. This has been a subject of recent debate, much of which has in effect held that attitudinal variables are useless epiphenomena. This was recently discussed by Fendrich (1967).

Such encouraging results do not, however, mitigate the need for (a) general experimental determination of the supposed effects of attitudes on behaviors, and (b) specific experimental determination of the effects of aspirations on attainments.

(3) The question may be raised as to the extent to which this system is inherently culture-bound. One might wonder whether attainment behavior within an institutionalized pattern of "sponsored" rather than "contest" achievement (Turner, 1960) would change the path model. Besides this (and

perhaps other institutionalized types of achievement patterns), there is also the question of the relevance of the model for ascribed occupational attainment systems. Obviously we do not have data bearing on these questions but we may at least discuss them. Let us suppose that the same eight variables are measured on youth in a "sponsored" achievement context. We speculate that if measured mental ability is the basis of selection of those who are to be advanced, then the direct path from mental ability to significant others' influence would increase because sponsors are significant others. (This would require a more general measure of significant others' influence than was used here.) If a variable other than mental ability or socioeconomic status is important to the sponsors, then the residual effect of unmeasured variables on significant others' influence would increase. Since one's sponsors presumably influence one's aspirations and aspirations in turn mediate attainment, the rest of the model probably would not change much.

Consider the case of ascribed attainment. Here one's parents' position determines what one's significant others will expect of one; mental ability is either irrelevant or controlled by family position; and one's aspirations are controlled by the family. The importance of higher education may vary among basically ascribed systems: in one it may be unimportant, in another it may merely validate one's status, or in still another it may train ascribed elites to fulfill the key social roles in the society. If educational attainment is important within the social system, aspirations will mediate the influence of significant others upon it, and it in turn will mediate occupational attainment. If not, occupational aspirations will mediate occupational attainment and educational attainment will drop out of the path model. In short, by allowing for variations in the path coefficients, the same basic social psychological model might work well to describe attainment in stratification and mobility systems quite different from that of the present sample.

(4) The linear model used here seems to be an appropriate way to operationalize social psychological positions holding that the function of "intervening" attitudinal variables is to mediate the influence of more fundamental social structural and psychological variables on behavior. By assuming linear relations among variables and applying a path system to the analysis, we have cast the attainment problem in such a framework. It seems to have worked quite well. We are sufficiently encouraged by this attempt to recommend that a parallel tack might be made on problems in which the overt behavior variables are quite different from educational and occupational attainment.

(5) Nonetheless, satisfactory as such a linear model and its accompanying theory seems to be, there is still the possibility that other techniques flowing from somewhat different social psychological assumptions might be better. It is possible that, in the action situation, enduring attitudes (such as educational and occupational aspirations) may function as independent forces which express themselves in relevant overt behaviors to the degree that other personality and situational variables permit. Linear models would thus be effective to the degree that the persons modify their aspirations to bring them in line with potentials for action offered by the latter variables. More importantly, the combined effects of aspirational and facilitational variables would produce nonlinear accelerating curves of influence on behavior variables. For the present types of data, this would imply that parental stratification position, mental ability, and significant others' influence not only produce aspirations, but also, to the extent to which these influences continue more or less unchanged on into early adulthood, they function as differential facilitators for the expression of aspirations in attainments. If this is true, a nonlinear system of statistical analysis handling interaction effects would be even more powerful than the one used in this paper.

(6) It should be remembered that the most highly educated of these young men had just begun their careers when the final data were collected. If the distance between them and the less educated widens, the occupational attainment variance accounted for by the model may well increase. The direct relations of some of the antecedents to occupational attainment may also change. In particular, mental ability may show a higher path to occupational attainment.

(7) Finally, although the results reported in this paper indicate that the proposed model has considerable promise for explaining educational and early occupational attainment of farm boys, its adequacy should now be tested on populations with a more differentiated socioeconomic background. It is quite possible that in such populations the effects of socioeconomic status on subsequent variables may be significantly increased. The effects of other variables in the system may also be altered when the model is applied to less homogeneous populations.

The present research appears to have extended knowledge of the causal mechanism influencing occupational attainment. Most of this was accomplished by providing a consistent social psychological model which adds to our ability to explain what is surely one of its key proximal antecedents, educational attainment.

NOTES

Revision of paper originally prepared for delivery at the joint sessions of the Rural Sociological Society and the American Sociological Association, San Francisco, August 1967. The research reported here was supported by the University of Wisconsin Graduate School, by the Cooperative State Research Service, and the University's College of Agriculture for North Central Regional Research Committee NC–86, by funds to the Institute for Research on Poverty at the University of Wisconsin provided by the Office of Economic Opportunity pursuant to the provisions of the Economic Opportunity Act of 1964, and by a grant from the National Institute of Health, U. S. Public Health Service (M–6275). The writers wish to thank Otis Dudley Duncan for his careful reading and incisive criticisms and Vimal P. Shah for help in the statistical analysis. The conclusions are the full responsibility of the authors.

[1] It is important to note that the timing of the follow-up was such as to allow most individuals to complete their education up to the bachelor's degree and beyond. It is unlikely that the educational attainment of the sample as a whole will change much in the years to come. On the other hand, while the span of seven years allowed those individuals who did not continue their education to find a stable position in the occupational structure and even improve upon it, there was not enough time for those who continued their education to do the same. A few of the latter were still in school; most had just begun their occupational careers. It is therefore possible that a follow-up taken five or ten years from now would show greater differentiation in attainments as the educated group gathers momentum and moves up in the occupational world.

[2] Naturally, father's occupation is a constant in this subsample of farm-reared males. It is important to note that the SES mean and standard deviations for this subsample are considerably lower than for the total sample. The low and homogeneous SES levels of this subsample may yield atypical relations among the variables.

[3] Our previous research (Sewell and Armer, 1966; Haller and Sewell, 1967) has led us to be skeptical of claims that local ecological and school class compositional factors influence aspirations and attainments. Nevertheless the zero-order intercorrelations of five such variables and their correlations with X_1–X_8 are available (although they are not presented here). Two of these pertain to the county in which the youth attended high school: county level of living and degree of urbanization. Three pertain to his high school senior class: average SES of the class, percentage of the class members whose fathers attended college, and percentage of the class members whose fathers had professional-level occupations. Though substantially correlated with each other, the variables are uncorrelated with the variables in the above model.

[4] Some readers will be interested in the path coefficients as calculated only for the lines hypothesized in the diagram. For this reason and because of the diagram's parsimony, we have calculated the values for each of its eight paths (or ten, including dubious ones). The restricted model explains 47 and 33 percent of the variance in X_2 and X_1, respectively. Data not presented here show that the model reproduces the zero-order correlation matrix quite well. For this reason and because the model is an effective predictor of X_2 and X_1, it may be considered to be fairly valid. Nonetheless, it seems more prudent to rest our case on the less presumptuous data already presented in Table 17.3. This is why the coefficients presented in the diagram are not discussed here.

REFERENCES

Alexander, C. Norman, Jr., and Ernest Q. Campbell. 1964. "Peer influences on adolescent educational aspirations and attainments." American Sociological Review 29 (August):568–575.

Blau, Peter M., and Otis Dudley Duncan. 1967. The American Occupational Structure. New York: Wiley.

Bordua, David J. 1960. "Educational aspirations and parental stress on college." Social Forces 38 (March):262–269.

Brookover, Wilbur B., Jean M. LePere, Don E. Hamachek, Shailer Thomas, and Edsel L. Erickson. 1965. Self-Concept of Ability and School Achievement. East Lansing: Michigan State University, Bureau of Educational Research Services.

Campbell, Ernest Q., and C. Norman Alexander. 1965. "Structural effects and interpersonal relationships." American Journal of Sociology 71 (November):284–289.

Cramer, M. R. 1967. "The relationship between educational and occupational plans of high school students." Paper presented at the meeting of the Southern Sociological Society, Atlanta (unpublished).

Duncan, Otis Dudley. 1961. "A socioeconomic index for all occupations." Pp. 109–138 in Albert J. Reiss, Jr. (ed.), Occupations and Social Status. New York: Free Press.

———. 1968a. "Ability and achievement." Eugenics Quarterly 15 (March):1–11.

———. 1969. "Contingencies in the construction of causal models." Edgar F. Borgatta, (ed.), Sociological Methodology. San Francisco: Jossey-Bass.

Duncan, Otis Dudley, Archibald O. Haller, and Alejandro Portes. 1968. "Peer influences on aspirations: a reinterpretation." American Journal of Sociology 74 (September):119–137.

Fendrich, James M. 1967. "Perceived reference group support: racial attitudes and overt behavior." American Sociological Review 32 (December):960–970.

Gerth, Hans, and C. Wright Mills. 1953. Character and Social Structure. New York: Harcourt, Brace and World.

Gross, Neal, Ward S. Mason, and Alexander W. McEachern. 1958. Explorations in Role Analysis. New York: Wiley.

Haller, Archibald O. 1966. "Occupational choices of rural youth." Journal of Cooperative Extension 4 (Summer):93–102.

Haller, Archibald O., and Charles E. Butterworth. 1960. "Peer influences on levels of occupational and educational aspiration." Social Forces 38 (May):289–295.

Haller, Archibald O., and Irwin W. Miller. 1963. The Occupational Aspiration Scale: Theory, Structure and Correlates. East Lansing: Michigan Agricultural Experiment Station Bulletin 288.

Haller, Archibald O., and William H. Sewell. 1967. "Occupational choices of Wisconsin farm boys." Rural Sociology 32 (March):37–55.

Havighurst, Robert J., and Bernice L. Neugarten. 1957. Society and Education. Boston: Allyn and Bacon.

Heise, David R. 1969. "Problems in path analysis and causal inference." Edgar F. Borgatta, (ed.), Sociological Methodology. San Francisco: Jossey-Bass.

Henmon, V. A. C., and M. J. Nelson. 1942. The Henmon-Nelson Test of Mental Ability. Boston: Houghton Mifflin Company.

Herriott, Robert E. 1963. "Some social determinants of educational aspiration." Harvard Educational Review 33 (Spring):157–177.

Kelley, Harold H. 1952. "Two functions of reference groups." Pp. 410–414 in Guy E. Swanson et al. (eds.), Readings in Social Psychology. New York: Henry Holt and Company.

Kuvlesky, William P., and George W. Ohlendorf. 1967. A Bibliography of Literature on Status Projections of Youth: I. Occupational Aspirations and Expectations. College Station: Texas A&M University, Department of Agricultural Economics and Sociology.

Lipset, Seymour M., and Reinhard Bendix. 1959. Social Mobility in Industrial Society. Berkeley: University of California Press.

Merton, Robert K. 1957. Social Theory and Social Structure. New York: Free Press.

Miller, I. W., and Archibald O. Haller. 1964. "The measurement of level of occupational aspiration." Personnel and Guidance Journal 42 (January):448–455.

Ohlendorf, George W., Sherry Wages, and William P. Kuvlesky. 1967. A Bibliography of Literature on Status Projections of Youth: II. Educational Aspirations and Expectations. College Station: Texas A & M University, Department of Agricultural Economics and Sociology.

Parsons, Talcott. 1959. "The school class as a social system." Harvard Educational Review 29 (Summer):297–318.

Portes, Alejandro, Archibald O. Haller, and William H. Sewell. 1968. "Professional-executive vs. farming as unique occupational choices." Rural Sociology 33 (June):153–159.

Sewell, William H. 1964. "Community of residence and college plans." American Sociological Review 29 (February):24–38.

Sewell, William H., and J. Michael Armer. 1966. "Neighborhood context and college plans." American Sociological Review 31 (April): 159–168.

Sewell, William H., Archibald O. Haller, and Murray A. Straus. 1957. "Social status and educational and occupational aspiration." American Sociological Review 22 (February):67–73.

Sewell, William H., and Alan M. Orenstein. 1965. "Community of residence and occupational choice." American Journal of Sociology 70 (March):551–563.

Sewell, William H., and Vimal P. Shah. 1967. "Socioeconomic status, intelligence, and the attainment of higher education." Sociology of Education 40 (Winter):1–23.

_____. 1968. "Social class, parental encouragement, and educational aspirations." American Journal of Sociology 73 (March):559–572.

Sherif, Muzafer. 1935. "A study of some social factors in perception." Archives of Psychology Number 187.

Super, Donald E. 1957. The Psychology of Careers. New York: Harper.

Turner, Ralph H. 1960. "Sponsored and contest mobility and the school system." American Sociological Review 25 (December):855–867.

Woelfel, Joseph. 1967. "A paradigm for research on significant others." Paper presented at the Joint Session of the Society for the Study of Social Problems and the American Sociological Association, San Francisco (unpublished).

Wright, Sewall. 1934. "The method of path coefficients." Annals of Mathematical Statistics 5 (September):161–215.

_____. 1960. "Path coefficients and regression coefficients: alternative or complementary concept?" Biometrics 16 (June):189–202.

18

CULTURAL REPRODUCTION AND SOCIAL REPRODUCTION

Pierre Bourdieu

◆◆◆

The specific role of the sociology of education is assumed once it has established itself as the science of the relations between cultural reproduction and social reproduction. This occurs when it endeavours to determine the contribution made by the educational system to the reproduction of the structure of power relationships and symbolic relationships between classes, by contributing to the reproduction of the structure of the distribution of cultural capital among these classes. The science of the reproduction of structures, understood as a system of objective relations which impart their relational properties to individuals whom they preexist and survive, has nothing in common with the analytical recording of relations existing within a given population, be it a question of the relations between the academic success of children and the social position of their family or of the relations between the

Pierre Bourdieu, "Cultural Reproduction and Social Reproduction," in *Knowledge, Education, and Cultural Change*, edited by Richard Brown, pp. 71-84. Copyright 1973 by Tavistock. We have omitted the tables and figures appearing in the appendix of the original text.

positions filled by children and their parents. The substantialist mode of thought which stops short at directly accessible elements, that is to say individuals, claims a certain fidelity to reality by disregarding the structure of relations whence these elements derive all their sociologically relevant determinations, and thus finds itself having to analyse intra- or inter-generational mobility processes to the detriment of the study of mechanisms which tend to ensure the reproduction of the structure of relations between classes; it is unaware that the controlled mobility of a limited category of individuals, carefully selected and modified by and for individual ascent, is not incompatible with the permanence of structures, and that it is even capable of contributing to social stability in the only way conceivable in societies based upon democratic ideals and thereby may help to perpetuate the structure of class relations.

Any break with substantialist atomism, even if it does not mean going as far as certain structuralists and seeing agents as the simple "supports" of structures invested with the mysterious power of determining other structures, implies taking as our theme the process of education. This means that our object becomes the production of the habitus, that system of dispositions which acts as a mediation between structures and practice; more specifically, it becomes necessary to study the laws that determine the tendency of structures to reproduce themselves by producing agents endowed with the system of predispositions which is capable of engendering practices adapted to the structures and thereby contributing to the reproduction of the structures. If it is conceived within a theoretical framework such as this, the sociology of educational institutions and, in particular, of institutions of higher education, is capable of making a decisive contribution to the science of the structural dynamics of class relations, which is an often neglected aspect of the sociology of power. Indeed, among all the solutions put forward throughout history to the problem of the transmission of power and privileges, there surely does not exist one that is better adapted to societies which tend to refuse the most patent forms of the hereditary transmission of power and privileges, than that solution which the educational system provides by contributing to the reproduction of the structure of class relations and by concealing, by an apparently neutral attitude, the fact that it fills this function.

By traditionally defining the educational system as the group of institutional or routine mechanisms by means of which is operated what Durkheim calls "the conservation of a culture inherited from the past," i.e. the transmission from generation to generation of accumulated information, classical theories tend to dissociate the function of cultural reproduction proper to all educational systems from their function of social reproduction. Transposing, as they do, the representation of culture and of cultural transmission, commonly accepted by the ethnologists, to the case of societies divided into classes, these theories are based upon the implicit assumption that the different pedagogic actions which are carried out within the framework of the social structure, that is to say, those which are carried out by families from the different social classes as well as that which is practised by the school, work together in a harmonious way to transmit a cultural heritage which is considered as being the undivided property of the whole society.

In fact the statistics of theatre, concert, and above all, museum attendance (since, in the last case, the effect of economic obstacles is more or less nil) are sufficient reminder that the inheritance of cultural wealth which has been accumulated and bequeathed by previous generations only really belongs (although it is *theoretically* offered to everyone) to those endowed with the means of appropriating it for themselves. In view of the fact that the apprehension and possession of cultural goods as symbolic goods (along with the symbolic satisfactions which accompany an appropriation of this kind) are possible only for those who hold the code making it possible to decipher them or, in other words, that the appropriation of symbolic goods presupposes the possession of the instruments of appropriation, it is sufficient to give free play to the laws of cultural transmission for cultural capital and for the structure of the distribution of cultural capital between social classes to be thereby reproduced. By this is meant the structure of the distribution of instruments for the appropriation of symbolic wealth socially designated as worthy of being sought and possessed.

In order to be persuaded of the truth of this, it must first be seen that the structure of the distribution of classes or sections ("fractions") of a class according to the extent to which they are consumers of culture corresponds, with a few slight differences such as the fact that heads of industry and commerce occupy a lower position than do higher office staff, professionals, and even intermediate office staff, to the structure of distribution according to the hierarchy of economic capital and power (see Table 18.1).

The different classes or sections of a class are organized around three major positions: the lower position, occupied by the agricultural professions, workers, and small tradespeople, which are, in fact, categories excluded from participation in "high" culture; the intermediate position, occupied on the one hand by the heads and employees of industry and business and, on the

Annual budget coefficients	Agricultural workers	Farmers	Workers	Small tradespeople	White-collar workers	Intermediate office staff	Heads of industry and commerce	Professionals and higher office staff
Durable goods	0.6	0.5	0.8	0.8	1.4	2.8	1.5	3.6
Other expenditure	1.6	1.9	2.2	2.2	3.2	3.6	3.3	6.2

Household consumption, INSEE–CREDOC survey carried out in 1956 of 20,000 households—tables of household consumption by socio-professional categories.

Table 18.1 Expenditure on Culture

Purchasers of books during last month[1]	Readers of books[2]	Regular theatre, concert, cinema attendance in the Parisian region[3]				Have been to the theatre at least once in year 1964[4] (all of France)
Farmers — 14	Farmers, agricultural workers — 15.5	Farmers				Farmers — 18
Workers — 22	Workers — 33	Workers	21	8	70	Workers — 17
Heads of industry & commerce — 31	White-collar workers — 53.5	Tradespeople & craftsmen	46	14	71	Tradespeople & craftsmen — 22
White-collar workers, intermediate office staff — 39	Craftsmen & tradespeople, intermediate office staff — 51.5	White-collar workers, intermediate office staff	47	22	80	White-collar workers, intermediate office staff — 32
Professionals, higher office staff — 50	Heads of industry, professionals, higher office staff — 72	Heads of industry, professionals, higher office staff	65	33	81	Heads of industry, professionals, higher office staff — 63

[1] Syndicat national des éditeurs (National Union of Publishers), "La clientèle du livre," July 1967, survey carried out by the IFOP.

[2] Syndicat national des éditeurs, "La lecture et le livre en France," January–April 1960, survey carried out by the IFOP.

[3] Survey of theatre attendance in the Parisian region carried out by the IFOP, 1964.

[4] Survey of theatre attendance, SOFRES, June 1964.

Table 18.2   Cultural Activities of Different Occupational Categories

	Have purchased a book in the last month[1]	Readers of books[2]	Regular attendance at:				Have been to the theatre:	
			Theatre[3]	Concert[3]	Cinema[3]	Art Cinema	at least once in 1964	4 times or more
Primary	15	28	18	7	62	3	15	2
Primary, Higher, Commercial & technical		60	41	15	76		24	5
Secondary	44	Secondary & Higher 80	57	25	79	15	38	12
Higher	64		69	43	88	32	49	21

[1] Syndicat national des éditeurs (National Union of Publishers), "La clientèle du livre," July 1967, survey carried out by the IFOP.

[2] Syndicat national des éditeurs, "La lecture et le livre en France," January–April 1960, survey carried out by the IFOP.

[3] Survey of theatre attendance in the Parisian region carried out by the IFOP, 1964.

Table 18.3   Cultural Activities and Level of Education

other hand, by the intermediate office staff (who are just about as removed from the two other categories as these categories are from the lower categories); and, lastly, the higher position, which is occupied by higher office staff and professionals.

The same structure is to be seen each time an assessment is made of cultural habits and, in particular, of those that demand a cultured disposition, such as reading, and theatre, concert, art-cinema, and museum attendance. In such cases, the only distortions are those that introduce the use of different principles of classification (Table 18.2).

Although statistics based like these upon the statements of those being questioned and not upon direct observation tend to overestimate the extent to which an activity is practised by reason of the propensity of the persons questioned to align themselves, at least when talking, to the activity that is recognized as legitimate, they do make it possible to make out the real structure of the distribution of cultural capital. In order to achieve this, it is sufficient to note that the statistics for the purchase of books omit all distinction between small self-employed craftsmen and tradespeople, whose activities are known to be very similar to those of the workers, and industrial and business management, whose cultural consumption is close to that of intermediate office staff; it is also to be noticed that the statistics for the readers of books (books which have been purchased, but doubtless also books which have been borrowed or read in libraries, which explains the movement of the structure towards the upper part) group together small self-employed craftsmen and tradespeople, who seldom practise a cultural activity, and intermediate office staff, who practise cultural activities to a greater extent than do white-collar workers.

Although they remain relatively disparate, the categories made use of in terms of level of education make possible a more direct comparison, and all throw light upon the existence of an extremely pronounced relationship between the different "legitimate" activities and the level of education (Table 18.3).

If, of all cultural activities, cinema attendance in its common form is the one that is least closely linked to level of education, as opposed to concert-going, which is a rarer activity than reading or theatre-going, the fact remains that, as is shown by the statistics for art-cinema attendance, the cinema has a tendency to acquire the power of *social distinction* that belongs to traditionally approved arts.

The greater reliability of the survey carried out by the Centre of European Sociology (Centre de Sociologie Européenne) of the European museum

	Mathematical expectation of visits over a period of a year expressed as a percentage					
	Without diploma	Certificate of primary studies	Certificate of secondary studies	Baccalaureat	Licence (=BA, BSc) and beyond	Total
Farmers	0.2	0.4	20.4			0.5
Workers	0.3	1.3	21.3			1
Craftsmen & tradespeople	1.9	2.8	30.7	59.4		4.9
White-collar workers, intermediate office staff		2.8	19.9	73.6		9.8
Higher office staff, heads of industry, professionals		2.0	12.3	64.4	77.6	43.3
Teachers, art specialists			(68.1)	153.7	(163.8)	151.5
Total	1	2.3	24	70.1	80.1	6.2
Men	1	2.3	24.4	64.5	65.1	6.1
Women	1.1	2.3	23.2	87.9	122.8	6.3

Cf. P. Bourdieu & A. Darbel (1969: 40).

Table 18.4   Annual Attendance Rates for the French Museums According to Occupational Categories

public is due to the fact that it was based upon the degree of effective practice and not on the statements of those being questioned. It makes it possible, moreover, to construct the system of social conditions for the production of the "consumers" of cultural goods considered as the most worthy of being consumed, i.e. the mechanisms of reproduction of the structure or the distribution of cultural capital which is seen in the structure of the distribution of the consumers of the museum, the theatre, the concert, the art cinema, and, more generally, of all the symbolic wealth that constitutes "legitimate" culture. Museum attendance, which increases to a large extent as the level of education rises, is almost exclusively to be found among the privileged classes. The proportions of the different socio-professional categories figuring in the public of the French museums are almost exactly the inverse ratio of their proportions in the overall population. Given that the typical visitor to French museums holds academic qualifications (since 55 per cent of visitors have at least the *baccalauréat*, the French school-leaving certificate), it is not surprising that the structure of the public distributed according to social category is very similar to the structure of the population of the students of the French faculties distributed according to social origin: the proportion of farmers is 1 per cent, that of workers 4 per cent, that of skilled workers and tradesmen is 5 per cent, that of white-collar workers and intermediate office staff is 23 per cent (of whom 5 per cent are primary-school teachers), and the proportion of the upper classes is 45 per cent. If, for the rate of attendance of the different categories of visitors in the whole of the museum public, we substitute the probability of their going into a museum, it will be seen (in Table 18.4) that, once the level of education is established, knowledge of the sex or socio-professional category of the visitors generally provides only a small amount of additional information (although it may be noted in passing that, when the level of education is the same, teachers and art specialists practise this activity to a distinctly greater extent than do other categories and, particularly, other sections of the dominant classes).

In short, all of the relations observed between museum attendance and such variables as class or section of a class, age, income, or residence come down, more or less, to the relation between the level of education and attendance. The existence of such a powerful and exclusive relationship between the level of education and cultural practice should not conceal the fact that, in view of the implicit presuppositions that govern it, the action of the educational system can attain full effectiveness only to the extent that it bears upon individuals who have been previously granted a certain familiarity with the world of art by their family upbringing. Indeed, it would seem that the action of the school, whose effect is unequal (if only from the point of view of duration) among children from different social classes, and whose success varies considerably among those upon whom it has an effect, tends to reinforce and to consecrate by its sanctions the initial inequalities. As may be seen in the fact that the proportion of those who have received from their families an early initiation into art increases to a very marked extent along with the level of education, what is measured by means of the level of education is nothing other than the accumulation of the effects of training acquired within the family and the academic apprenticeships which themselves presupposed this previous training.

If this is the case, the main reasons are, first, that the appropriation of works of art depends in its intensity, its modality, and its very existence upon the mastery that the spectator has of the available instruments of appropriation and, more specifically, of the generic and particular code of the work or, if it is preferred, of the peculiarly artistic lines of interpretation that are directly appropriate to each particular work and are the necessary condition for the deciphering of the work; second, that, in the specific case of works of "high" culture, mastery of the code cannot be totally acquired by means of the simple and diffuse apprenticeships provided by daily existence but presupposes an education methodically organized by an institution specially equipped for this purpose. It is to be noted, however, that the yield of pedagogic communication, entrusted, among other functions, with the responsibility of transmitting the code of works of "high" culture, along with the code according to which this transmission is carried out, is itself a function of the cultural competence that the receiver owes to his family up bringing, which is more or less close to the "high" culture transmitted by the colleges and to the linguistic and cultural models according to which this transmission is carried out. In view of the fact that reception of the pictorial message and the institutionally organized acquisition of cultural competence, which is the condition for the reception of this message, are subject to the same laws, it is not surprising that it is difficult to break the circle in which cultural capital is added to cultural capital. The museum that demarcates its public and legitimizes its social quality by the mere effect of its "level of emission,"[1] i.e. by the simple fact that it presupposes the possession of the fairly complex, and therefore fairly rare, cultural code which is necessary in order to decipher the works exhibited, may be seen as the limit towards which an educational action is directed (it might be possible to use the words "pedagogic action" here were it not for the fact that it is rather, in this case, a non-pedagogic action), implicitly requiring of those on whom it bears that they possess the conditions necessary to its full productivity.

The educational system reproduces all the more perfectly the structure of the distribution of cultural capital among classes (and sections of a class) in that the culture which it transmits is closer to the dominant culture and that the mode of inculcation to which it has recourse is less removed from the mode of inculcation practised by the family. Inasmuch as it operates in and through a relationship of communication, pedagogic action directed at inculcating the dominant culture can in fact escape (even if it is only in part) the general laws of cultural transmission, according to which the appropriation of the proposed culture (and, consequently, the success of the apprenticeship which is crowned by academic qualification) depends upon the previous possession of the instruments of appropriation, to the extent and only to the extent that it explicitly and deliberately hands over, in the pedagogic communication itself, those instruments which are indispensable to the success of the communication and which, in a society divided into classes, are very unequally distributed among children from the different social classes. An educational system which puts into practice an implicit pedagogic action, requiring initial familiarity with the dominant culture, and which proceeds by imperceptible familiarization, offers information and training which can be received and acquired only by subjects endowed with the system of predispositions that is the condition for the success of the transmission and of the inculcation of the culture. By doing away with giving explicitly to everyone what it implicitly demands of everyone, the educational system demands of everyone alike that they have what it does not give. This consists mainly of linguistic and cultural competence and that relationship of familiarity with culture which can only be produced by family upbringing when it transmits the dominant culture.

In short, an institution officially entrusted with the transmission of the instruments of appropriation of the dominant culture which neglects methodically to transmit the instruments indispensable to the success of its undertaking is bound to become the monopoly of those social classes capable of transmitting by their own means, that is to say by that diffuse and implicit continuous educational action which operates within cultured families (often unknown to those responsible for it and to those who are subjected to it), the instruments necessary for the reception of its message, and thereby to confirm their monopoly of the instruments of appropriation

of the dominant culture and thus their monopoly of that culture.[2] The closer
that educational action gets to that limit, the more the value that the educational system attributes to the products of the educational work carried out
by families of the different social classes is directly a function of the value as
cultural capital which is attributed, on a market dominated by the products
of the educational work of the families of the dominant classes, to the linguistic and cultural competence which the different classes or sections of a
class are in a position to transmit, mainly in terms of the culture that they
possess and of the time that they are able to devote to its explicit or implicit
transmission. That is to say that the transmission of this competence is in direct relation to the distance between the linguistic and cultural competence
implicitly demanded by the educational transmission of educational culture
(which is itself quite unevenly removed from the dominant culture) and the
linguistic and cultural competence, inculcated by primary education in the
different social classes.

The laws of the educational market may be read in the statistics which establish that, from the moment of entering into secondary education right up
to the *grandes écoles*, the hierarchy of the educational establishments and
even, within these establishments, the hierarchy of the sections and of the
fields of study arranged according to their prestige and to the education
value they impart to their public, correspond exactly to the hierarchy of the
institutions according to the social structure of their public, on account of
the fact that those classes or sections of a class which are richest in cultural
capital become more and more over-represented as there is an increase in the
rarity and hence in the educational value and social yield of academic qualifications. If such is the case, the reason is that, by virtue of the small real
autonomy of an educational system which is incapable of affirming the
specificity of its principles of evaluation and of its own mode of production
of cultured dispositions, the relationship between the pedagogic actions carried out by the dominated classes and by the dominant classes may be
understood by analogy with the relationship which is set up, in the economic
field, between modes of production of different epochs when for example, in
a dualist economy, the products of a traditional local craft industry are submitted to the laws of a market dominated by the chain-produced products of
a highly developed industry: the symbolic products of the educational work
of the different social classes, i.e. apart from knowledge and know-how, styles
of being, of speaking, or of doing, have less value on the educational market
and, more widely, on the symbolic market (in matrimonial exchanges, for in-

stance) and on the economic market (at least to the extent that its sanctions depend upon academic ratification) in that the mode of symbolic production of which they are the product is more removed from the dominant mode of production or, in other words, from the educational norms of those social classes capable of imposing the domination of criteria of evaluation which are the most favourable to their products. It is in terms of this logic that must be understood the prominent value accorded by the French educational system to such subtle modalities in the relationship to culture and language as affluence, elegance, naturalness, or distinction, all of which are ways of making use of the symbolic products whose role of representing excellence in the field of culture (to the detriment of the dispositions produced by the school and paradoxically devalued, by the school itself, as being "academic") is due to the fact that they belong only to those who have acquired culture or, at least, the dispositions necessary for the acquisition of academic culture, by means of familiarization, i.e. imperceptible apprenticeships from the family upbringing, which is the mode of acquisition of the instruments of appropriation of the dominant culture of which the dominant classes hold the monopoly.

The sanctions of the academic market owe their specific effectiveness to the fact that they are brought to bear with every appearance of legitimacy: it is, in fact, as though the agents proportioned the investments that are placed in production for the academic market—investments of time and enthusiasm for education on the part of the pupils, investments of time, effort, and money on the part of families—to the profits which they may hope to obtain, over a more or less long term, on this market, as thought the price that they attribute to the sanctions of the academic market were in direct relation to the price attributed to them by the sanctions of this market and to the extent to which their economic and symbolic value depends on the value which they are recognized to possess by the academic market. It follows from this that the negative predispositions towards the school which result in the self-elimination of most children from the most culturally unfavoured classes and sections of a class—such as self-depreciation, devaluation of the school and its sanctions, or a resigned attitude to failure and exclusion—must be understood as an anticipation, based upon the unconscious estimation of the objective probabilities of success possessed by the whole category, of the sanctions objectively reserved by the school for those classes or sections of a class deprived of cultural capital. Owing to the fact that it is the product of the internalization of value that the academic market (anticipating by its formally neutral sanctions the sanctions of the symbolic or economic market) confers upon the products of the family upbringing of the different social classes, and of the value which, by their objective sanctions, the economic and symbolic markets confer upon the products of educational action according to the social class from which they originate, the system of dispositions towards the school, understood as a propensity to consent to the investments in time, effort, and money necessary to conserve or increase cultural capital, tends to redouble the symbolic and economic effects of the uneven distribution of cultural capital, all the while concealing it and, at the same time, legitimating it. The functionalist sociologists who announce the brave new world when, at the conclusion of a longitudinal study of academic and social careers, they discover that, as though by a pre-established harmony, individuals have hoped for nothing that they have not obtained and obtained nothing that they have not hoped for, are simply the least forgivable victims of the ideological effect which is produced by the school when it cuts off from their social conditions of production all predispositions regarding the school such as "expectations," "aspirations," "inclinations," or "desire," and thus tends to cover up the fact that objective conditions—and in the individual case, the laws of the academic market—determine aspirations by determining the extent to which they can be satisfied.

This is only one of the mechanisms by which the academic market succeeds in imposing upon those very persons who are its victims recognition of the existence of its sanctions by concealing from them the objective truth of the mechanisms and social motives that determine them. To the extent to which it is enough for it to be allowed to run its own course, that is to say to give free play to the laws of cultural transmission, in order to ensure the reproduction of the structure of distribution of cultural capital, the educational system which merely records immediate or deferred self-elimination (in the form of the self-relegation of children from the underprivileged classes to the lower educational streams) or encourages elimination simply by the effectiveness of a non-existent pedagogical practice (able to conceal behind patently obvious procedures of selection the action of mechanisms tending to ensure in an almost automatic way—that is to say, in a way which conforms to the laws governing all forms of cultural transmission—the exclusion of certain categories of recipients of the pedagogic message), this educational system masks more thoroughly than any other legitimation mechanism (imagine for example what would be the social effects of an arbitrary limitation of the public carried out in the name of ethnic or social criteria) the arbitrary nature of the actual demarcation of its public, thereby imposing more subtly the legitimacy of its products and of its hierarchies.

By making social hierarchies and the reproduction of these hierarchies appear to be based upon the hierarchy of "gifts," merits, or skills established and ratified by its sanctions, or, in a word, by converting social hierarchies into academic hierarchies, the educational system fulfils a function of legitimation which is more and more necessary to the perpetuation of the "social order" as the evolution of the power relationship between classes tends more completely to exclude the imposition of a hierarchy based upon the crude and ruthless affirmation of the power relationship.

NOTES

[1] Concerning this concept, see Bourdieu & Darbel (1969: 104–10).

[2] The extremely close relationship that may be observed between museum attendance and level of education, on the one hand, and early attendance at museums, on the other hand, follows the same logic.

REFERENCES

Bourdieu, P. & Darbel, A. 1969. *L'Amour de l'art: les musées d'art européens et leur public.* Paris: Les Editions de Minuit.

SOFRES. 1964. *Le Marché des cadres supérieurs francais.* Paris.

Syndicat national des éditeurs (National Union of Publishers). 1960. La lecture et le livre en France (January–April 1960, survey carried out by the IFOP).

Syndicat national des éditeurs. 1967. La clientele du livre (July 1967, survey carried out by the IFOP).

19

THE THEORY OF THE LEISURE CLASS

Thorstein Veblen

♦♦♦

PECUNIARY EMULATION

The end of acquisition and accumulation is conventionally held to be the consumption of the goods accumulated—whether it is consumption directly by the owner of the goods or by the household attached to him and for this purpose identified with him in theory. This is at least felt to be the economically legitimate end of acquisition, which alone it is incumbent on the theory to take account of. Such consumption may of course be conceived to serve the consumer's physical wants—his physical comfort—or his so-called higher wants—spiritual, æsthetic, intellectual, or what not; the latter class of wants being served indirectly by an expenditure of goods, after the fashion familiar to all economic readers.

But it is only when taken in a sense far removed from its naïve meaning that consumption of goods can be said to afford the incentive from which

Thorstein Veblen, *The Theory of the Leisure Class*, pp. 35–36, 38–43, 61, 65–72, 94, 98. Copyright 1973 by Houghton Mifflin Company. Used by permission of Houghton Mifflin.

accumulation invariably proceeds. The motive that lies at the root of owner-ship is emulation; and the same motive of emulation continues active in the further development of the institution to which it has given rise and in the development of all those features of the social structure which this institution of ownership touches. The possession of wealth confers honor; it is an invid-ious distinction. Nothing equally cogent can be said for the consumption of goods, nor for any other conceivable incentive to acquisition, and especially not for any incentive to the accumulation of wealth.

It is of course not to be overlooked that in a community where nearly all goods are private property the necessity of earning a livelihood is a powerful and ever-present incentive for the poorer members of the community. The need of subsistence and of an increase of physical comfort may for a time be the dominant motive of acquisition for those classes who are habitually em-ployed at manual labor, whose subsistence is on a precarious footing, who possess little and ordinarily accumulate little; but it will appear in the course of the discussion that even in the case of these impecunious classes the pre-dominance of the motive of physical want is not so decided as has sometimes been assumed. On the other hand, so far as regards those members and classes of the community who are chiefly concerned in the accumulation of wealth, the incentive of subsistence or of physical comfort never plays a con-siderable part. Ownership began and grew into a human institution on grounds unrelated to the subsistence minimum. The dominant incentive was from the outset the invidious distinction attaching to wealth, and, save tem-porarily and by exception, no other motive has usurped the primacy at any later stage of the development. . . .

In any community where goods are held in severalty it is necessary, in order to ensure his own peace of mind, that an individual should possess as large a portion of goods as others with whom he is accustomed to class himself; and it is extremely gratifying to possess something more than others. But as fast as a person makes new acquisitions, and becomes accustomed to the resulting new standard of wealth, the new standard forthwith ceases to afford apprecia-bly greater satisfaction than the earlier standard did. The tendency in any case is constantly to make the present pecuniary standard the point of departure for a fresh increase of wealth; and this in turn gives rise to a new standard of suffi-ciency and a new pecuniary classification of one's self as compared with one's neighbors. So far as concerns the present question, the end sought by accumu-lation is to rank high in comparison with the rest of the community in point of pecuniary strength. So long as the comparison is distinctly unfavorable to himself, the normal, average individual will live in chronic dissatisfaction with his present lot; and when he has reached what may be called the normal pecuniary standard of the community, or of his class in the community, this chronic dissatisfaction will give place to a restless straining to place a wider and ever-widening pecuniary interval between himself and this average standard. The invidious comparison can never become so favorable to the individual making it that he would not gladly rate himself still higher relatively to his competitors in the struggle for pecuniary reputability.

In the nature of the case, the desire for wealth can scarcely be satiated in any individual instance, and evidently a satiation of the average or general desire for wealth is out of the question. However widely, or equally, or "fairly," it may be distributed, no general increase of the community's wealth can make any approach to satiating this need, the ground of which is the desire of everyone to excel everyone else in the accumulation of goods. If, as is sometimes assumed, the incentive to accumulation were the want of subsistence or of physical comfort, then the aggregate economic wants of a community might conceivably be satisfied at some point in the advance of industrial efficiency; but since the struggle is substantially a race for reputability on the basis of an invidious comparison, no approach to a definitive attainment is possible.

What has just been said must not be taken to mean that there are no other incentives to acquisition and accumulation than this desire to excel in pecuniary standing and so gain the esteem and envy of one's fellowmen. The desire for added comfort and security from want is present as a motive at every stage of the process of accumulation in a modern industrial community; although the standard of sufficiency in these respects is in turn greatly affected by the habit of pecuniary emulation. To a great extent this emulation shapes the methods and selects the objects of expenditure for personal comfort and decent livelihood.

Besides this, the power conferred by wealth also affords a motive to accumulation. That propensity for purposeful activity and that repugnance to all futility of effort which belong to man by virtue of his character as an agent do not desert him when he emerges from the naïve communal culture where the dominant note of life is the unanalyzed and undifferentiated solidarity of the individual with the group with which his life is bound up. When he enters upon the predatory stage, where self-seeking in the narrower sense becomes the dominant note, this propensity goes with him still, as the pervasive trait that shapes his scheme of life. The propensity for achievement and the repugnance to futility remain the underlying economic motive. The propensity changes only in the form of its expression and in the proximate objects to which it directs the man's activity. Under the regime of individual ownership the most available means of visibly achieving a purpose is that afforded by the acquisition and accumulation of goods; and as the self-regarding antithesis between man and man reaches fuller consciousness, the propensity for achievement—the instinct of workmanship—tends more and more to shape itself into a straining to excel others in pecuniary achievement. Relative success, tested by an invidious pecuniary comparison with other men, becomes the conventional end of action. The currently accepted legitimate end of effort becomes the achievement of a favorable comparison with other men; and therefore the repugnance to futility to a good extent coalesces with the incentive of emulation. It acts to accentuate the struggle for pecuniary reputability by visiting with a sharper disapproval all shortcoming and all evidence of shortcoming in point of pecuniary success. Purposeful effort comes to mean, primarily, effort directed to or resulting in a more creditable showing of accumulated wealth. Among the motives which lead men to accumulate wealth, the primacy, both in scope and intensity, therefore, continues to belong to this motive of pecuniary emulation.

In making use of the term "invidious," it may perhaps be unnecessary to remark, there is no intention to extol or depreciate, or to commend or deplore any of the phenomena which the word is used to characterize. The term is used in a technical sense as describing a comparison of persons with a view to rating and grading them in respect of relative worth or value—in an æsthetic or moral sense—and so awarding and defining the relative degrees of complacency with which they may legitimately be contemplated by themselves and by others. An invidious comparison is a process of valuation of persons in respect of worth.

CONSPICUOUS LEISURE

If its working were not disturbed by other economic forces or other features of the emulative process, the immediate effect of such a pecuniary struggle as has just been described in outline would be to make men industrious and frugal. This result actually follows, in some measure, so far as regards the lower classes, whose ordinary means of acquiring goods is productive labor. This is more especially true of the laboring classes in a sedentary community which is at an agricultural stage of industry, in which there is a considerable subdivision of property, and whose laws and customs secure to these classes a more or less definite share of the product of their industry. These lower classes can in any case not avoid labor, and the imputation of labor is therefore not greatly derogatory to them, at least not within their class. Rather, since labor is their recognized and accepted mode of life, they take some emulative pride in a reputation for efficiency in their work, this being often the only line of emulation that is open to them. For those for whom acquisition and emulation is possible only within the field of productive efficiency and thrift, the struggle for pecuniary reputability will in some measure work out in an increase of diligence and parsimony. But certain secondary features of the emulative process, yet to be spoken of, come in to very materially circumscribe and modify emulation in these directions among the pecuniarily inferior classes as well as among the superior class.

But it is otherwise with the superior pecuniary class, with which we are here immediately concerned. For this class also the incentive to diligence and thrift is not absent; but its action is so greatly qualified by the secondary demands of pecuniary emulation, that any inclination in this direction is practically overborne and any incentive to diligence tends to be of no effect. The most imperative of these secondary demands of emulation, as well as the one of widest scope, is the requirement of abstention from productive work. . . . During the predatory culture labor comes to be associated in men's habits of thought with weakness and subjection to a master. It is therefore a mark of inferiority, and therefore comes to be accounted unworthy of man in his best estate. By virtue of this tradition labor is felt to be debasing, and this tradition has never died out. On the contrary, with the advance of social differentiation it has acquired the axiomatic force due to ancient and unquestioned prescription.

In order to gain and to hold the esteem of men it is not sufficient merely to possess wealth or power. The wealth or power must be put in evidence, for esteem is awarded only on evidence. And not only does the evidence of wealth serve to impress one's importance on others and to keep their sense of importance alive and alert, but it is of scarcely less use in building up and preserving one's self-complacency. In all but the lowest stages of culture the normally constituted man is comforted and upheld in his self-respect by "decent surroundings" and by exemption from "menial offices." Enforced departure from his habitual standard of decency, either in the paraphernalia of life or in the kind and amount of his everyday activity, is felt to be a slight upon his human dignity, even apart from all conscious consideration of the approval or disapproval of his fellows.

The archaic theoretical distinction between the base and the honorable in the manner of a man's life retains very much of its ancient force even today. So much so that there are few of the better class who are not possessed of an instinctive repugnance for the vulgar forms of labor. We have a realizing sense of ceremonial uncleanness attaching in an especial degree to the occupations which are associated in our habits of thought with menial service. It is felt by all persons of refined taste that a spiritual contamination is inseparable from certain offices that are conventionally required of servants. Vulgar surroundings, mean (that is to say, inexpensive) habitations, and vulgarly productive occupations are unhesitatingly condemned and avoided. They are incompatible with life on a satisfactory spiritual plane—with "high thinking." From the days of the Greek philosophers to the present, a degree of leisure and of exemption from contact with such industrial processes as serve the immediate everyday purposes of human life has ever been recognized by thoughtful men as a prerequisite to a worthy or beautiful, or even a blameless, human life. In itself and in its consequences the life of leisure is beautiful and ennobling in all civilized men's eyes.

This direct, subjective value of leisure and of other evidences of wealth is no doubt in great part secondary and derivative. It is in part a reflex of the utility of leisure as a means of gaining the respect of others, and in part it is the result of a mental substitution. The performance of labor has been accepted as a conventional evidence of inferior force; therefore it comes itself, by a mental shortcut, to be regarded as intrinsically base. . . .

CONSPICUOUS CONSUMPTION

In the earlier phases of the predatory culture the only economic differentiation is a broad distinction between an honorable superior class made up of the able-bodied men on the one side, and a base inferior class of laboring women on the other. According to the ideal scheme of life in force at that time it is the office of the men to consume what the women produce. Such consumption as falls to the women is merely incidental to their work; it is a means to their continued labor, and not a consumption directed to their own comfort and fullness of life. Unproductive consumption of goods is honorable, primarily as a mark of prowess and a perquisite of human dignity; secondarily it becomes substantially honorable in itself, especially the consumption of the more desirable things. The consumption of choice articles of food, and frequently also of rare articles of adornment, becomes tabu to the women and children; and if there is a base (servile) class of men, the tabu holds also for them. With a further advance in culture this tabu may change into simple custom of a more or less rigorous character; but whatever be the theoretical basis of the distinction which is maintained, whether it be a tabu or a larger conventionality, the features of the conventional scheme of consumption do not change easily. When the quasi-peaceable stage of industry is reached, with its fundamental institution of chattel slavery, the general principle, more or less rigorously applied, is that the base, industrious class should consume only what may be necessary to their subsistence. In the nature of things, luxuries and the comforts of life belong to the leisure class. Under the tabu, certain victuals, and more particularly certain beverages, are strictly reserved for the use of the superior class. . . .

As wealth accumulates, the leisure class develops further in function and structure, and there arises a differentiation within the class. There is a more or less elaborate system of rank and grades. This differentiation is furthered by the inheritance of wealth and the consequent inheritance of gentility. With the inheritance of gentility goes the inheritance of obligatory leisure; and gentility of a sufficient potency to entail a life of leisure may be inherited without the complement of wealth required to maintain a dignified leisure. Gentle blood may be transmitted without goods enough to afford a reputably free consumption at one's ease. Hence results a class of impecunious gentlemen of leisure. These half-caste gentlemen of leisure fall into a system of hierarchical gradations. Those who stand near the higher and the highest grades of the wealthy leisure class, in point of birth, or in point of wealth, or both, outrank the remoter-born and the pecuniarily weaker. These lower grades, especially the impecunious, or marginal, gentlemen of leisure, affiliate themselves by a system of dependence or fealty to the great ones; by so doing they gain an increment of repute, or of the means with which to lead a life of leisure, from their patron. They become his courtiers or retainers, servants; and being fed and countenanced by their patron they are indices of his rank and vicarious consumers of his superfluous wealth. Many of these affiliated gentlemen of leisure are at the same time lesser men of substance in their own right; so that some of them are scarcely at all, others only partially, to be rated as vicarious consumers. So many of them, however, as make up the retainers and hangers-on of the patron may be classed as vicarious consumers without qualification. Many of these again, and also many of the other aristocracy of less degree, have in turn attached to their persons a more or less comprehensive group of vicarious consumers in the persons of their wives and children, their servants, retainers, etc.

Throughout this graduated scheme of vicarious leisure and vicarious consumption the rule holds that these offices must be performed in some such manner, or under some such circumstance or insignia, as shall point plainly to the master to whom this leisure or consumption pertains, and to whom therefore the resulting increment of good repute of right inures. The consumption and leisure executed by these persons for their master or patron represents an investment on his part with a view to an increase of good fame. . . .

With the disappearance of servitude, the number of vicarious consumers attached to any one gentleman tends, on the whole, to decrease. The like is of course true, and perhaps in a still higher degree, of the number of dependents who perform vicarious leisure for him. In a general way, though not wholly nor consistently, these two groups coincide. The dependent who was first delegated for these duties was the wife, or the chief wife; and, as would be expected, in the later development of the institution, when the number of persons by whom these duties are customarily performed gradually narrows, the wife remains the last. In the higher grades of society a large volume of both these kinds of service is required; and here the wife is of course still assisted in the work by a more or less numerous corps of menials. But as we descend the social scale, the point is presently reached where the duties of vicarious leisure and consumption devolve upon the wife alone. In the communities of the Western culture, this point is at present found among the lower middle class.

And here occurs a curious inversion. It is a fact of common observance that in this lower middle class there is no pretense of leisure on the part of the head of the household. Through force of circumstances it has fallen into disuse. But the middle-class wife still carries on the business of vicarious leisure, for the good name of the household and its master. In descending the social scale in any modern industrial community, the primary fact—the conspicuous leisure of the master of the household—disappears at a relatively high point. The head of the middle-class household has been reduced by economic circumstances to turn his hand to gaining a livelihood by occupations which often partake largely of the character of industry, as in the case of the ordinary business man of today. But the derivative fact—the vicarious leisure and consumption rendered by the wife, and the auxiliary vicarious performance of leisure by menials—remains in vogue as a conventionality which the demands of reputability will not suffer to be slighted. It is by no means an uncommon spectacle to find a man applying himself to work with the utmost assiduity, in order that his wife may in due form render for him that degree of vicarious leisure which the common sense of the time demands.

The leisure rendered by the wife in such cases is, of course, not a simple manifestation of idleness or indolence. It almost invariably occurs disguised under some form of work or household duties or social amenities, which prove on analysis to serve little or no ulterior end beyond showing that she does not occupy herself with anything that is gainful or that is of substantial use. The greater part of the customary round of domestic cares to which the middle-class housewife gives her time and effort is of this character. Not that the results of her attention to household matters, of a decorative and mundificatory character, are not pleasing to the sense of men trained in middle-class proprieties; but the taste to which these effects of household adornment and tidiness appeal is a taste which has been formed under the selective guidance of a canon of propriety that demands just these evidences of wasted effort. The effects are pleasing to us chiefly because we have been taught to find them pleasing. There goes into these domestic duties much solicitude for a proper combination of form and color, and for other ends that are to be classed as æsthetic in the proper sense of the term; and it is not denied that effects having some substantial æsthetic value are sometimes attained. Pretty much all that is here insisted on is that, as regards these amenities of life, the housewife's efforts are under the guidance of traditions that have been shaped by the law of conspicuously wasteful expenditure of time and substance. If beauty or comfort is achieved—and it is a more or less fortuitous circumstance if they are—they must be achieved by means and methods that commend themselves to the great economic law of wasted effort. The more reputable, "presentable" portion of middle-class household paraphernalia are, on the one hand, items of conspicuous consumption, and on the other hand, apparatus for putting in evidence the vicarious leisure rendered by the housewife.

The requirement of vicarious consumption at the hands of the wife continues in force even at a lower point in the pecuniary scale than the requirement of vicarious leisure. At a point below which little if any pretense of wasted effort, in ceremonial cleanness and the like, is observable, and where there is assuredly no conscious attempt at ostensible leisure, decency still requires the wife to consume some goods conspicuously for the reputability of the household and its head. So that, as the latter-day outcome of this evolution of an archaic institution, the wife, who was at the outset the drudge and chattel of the man, both in fact and in theory—the producer of goods for him to consume—has become the ceremonial consumer of goods which he produces. But she still quite unmistakably remains his chattel in theory; for the habitual rendering of vicarious leisure and consumption is the abiding mark of the unfree servant.

This vicarious consumption practiced by the household of the middle and lower classes cannot be counted as a direct expression of the leisure-class scheme of life, since the household of this pecuniary grade does not belong within the leisure class. It is rather that the leisure-class scheme of life here comes to an expression at the second remove. The leisure class stands at the head of the social structure in point of reputability; and its manner of life and its standards of worth therefore afford the norm of reputability for the community. The observance of these standards, in some degree of approximation, becomes incumbent upon all classes lower in the scale. In modern civilized communities the lines of demarcation between social classes have grown vague and transient, and wherever this happens the norm of reputability imposed by the upper class extends its coercive influence with but slight hindrance down through the social structure to the lowest strata. The result is that the members of each stratum accept as their ideal of decency the scheme of life in vogue in the next higher stratum, and bend their energies to live up to that ideal. On pain of forfeiting their good name and their self-respect in case of failure, they must conform to the accepted code, at least in appearance.

The basis on which good repute in any highly organized industrial community ultimately rests is pecuniary strength; and the means of showing pecuniary strength, and so of gaining or retaining a good name, are leisure and a conspicuous consumption of goods. Accordingly, both of these methods are in vogue as far down the scale as it remains possible; and in the lower strata in which the two methods are employed, both offices are in great part delegated to the wife and children of the household. Lower still, where any degree of leisure, even ostensible, has become impracticable for the wife, the conspicuous consumption of goods remains and is carried on by the wife and children. The man of the household also can do something in this direction, and indeed, he commonly does; but with a still lower descent into the levels of indigence—along the margin of the slums—the man, and presently also the children, virtually cease to consume valuable goods for appearances, and the woman remains virtually the sole exponent of the household's pecuniary decency. No class of society, not even the most abjectly poor, forgoes all customary conspicuous consumption. The last items of this category of consumption are not given up except under stress of the direst necessity. Very much of squalor and discomfort will be endured before the last trinket or the last pretense of pecuniary decency is put away. There is no class and no country that has yielded so abjectly before the pressure of physical want as to deny themselves all gratification of this higher or spiritual need.

From the foregoing survey of the growth of conspicuous leisure and consumption, it appears that the utility of both alike for the purposes of reputability lies in the element of waste that is common to both. In the one case it is a waste of time and effort, in the other it is a waste of goods. Both are methods of demonstrating the possession of wealth, and the two are conventionally accepted as equivalents. The choice between them is a question of advertising expediency simply, except so far as it may be affected by other standards of propriety, springing from a different source. On grounds of expediency the preference may be given to the one or the other at different stages of the economic development. The question is, which of the two methods will most effectively reach the persons whose convictions it is desired to affect. Usage has answered this question in different ways under different circumstances.

So long as the community or social group is small enough and compact enough to be effectually reached by common notoriety alone—that is to say, so long as the human environment to which the individual is required to adapt himself in respect of reputability is comprised within his sphere of personal acquaintance and neighborhood gossip—so long the one method is about as effective as the other. Each will therefore serve about equally well during the earlier stages of social growth. But when the differentiation has gone farther and it becomes necessary to reach a wider human environment, consumption begins to hold over leisure as an ordinary means of decency. This is especially true during the later, peaceable economic stage. The means of communication and the mobility of the population now expose the individual to the observation of many persons who have no other means of judging of his reputability than the display of goods (and perhaps of breeding) which he is able to make while he is under their direct observation.

The modern organization of industry works in the same direction also by another line. The exigencies of the modern industrial system frequently place individuals and households in juxtaposition between whom there is little contact in any other sense than that of juxtaposition. One's neighbors, mechanically speaking, often are socially not one's neighbors, or even acquaintances; and still their transient good opinion has a high degree of utility. The only practicable means of impressing one's pecuniary ability on these unsympathetic observers of one's everyday life is an unremitting demonstration of ability to pay. In the modern community there is also a more frequent attendance at large gatherings of people to whom one's everyday life is unknown; in such places as churches, theaters, ballrooms, hotels, parks, shops, and the like. In order to impress these transient observers, and to retain one's self-complacency under their observation, the signature of one's pecuniary strength should be written in characters which he who runs may read. It is evident, therefore, that the present trend of the development is in the direction of heightening the utility of conspicuous consumption as compared with leisure. . . .

Pecuniary Canons of Taste

The requirements of pecuniary decency have, to a very appreciable extent, influenced the sense of beauty and of utility in articles of use or beauty. Articles are to an extent preferred for use on account of their being conspicuously wasteful; they are felt to be serviceable somewhat in proportion as they are wasteful and ill adapted to their ostensible use. . . .

By habituation to an appreciative perception of the marks of expensiveness in goods, and by habitually identifying beauty with reputability, it comes about that a beautiful article which is not expensive is accounted not beautiful. In this way it has happened, for instance, that some beautiful flowers pass conventionally for offensive weeds; others that can be cultivated with relative ease are accepted and admired by the lower middle class, who can afford no more expensive luxuries of this kind; but these varieties are rejected as vulgar by those people who are better able to pay for expensive flowers and who are educated to a higher schedule of pecuniary beauty in the florist's products; while still other flowers, of no greater intrinsic beauty than these, are cultivated at great cost and call out much admiration from flower-lovers whose tastes have been matured under the critical guidance of a polite environment.

The same variation in matters of taste, from one class of society to another, is visible also as regards many other kinds of consumable goods, as, for example, is the case with furniture, houses, parks, and gardens. This diversity of views as to what is beautiful in these various classes of goods is not a diversity of the norm according to which the unsophisticated sense of the beautiful works. It is not a constitutional difference of endowments in the æsthetic respect, but rather a difference in the code of reputability which specifies what objects properly lie within the scope of honorific consumption for the class to which the critic belongs. It is a difference in the traditions of propriety with respect to the kinds of things which may, without derogation to the consumer, be consumed under the head of objects of taste and art. With a certain allowance for variations to be accounted for on other grounds, these traditions are determined, more or less rigidly, by the pecuniary plane of life of the class.

20

DISTINCTION

A SOCIAL CRITIQUE OF THE JUDGEMENT OF TASTE

Pierre Bourdieu

◆◆◆

THE SOCIAL SPACE

The distribution of the different classes (and class fractions) runs from those who are best provided with both economic and cultural capital to those who are most deprived in both respects (see Figures 20.1 and 20.2). The members of the professions, who have high incomes and high qualifications, who very often (52.9 percent) originate from the dominant class (professions or senior executives), who receive and consume a large quantity of both material and cultural goods, are opposed in almost all respects to the office workers, who

Pierre Bourdieu, *Distinction: A Social Critique of the Judgement of Taste*, pp. 114–115, 128–129, 169–180, 183–189, 193–197, 199–202, 206–209, 503, 519–521, 523, 572–576. Copyright 1984 by the President and Fellows of Harvard University Press and Routledge and Kegan Paul, Ltd. Reprinted by permission of the publishers and of Routledge and Kegan Paul, Ltd. This chapter is based on survey data collected by Pierre Bourdieu and on additional complementary data sources (denoted in the text by C.S. I – C.S. V). For the purpose of conserving space, we have omitted all the special passages, set off in distinct type in the original, that were devoted to "illustrative examples or discussion of ancillary issues" (Bourdieu, *Distinction*, p. xiii). We have also omitted some of the more detailed tables.

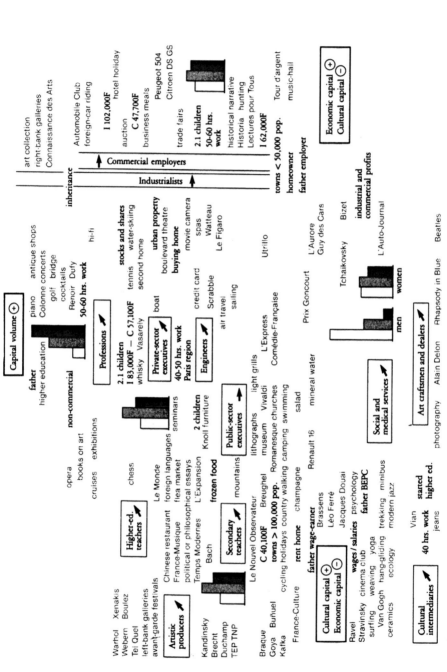

Figure 20.1   The Space of Social Positions (shown in black)

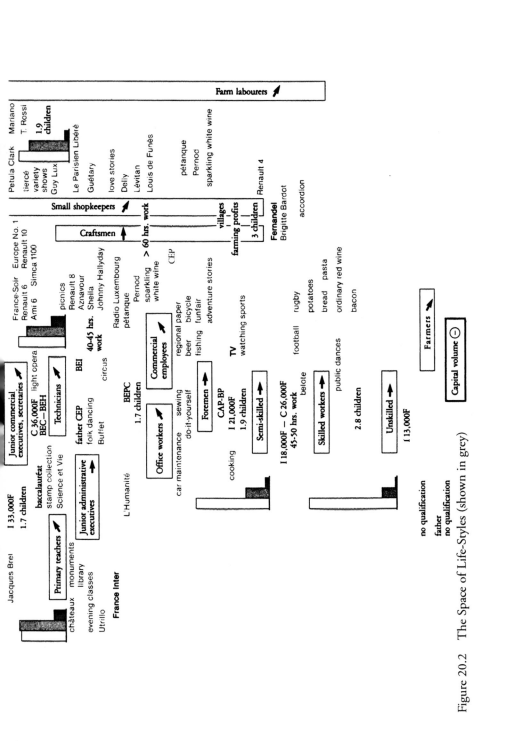

Figure 20.2   The Space of Life-Styles (shown in grey)

have low qualifications, often originate from the working or middle classes, who receive little and consume little, devoting a high proportion of their time to care maintenance and home improvement; and they are even more opposed to the skilled or semi-skilled workers, and still more to unskilled workers or farm labourers, who have the lowest incomes, no qualifications, and originate almost exclusively (90.5 percent of farm labourers, 84.5 percent of unskilled workers) from the working classes.[1]

The differences stemming from the total volume of capital almost always conceal, both from common awareness and also from "scientific" knowledge, the secondary differences which, within each of the classes defined by over-all volume of capital, separate class fractions, defined by different asset structures, i.e., different distributions of their total capital among the different kinds of capital [economic and cultural].

Once one takes account of the structure of total assets—and not only, as has always been done implicitly, of the dominant kind in a given structure, "birth," "fortune" or "talents," as the nineteenth century put it—one has the means of making more precise divisions and also of observing the specific effects of the structure of distribution between the different kinds of capital. This may, for example, be symmetrical (as in the case of the professions, which combine very high income with very high cultural capital) or asymmetrical (in the case of higher-education and secondary teachers or employers, with cultural capital dominant in one case, economic capital in the other). One thus discovers two sets of homologous positions. The fractions whose reproduction depends on economic capital, usually inherited—industrial and commercial employers at the higher level, craftsmen and shopkeepers at the intermediate level—are opposed to the fractions which are least endowed (relatively, of course) with economic capital, and whose reproduction mainly depends on cultural capital—higher-education and secondary teachers at the higher level, primary teachers at the intermediate level. . . .

The Habitus

The mere fact that the social space described here can be presented as a diagram indicates that it is an abstract representation, deliberately constructed, like a map, to give a bird's-eye view, a point of view on the whole set of points from which ordinary agents (including the sociologist and his reader,

in their ordinary behaviour) see the social world. Bringing together in simul-
taneity, in the scope of a single glance—this is its heuristic value—positions
which the agents can never apprehend in their totality and in their multiple
relationships, social space is to the practical space of everyday life, with its
distances which are kept or signalled, and neighbours who may be more remote than strangers, what geometrical space is to the "travelling space"
(*espace hodologique*) of ordinary experience, with its gaps and discontinuities.

But the most crucial thing to note is that the question of this space is
raised within the space itself—that the agents have points of view on this objective space which depend on their position within it and in which their will
to transform or conserve it is often expressed. Thus many of the words which
sociology uses to designate the classes it constructs are borrowed from ordinary usage, where they serve to express the (generally polemical) view that
one group has of another. As if carried away by their quest for greater objec-
tivity, sociologists almost always forget that the "objects" they classify
produce not only objectively classifiable practices but also classifying operations that are no less objective and are themselves classifiable. The division
into classes performed by sociology leads to the common root of the classifiable practices which agents produce and of the classificatory judgements they
make of other agents' practices and their own. The habitus is both the generative principle of objectively classifiable judgements and the system of
classification (*principium divisionis*) of these practices. It is in the relationship
between the two capacities which define the habitus, the capacity to produce
classifiable practices and works, and the capacity to differentiate and appreciate these practices and products (taste), that the represented social world,
i.e., the space of lifestyles, is constituted.

The relationship that is actually established between the pertinent characteristics of economic and social condition (capital volume and composition,
in both synchronic and diachronic aspects) and the distinctive features associated with the corresponding position in the universe of life-styles only
becomes intelligible when the habitus is constructed as the generative formula which makes it possible to account both for the classifiable practices
and products and for the judgements, themselves classified, which make
these practices and works into a system of distinctive signs. When one speaks
of the aristocratic asceticism of teachers or the pretension of the petite bourgeoisie, one is not only describing these groups by one, or even the most
important, of their properties, but also endeavouring to name the principle
which generates all their properties and all their judgements of their, or other

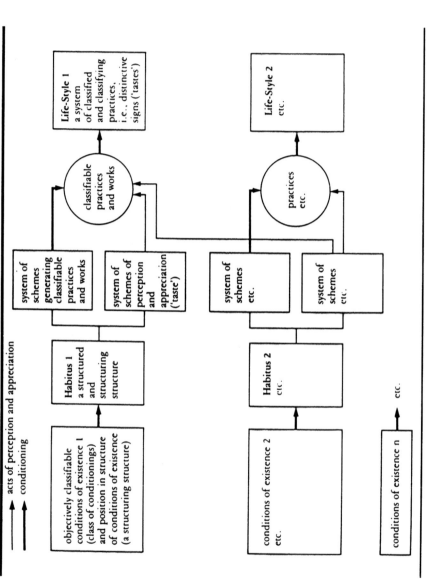

Figure 20.3　Conditions of Existence, Habitus, and Life-Style

people's, properties. The habitus is necessity internalized and converted into a disposition that generates meaningful practices and meaning-giving perceptions; it is a general, transposable disposition which carries out a systematic, universal application—beyond the limits of what has been directly learnt—of the necessity inherent in the learning conditions. That is why an agent's whole set of practices (or those of a whole set of agents produced by similar conditions) are both systematic, inasmuch as they are the product of the application of identical (or interchangeable) schemes, and systematically distinct from the practices constituting another life-style.

Because different conditions of existence produce different habitus—systems of generative schemes applicable, by simple transfer, to the most varied areas of practice—the practices engendered by the different habitus appear as systematic configurations of properties expressing the differences objectively inscribed in conditions of existence in the form of systems of differential deviations which, when perceived by agents endowed with the schemes of perception and appreciation necessary in order to identify, interpret and evaluate their pertinent features, function as life-styles (see Figure 20.3).[2]

The habitus is not only a structuring structure, which organizes practices and the perception of practices, but also a structured structure: the principle of division into logical classes which organizes the perception of the social world is itself the product of internalization of the division into social classes. Each class condition is defined, simultaneously, by its intrinsic properties and by the relational properties which it derives from its position in the system of class conditions, which is also a system of differences, differential positions, i.e., by everything which distinguishes it from what it is not and especially from everything it is opposed to; social identity is defined and asserted through difference. This means that inevitably inscribed within the dispositions of the habitus is the whole structure of the system of conditions, as it presents itself in the experience of a life-condition occupying a particular position within that structure. The most fundamental oppositions in the structure (high/low, rich/poor etc.) tend to establish themselves as the fundamental structuring principles of practices and the perception of practices. As a system of practice-generating schemes which expresses systematically the necessity and freedom inherent in its class condition and the difference constituting that position, the habitus apprehends differences between conditions, which it grasps in the form of differences between classified, classifying practices (products of other habitus), in accordance with principles of differentiation which, being themselves the product of these differences, are objectively attuned to them and therefore tend to perceive them as natural.

While it must be reasserted, against all forms of mechanism, that ordinary experience of the social world is a cognition, it is equally important to realize—contrary to the illusion of the spontaneous generation of consciousness which so many theories of the "awakening of class consciousness:" (*prise de conscience*) amount to—that primary cognition is misrecognition, recognition of an order which is also established in the mind. Life-styles are thus the systematic products of habitus, which, perceived in their mutual relations through the schemes of the habitus, become sign systems that are socially qualified (as "distinguished," "vulgar" etc.). The dialectic of conditions and habitus is the basis of an alchemy which transforms the distribution of capital, the balance-sheet of a power relation, into a system of perceived differences, distinctive properties, that is, a distribution of symbolic capital, legitimate capital, whose objective truth is misrecognized.

As structured products (*opus operatum*) which a structuring structure (*modus operandi*) produces through retranslations according to the specific logic of the different *fields,* all the practices and products of a given agent are objectively harmonized among themselves, without any deliberate pursuit of coherence, and objectively orchestrated, without any conscious concertation, with those of all members of the same class. The habitus continuously generates practical metaphors, that is to say, transfers (of which the transfer of motor habits is only one example) or, more precisely, systematic transpositions required by the particular conditions in which the habitus is "put into practice" (so that, for example, the ascetic ethos which might be expected always to express itself in saving may, in a given context, express itself in a particular way of using credit). The practices of the same agent, and, more generally, the practices of all agents of the same class, owe the stylistic affinity which makes each of them a metaphor of any of the others to the fact that they are the product of transfers of the same schemes of action from one field to another. An obvious paradigm would be the disposition called "handwriting", a singular way of tracing letters which always produces the same writing, i.e., graphic forms which, in spite of all the differences of size, material or colour due to the surface (paper or blackboard) or the instrument (pen or chalk)—in spite, therefore, of the different use of muscles—present an immediately perceptible family resemblance, like all the features of style or manner whereby a painter or writer can be recognized as infallibly as a man by his walk.

Systematicity is found in the opus operatum because it is in the modus operandi.[3] It is found in all the properties—and property—with which individuals and groups surround themselves, houses, furniture, paintings, books, cars, spirits, cigarettes, perfume, clothes, and in the practices in which they manifest their distinction, sports, games, entertainments, only because it is in the synthetic unity of the habitus, the unifying, generative principle of all practices. Taste, the propensity and capacity to appropriate (materially or symbolically) a given class of classified, classifying objects or practices, is the generative formula of life-style, a unitary set of distinctive preferences which express the same expressive intention in the specific logic of each of the symbolic subspaces, furniture, clothing, language or body hexis. Each dimension of life-style "symbolizes with" the others, in Leibniz's phrase, and symbolizes them. An old cabinetmaker's world view, the way he manages his budget, his time or his body, his use of language and choice of clothing are fully present in his ethic of scrupulous, impeccable craftsmanship and in the aesthetic of work for work's sake which leads him to measure the beauty of his products by the care and patience that have gone into them.

The system of matching properties, which includes people—one speaks of a "well-matched couple", and friends like to say they have the same tastes—is organized by taste, a system of classificatory schemes which may only very partially become conscious although, as one rises in the social hierarchy, life-style is increasingly a matter of what Weber calls the "stylization of life". Taste is the basis of the mutual adjustment of all the features associated with a person, which the old aesthetic recommended for the sake of the mutual reinforcement they give one another; the countless pieces of information a person consciously or unconsciously imparts endlessly underline and confirm one another, offering the alert observer the same pleasure an art-lover derives from the symmetries and correspondences produced by a harmonious distribution of redundancies. The over-determination that results from these redundancies is felt the more strongly because the different features which have to be isolated for observation or measurement strongly interpenetrate in ordinary perception; each item of information imparted in practice (e.g., a judgement of a painting) is contaminated—and, if it deviates from the probable feature, corrected—by the effect of the whole set of features previously or simultaneously perceived. That is why a survey which tends to isolate features—for example, by dissociating the things said from the way they are said—and detach them from the system of correlative features tends to minimize the deviation, on each point, between the classes, especially that between the petit bourgeois and the bourgeois. In the ordinary situations of bourgeois life, banalities about art, literature or cinema are inseparable from the steady tone, the slow, casual diction, the distant or self-assured smile, the measured gesture, the well-tailored suit and the bourgeois salon of the person who pronounces them.

Taste is the practical operator of the transmutation of things into distinct and distinctive signs, of continuous distributions into discontinuous oppositions; it raises the differences inscribed in the physical order of bodies to the symbolic order of significant distinctions. It transforms objectively classified practices, in which a class condition signifies itself (through taste), into classifying practices, that is, into a symbolic expression of class position, by perceiving them in their mutual relations and in terms of social classificatory schemes. Taste is thus the source of the system of distinctive features which cannot fail to be perceived as a systematic expression of a particular class of conditions of existence, i.e., as a distinctive life-style, by anyone who possesses practical knowledge of the relationships between distinctive signs and positions in the distributions—between the universe of objective properties, which is brought to light by scientific construction, and the no less objective universe of life-styles, which exists as such for and through ordinary experience.

This classificatory system, which is the product of the internalization of the structure of social space, in the form in which it impinges through the experience of a particular position in that space, is, within the limits of economic possibilities and impossibilities (which it tends to reproduce in its own logic), the generator of practices adjusted to the regularities inherent in a condition. It continuously transforms necessities into strategies, constraints into preferences, and, without any mechanical determination, it generates the set of "choices" constituting life-styles, which derive their meaning, i.e., their value, from their position in a system of oppositions and correlations.[4] It is a virtue made of necessity which continuously transforms necessity into virtue by inducing "choices" which correspond to the condition of which it is the product. As can be seen whenever a change in social position puts the habitus into new conditions, so that its specific efficacy can be isolated, it is taste—the taste of necessity or the taste of luxury—and not high or low income which commands the practices objectively adjusted to these resources. Through taste, an agent has what he likes because he likes what he has, that is, the properties actually given to him in the distributions and legitimately assigned to him in the classifications.[5]

THE HOMOLOGY BETWEEN THE SPACES

Bearing in mind all that precedes, in particular the fact that the generative schemes of the habitus are applied, by simple transfer, to the most dissimilar areas of practice, one can immediately understand that the practices or goods associated with the different classes in the different areas of practice are organized in accordance with structures of opposition which are homologous to one another because they are all homologous to the structure of objective oppositions between class conditions. Without presuming to demonstrate here in a few pages what the whole of the rest of this work will endeavour to establish—but lest the reader fail to see the wood for the trees of detailed analysis—I shall merely indicate, very schematically, how the two major organizing principles of the social space govern the structure and modification of the space of cultural consumption, and, more generally, the whole universe of life-styles.

In cultural consumption, the main opposition, by overall capital value, is between the practices designated by their rarity as distinguished, those of the fractions richest in both economic and cultural capital, and the practices socially identified as vulgar because they are both easy and common, those of the fractions poorest in both these respects. In the intermediate position are the practices which are perceived as pretentious, because of the manifest discrepancy between ambition and possibilities. In opposition to the dominated condition, characterized, from the point of view of the dominant, by the combination of forced poverty and unjustified laxity, the dominant aesthetic—of which the work of art and the aesthetic disposition are the most complete embodiments—proposes the combination of ease and asceticism, i.e., self-imposed austerity, restraint, reserve, which are affirmed in that absolute manifestation of excellence, relaxation in tension.

This fundamental opposition is specified according to capital composition. Through the mediation of the means of appropriation available to them, exclusively or principally cultural on the one hand, mainly economic on the other, and the different forms of relation to works of art which result from them, the different fractions of the dominant class are oriented towards cultural practices so different in their style and object and sometimes so antagonistic (those of "artists" and "bourgeois")[6] that it is easy to forget that they are variants of the same fundamental relationship to necessity and to those who remain subject to it, and that each pursues the exclusive appropriation of legitimate cultural goods and the associated symbolic profits. Whereas the dominant fractions of the dominant class (the "bourgeoisie") demand of art a high degree of denial of the social world and incline towards a hedonistic aesthetic of ease and facility, symbolized by boulevard theatre or Impressionist painting, the dominated fractions (the "intellectuals" and "artists") have affinities with the ascetic aspect of aesthetics and are inclined to support all artistic revolutions conducted in the name of purity and purification, refusal of ostentation and the bourgeois taste for ornament; and the dispositions towards the social world which they owe to their status as poor relations incline them to welcome a pessimistic representation of the social world.

While it is clear that art offers it the greatest scope, there is no area of practice in which the intention of purifying, refining and sublimating facile impulses and primary needs cannot assert itself, or in which the stylization of life, i.e., the primacy of form over function, which leads to the denial of function, does not produce the same effects. In language, it gives the opposition between popular outspokenness and the highly censored language of the bourgeois, between the expressionist pursuit of the picturesque or the rhetorical effect and the choice of restraint and false simplicity (litotes). The same economy of means is found in body language: here too, agitation and haste, grimaces and gesticulation are opposed to slowness—"the slow gestures, the slow glance" of nobility, according to Nietzsche[7]—to the restraint and impassivity which signify elevation. Even the field of primary tastes is organized according to the fundamental opposition, with the antithesis between quantity and quality, belly and palate, matter and manners, substance and form.

Form and Substance

The fact that in the realm of food the main opposition broadly corresponds to differences in income has masked the secondary opposition which exists, both within the middle classes and within the dominant class, between the fractions richer in cultural capital and less rich in economic capital and those whose assets are structured in the opposite way. Observers tend to see a simple effect of income in the fact that, as one rises in the social hierarchy, the proportion of income spent on food diminishes, or that, within the food budget, the proportion spent on heavy, fatty, fattening foods, which are also cheap—pasta, potatoes, beans, bacon, pork—declines (C.S. III), as does that spent on wine, whereas an increasing proportion is spent on leaner, lighter (more digestible), non-fattening foods (beef, veal, mutton, lamb, and especially fresh fruit and vegetables).[8] Because the real principle of preferences is taste, a virtue made of necessity, the theory which makes consumption a simple function of income has all the appearances to support it, since income plays an important part in determining distance from necessity. However, it cannot account for cases in which the same income is associated with totally different consumption patterns. Thus, foremen remain attached to "popular" taste although they earn more than clerical and commercial employees, whose taste differs radically from that of manual workers and is closer to that of teachers.

For a real explanation of the variations which J. F. Engel's law merely records, one has to take account of all the characteristics of social condition which are (statistically) associated from earliest childhood with possession of high or low income and which tend to shape tastes adjusted to these conditions.[9] The true basis of the differences found in the area of consumption, and far beyond it, is the opposition between the tastes of luxury (or freedom) and the tastes of necessity. The former are the tastes of individuals who are the product of material conditions of existence defined by distance from necessity, by the freedoms or facilities stemming from possession of capital; the latter express, precisely in their adjustment, the necessities of which they are the product. Thus it is possible to deduce popular tastes for the foods that are simultaneously most "filling" and most economical[10] from the necessity of reproducing labour power at the lowest cost which is forced on the proletariat as its very definition. The idea of taste, typically bourgeois, since it presupposes absolute freedom of choice, is so closely associated with the idea of freedom that many people find it hard to grasp the paradoxes of the taste of necessity. Some simply sweep it aside, making practice a direct product of economic necessity (workers eat beans because they cannot afford anything else), failing to realize that necessity can only be fulfilled, most of the time, because the agents are inclined to fulfil it, because they have a taste for what they are anyway condemned to. Others turn it into a taste of freedom, forgetting the conditionings of which it is the product, and so reduce it to pathological or morbid preference for (basic) essentials, a sort of congenital coarseness, the pretext for a class racism which associates the populace with everything heavy, thick and fat.[11] Taste is *amor fati*, the choice of destiny, but a forced choice, produced by conditions of existence which rule out all alternatives as mere daydreams and leave no choice but the taste for the necessary.

The taste of necessity can only be the basis of a life-style "in-itself", which is defined as such only negatively, by an absence, by the relationship of privation between itself and the other life-styles. For some, there are elective emblems, for others stigmata which they bear in their very bodies. "As the chosen people bore in their features the sign that they were the property of Jehovah, so the division of labour brands the manufacturing worker as the property of capital".[12] The brand which Marx speaks of is nothing other than life-style, through which the most deprived immediately betray themselves, even in their use of spare time; in so doing they inevitably serve as a foil to every distinction and contribute, purely negatively, to the dialectic of pretension and distinction which fuels the incessant changing of taste. Not content with lacking virtually all the knowledge or manners which are valued in the markets of academic examination or polite conversation nor with only possessing skills which have no value there, they are the people "who don't know how to live", who sacrifice most to material foods, and to the heaviest, grossest and most fattening of them, bread, potatoes, fats, and the most vulgar, such as wine; who spend least on clothing and cosmetics, appearance and beauty; those who "don't know how to relax", "who always have to be doing something", who set off in their Renault 5 or Simca 1000 to join the great traffic jams of the holiday exodus, who picnic beside major roads, cram their tents into overcrowded campsites, fling themselves into the prefabricated leisure activities designed for them by the engineers of cultural mass production; those who by all these uninspired "choices" confirm class racism, if it needed to be confirmed, in its conviction that they only get what they deserve.

The art of eating and drinking remains one of the few areas in which the working classes explicitly challenge the legitimate art of living. In the face of the new ethic of sobriety for the sake of slimness, which is most recognized at the highest levels of the social hierarchy, peasants and especially industrial workers maintain an ethic of convivial indulgence. A bon vivant is not just someone who enjoys eating and drinking; he is someone capable of entering into the generous and familiar—that is, both simple and free—relationship that is encouraged and symbolized by eating and drinking together, in a conviviality which sweeps away restraints and reticence.

The boundary marking the break with the popular relation to food runs, without any doubt, between the manual workers and the clerical and commercial employees (C.S. II). Clerical workers spend less on food than skilled manual workers, both in absolute terms (9,376 francs as against 10,347 francs) and in relative terms (34.2 percent as against 38.3 percent); they consume less bread, pork, pork products (*charcuterie*), milk, cheese, rabbit, poultry, dried vegetables and fats, and, within a smaller food budget, spend as much on meat—beef, veal, mutton and lamb—and slightly more on fish, fresh fruit and aperitifs. These changes in the structure of spending on food are accompanied by increased spending on health and beauty care and clothing, and a slight increase in spending on cultural and leisure activities. When it is noted that the reduced spending on food, especially on the most earthly, earthy, down-to-earth foods, is accompanied by a lower birth-rate, it is reasonable to suppose that it constitutes one aspect of an overall transformation of the relationship to the world. The "modest" taste which can defer its gratifications is opposed to the spontaneous materialism of the working classes, who refuse to participate in the Benthamite calculation of pleasures and pains, benefits and costs (e.g., for health and beauty). In other words, these two relations to the "fruits of the earth" are grounded in two dispositions towards the future which are themselves related in circular causality to two objective futures. Against the imaginary anthropology of economics, which has never shrunk from formulating universal laws of "temporal preference", it has to be pointed out that the propensity to subordinate present desires to future desires depends on the extent to which this sacrifice is "reasonable", that is, on the likelihood, in any case, of obtaining future satisfactions superior to those sacrificed.[13]

Among the economic conditions of the propensity to sacrifice immediate satisfactions to expected satisfactions one must include the probability of these future satisfactions which is inscribed in the present condition. There is still a sort of economic calculation in the unwillingness to subject existence to economic calculation. The hedonism which seizes day by day the rare satisfactions ("good times") of the immediate present is the only philosophy conceivable to those who "have no future" and, in any case, little to expect from the future.[14] It becomes clearer why the practical materialism which is particularly manifested in the relation to food is one of the most fundamental components of the popular ethos and even the popular ethic. The being-in-the-present which is affirmed in the readiness to take advantage of the good times and take time as it comes is, in itself, an affirmation of solidarity with others (who are often the only present guarantee against the threats of the future), inasmuch as this temporal immanentism is a recognition of the limits which define the condition. This is why the sobriety of the petit bourgeois is felt as a break: in abstaining from having a good time and from having it with others, the would-be petit bourgeois betrays his ambition of escaping from the common present, when, that is, he does not

Type of spending	Teachers (higher and secondary)		Professionals		Industrial and commercial employers	
	Francs	% of total	Francs	% of total	Francs	% of total
Food[a]	9,969	24.4	13,956	24.4	16,578	37.4
Presentation[b]	4,912	12.0	12,680	22.2	5,616	12.7
Culture[c]	1,753	4.3	1,298	2.3	574	1.3

Source: C.S. II (1972).
a. Includes restaurant or canteen meals.
b. Clothes, shoes, repairs and cleaning, toiletries, hairdressing, domestic servants.
c. Books, newspapers and magazines, stationery, records, sport, toys, music, entertainments.

Table 20.1   Yearly Spending by Teachers, Professionals, and Industrial and Commercial Employers, 1972

construct his whole self-image around the opposition between his home and the café, abstinence and intemperance, in other words, between individual salvation and collective solidarities.

Three Styles of Distinction

The basic opposition between the tastes of luxury and the tastes of necessity is specified in as many oppositions as there are different ways of asserting one's distinction vis-à-vis the working class and its primary needs, or—which amounts to the same thing—different powers whereby necessity can be kept at a distance. Thus, within the dominant class, one can, for the sake of simplicity, distinguish three structures of the consumption distributed under three items: food, culture and presentation (clothing, beauty care, toiletries, domestic servants). These structures take strictly opposite forms—like the structures of their capital—among the teachers as against the industrial and commercial employers (see Table 20.1). Whereas the latter have exceptionally high expenditure on food (37 percent of the budget), low cultural costs and medium spending on presentation and representation, the former, whose total spending is lower on average, have low expenditure on food (relatively less than manual workers), limited expenditure on presentation (though their expenditure on health is one of the highest) and relatively high expenditure on culture (books, papers, entertainments, sport, toys, music, radio and record-player). Opposed to both these groups are the members of the professions, who devote the same proportion of their budget to food as the teachers (24.4

percent), but out of much greater total expenditure (57,122 francs as against 40,884 francs), and who spend much more on presentation and representation than all other fractions, especially if the costs of domestic service are included, whereas their cultural expenditure is lower than that of the teachers (or even the engineers and senior executives, who are situated between the teachers and the professionals, though nearer the latter, for almost all items).

The system of differences becomes clearer when one looks more closely at the patterns of spending on food. In this respect the industrial and commercial employers differ markedly from the professionals, and a fortiori from the teachers, by virtue of the importance they give to cereal-based products (especially cakes and pastries), wine, meat preserves (foie gras, etc.) and game, and their relatively low spending on meat, fresh fruit and vegetables. The teachers, whose food purchases are almost identically structured to those of office workers, spend more than all other fractions on bread, milk products, sugar, fruit preserves and non-alcoholic drinks, less on wine and spirits and distinctly less than the professions on expensive products such as meat—especially the most expensive meats, such as mutton and lamb—and fresh fruit and vegetables. The members of the professions are mainly distinguished by the high proportion of their spending which goes on expensive products, particularly meat (18.3 percent of their food budget), and especially the most expensive meat (veal, lamb, mutton), fresh fruit and vegetables, fish and shellfish, cheese and aperitifs.[15]

Thus, when one moves from the manual workers to the industrial and commercial employers, through foremen, craftsmen and small shopkeepers, economic constraints tend to relax without any fundamental change in the pattern of spending (see Table 20.2). The opposition between the two extremes is here established between the poor and the rich (nouveau riche), between *la bouffe* and *la grande bouffe*;[16] the food consumed is increasingly rich (both in cost and in calories) and increasingly heavy (game, foie gras). By contrast, the taste of the professionals or senior executives defines the popular taste, by negation, as the taste for the heavy, the fat and the coarse, by tending towards the light, the refined and the delicate (see Figure 20.4). The disappearance of economic constraints is accompanied by a strengthening of the social censorships which forbid coarseness and fatness, in favour of slimness and distinction. The taste for rare, aristocratic foods points to a traditional cuisine, rich in expensive or rare products (fresh vegetables, meat). Finally, the teachers, richer in cultural capital than in economic capital, and

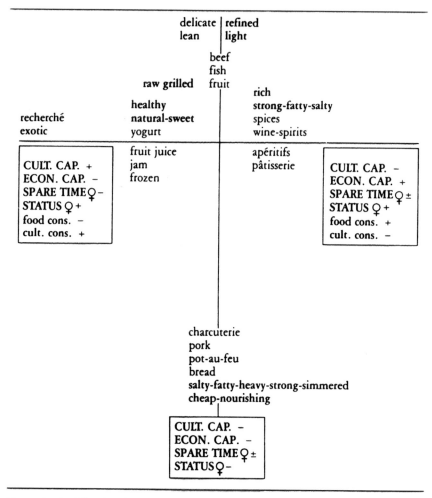

Figure 20.4   The Food Space

therefore inclined to ascetic consumption in all areas, pursue originality at the lowest economic cost and go in for exoticism (Italian, Chinese cooking etc.)[17] and culinary populism (peasant dishes). They are thus almost consciously opposed to the (new) rich with their rich food, the buyers and sellers of *grosse bouffe*, the "fat cats,"[18] gross in body and mind, who have the economic means to flaunt, with an arrogance perceived as "vulgar", a life-style which remains very close to that of the working classes as regards economic and cultural consumption.

Unpretentious or Uncouth?

It is clear that tastes in food cannot be considered in complete independence of the other dimensions of the relationship to the world, to others and to one's own body, through which the practical philosophy of each class is enacted. To demonstrate this, one would have to make a systematic comparison of the working-class and bourgeois ways of treating food, of serving, presenting and offering it, which are infinitely more revelatory than even the nature of the products involved (especially since most surveys of consumption ignore differences in quality). The analysis is a difficult one, because each life-style can only really be constructed in relation to the other, which is its objective and subjective negation, so that the meaning of behaviour is totally reversed depending on which point of view is adopted and on whether the common words which have to be used to name the conduct (e.g., "manners") are invested with popular or bourgeois connotations.

Plain speaking, plain eating: the working-class meal is characterized by plenty (which does not exclude restrictions and limits) and above all by freedom. "Elastic" and "abundant" dishes are brought to the table—soups or sauces, pasta or potatoes (almost always included among the vegetables)—and served with a ladle or spoon, to avoid too much measuring and counting, in contrast to everything that has to be cut and divided, such as roasts.[19] This impression of abundance, which is the norm on special occasions, and always applies, so far as is possible, for the men, whose plates are filled twice (a privilege which marks a boy's accession to manhood), is often balanced, on ordinary occasions, by restrictions which generally apply to the women, who will share one portion between two, or eat the leftovers of the previous day; a girl's accession to womanhood is marked by doing without. It is part of men's status to eat and to eat well (and also to drink well); it is particularly insisted that they should eat, on the grounds that "it won't keep", and there is something suspect about a refusal. On Sundays, while the women are on their feet, busily serving, clearing the table, washing up, the men remain seated, still eating and drinking. These strongly marked differences of social status (associated with sex and age) are accompanied by no practical differentiation (such as the bourgeois division between the dining room and the kitchen, where the servants eat and sometimes the children), and strict sequencing of the meal tends to be ignored. Everything may be put on the table at much the same time (which also saves walking), so that the women may have reached the dessert, and also the children, who will take their

Type of Food	Teachers (higher and secondary) Average exp. Francs	As % of all food exp.	Senior executives Average exp. Francs	As % of all food exp.	Professions Average exp. Francs	As % of all food exp.	Engineers Average exp. Francs	As % of all food exp.	Industrial and commercial employers Average exp. Francs	As % of all food exp.
Average number persons per household	3.11		3.6		3.5		3.6		3.6	
Average total household expenditure (francs)	40,844		52,156		57,122		49,822		44,339	
Average total household expenditure on food (francs)	9,969		13,158		13,956		12,666		16,578	
Expenditure on food as % of total expenditure	24.4		25.2		24.4		25.4		37.4	
Cereals	865	8.7	993	7.5	1,011	7.2	951	7.5	1,535	9.2
bread	322	3.2	347	2.6	326	2.3	312	2.5	454	2.5
cakes, pastries	452	4.5	552	4.1	548	4.0	539	4.2	989	5.6
rusks	16	0.2	27	0.2	33	0.2	28	0.2	29	0.1
rice	35	0.3	32	0.2	62	0.4	41	0.3	33	0.1
flour	40	0.4	35	0.2	41	0.3	31	0.2	28	0.1
Vegetables	766	7.7	1,015	7.7	1,100	7.9	899	7.1	1,222	7.4
potatoes	81	0.8	94	0.7	95	0.7	98	0.7	152	0.8
fresh vegetables	555	5.6	729	5.5	811	5.8	647	5.1	915	5.1
dried or canned	131	1.3	191	1.4	216	1.5	154	1.2	153	0.8
Fruit	632	6.3	871	6.6	990	7.2	864	6.8	877	5.2
fresh fruit	295	2.9	405	3.1	586	4.2	424	3.3	547	3.1
citrus fruit, bananas	236	2.4	343	2.6	303	2.2	324	2.5	256	1.4
dried	102	1.0	122	0.9	98	0.7	116	0.9	72	0.4
Butcher's meat	1,556	15.6	2,358	18.0	2,552	18.3	2,073	16.4	2,323	14.0
beef	814	8.1	1,291	9.8	1,212	8.7	1,144	9.0	1,273	7.2
veal	335	3.4	452	3.4	630	4.5	402	3.1	377	2.3
mutton, lamb	156	1.6	315	2.3	438	3.2	242	1.9	390	2.2
horse	31	0.3	49	0.3	31	0.2	37	0.3	94	0.5
pork (fresh)	221	2.2	251	1.7	239	1.7	247	1.9	187	1.3

Table 20.2 Annual Household Expenditures on Food: Fractions of the Dominant Class, 1972

Pork products	634	6.3	741	5.6	774	5.5	705	5.6	812	4.9
Meat preserves	336	3.4	350	2.6	233	1.7	310	2.4	1,362	8.0
Fish, shellfish	336	3.4	503	3.8	719	5.1	396	3.1	588	3.5
Poultry	235	2.3	311	2.4	399	2.8	310	2.4	333	2.0
Rabbit, game	36	0.3	97	0.7	148	1.1	89	0.7	289	1.7
Eggs	149	1.4	172	1.3	190	1.4	178	1.4	185	1.1
Milk	299	3.0	271	2.0	249	1.8	287	2.3	309	1.9
Cheese, yogurt	692	6.9	776	5.9	843	6.0	785	6.1	1,090	6.5
Fats	399	4.0	564	4.3	525	3.8	504	4.0	551	3.3
butter	320	3.2	408	3.1	379	2.7	371	2.9	405	2.4
oil	66	0.6	136	1.0	132	1.0	103	0.8	112	0.6
margarine	12	0.1	17	0.1	12	0.1	29	0.2	19	0.1
lard	1	0	2	0	1	0	1	0	13	0.1
Sugar, confectionery, cocoa	304	3.0	395	3.0	265	1.9	327	2.6	407	2.4
Alcohol	711	7.1	1,365	10.3	1,329	9.5	937	7.4	2,218	13.4
wine	457	4.6	869	6.6	899	6.4	392	3.1	1,881	11.8
beer	82	0.8	91	0.7	40	0.3	184	1.4	93	0.5
cider	13	0.1	12	0	0	0	8	0	5	0
apéritifs, liqueurs etc.	157	1.6	391	3.0	389	2.8	352	2.8	237	1.4
Non-alcoholic drinks	344	3.4	342	2.6	267	1.9	295	2.3	327	2.0
Coffee, tea	152	1.5	215	1.5	291	2.1	178	1.4	298	1.8
Restaurant meals	829	8.3	1,863	13.0	1,562	11.2	1,372	10.8	1,179	7.1
Canteen meals	745	7.5	562	4.0	221	1.6	773	6.1	299	1.8
Miscellaneous	264	2.6	379	2.7	258	1.8	432	3.4	324	1.9

Source: C.S. II (1972).

plates and watch television, while the men are still eating the main dish and the "lad", who has arrived late, is swallowing his soup.

This freedom, which may be perceived as disorder or slovenliness, is adapted to its function. Firstly, it is labour-saving, which is seen as an advantage. Because men take no part in housework, not least because the women would not allow it—it would be a dishonour to see men step outside their rôle—every economy of effort is welcome. Thus, when the coffee is served, a single spoon may be passed around to stir it. But these short cuts are only permissible because one is and feels at home, among the family, where ceremony would be an affectation. For example, to save washing up, the dessert may be handed out on improvised plates torn from the cake-box (with a joke about "taking the liberty", to mark the transgression), and the neighbour invited in for a meal will also receive his piece of cardboard (offering a plate would exclude him) as a sign of familiarity. Similarly, the plates are not changed between dishes. The soup plate, wiped with bread, can be used right through the meal. The hostess will certainly offer to "change the plates", pushing back her chair with one hand and reaching with the other for the plate next to her, but everyone will protest ("It all gets mixed up inside you") and if she were to insist it would look as if she wanted to show off her crockery (which she is allowed to if it is a new present) or to treat her guests as strangers, as is sometimes deliberately done to intruders or "scroungers" who never return the invitation. These unwanted guests may be frozen out by changing their plates despite their protests, not laughing at their jokes, or scolding the children for their behaviour ("No, no, *we* don't mind", say the guests; "They ought to know better by now", the parents respond). The common root of all these "liberties" is no doubt the sense that at least there will not be self-imposed controls, constraints and restrictions—especially not in eating, a primary need and a compensation—and especially not in the heart of domestic life, the one realm of freedom, when everywhere else, and at all other times, necessity prevails.

In opposition to the free-and-easy working-class meal, the bourgeoisie is concerned to eat with all due form. Form is first of all a matter of rhythm, which implies expectations, pauses, restraints; waiting until the last person served has started to eat, taking modest helpings, not appearing over-eager. A strict sequence is observed and all coexistence of dishes which the sequence separates, fish and meat, cheese and dessert, is excluded: for example, before the dessert is served, everything left on the table, even the salt-cellar, is removed, and the crumbs are swept up. This extension of rigorous rules into everyday life (the bourgeois male shaves and dresses first thing every morning, and not just to "go out"), refusing the division between home and the exterior, the quotidian and the extraquotidian, is not explained solely by the presence of strangers—servants and guests—in the familiar family world. It is the expression of a habitus of order, restraint and propriety which may not be abdicated. The relation to food—*the* primary need and pleasure—is only one dimension of the bourgeois relation to the social world. The opposition between the immediate and the deferred, the easy and the difficult, substance (or function) and form, which is exposed in a particularly striking fashion in bourgeois ways of eating, is the basis of all aestheticization of practice and every aesthetic. Through all the forms and formalisms imposed on the immediate appetite, what is demanded—and inculcated—is not only a disposition to discipline food consumption by a conventional structuring which is also a gentle, indirect, invisible censorship (quite different from enforced privations) and which is an element in an art of living (correct eating, for example, is a way of paying homage to one's hosts and to the mistress of the house, a tribute to her care and effort). It is also a whole relationship to animal nature, to primary needs and the populace who indulge them without restraint; it is a way of denying the meaning and primary function of consumption, which are essentially common, by making the meal a social ceremony, an affirmation of ethical tone and aesthetic refinement. The manner of presenting and consuming the food, the organization of the meal and setting of the places, strictly differentiated according to the sequence of dishes and arranged to please the eye, the presentation of the dishes, considered as much in terms of shape and colour (like works of art) as of their consumable substance, the etiquette governing posture and gesture, ways of serving oneself and others, of using the different utensils, the seating plan, strictly but discreetly hierarchical, the censorship of all bodily manifestations of the act or pleasure of eating (such as noise or haste), the very refinement of the things consumed, with quality more important than quantity—this whole commitment to stylization tends to shift the emphasis from substance and function to form and manner, and so to deny the crudely material reality of the act of eating and of the things consumed, or, which amounts to the same thing, the basely material vulgarity of those who indulge in the immediate satisfactions of food and drink.[20]

Given the basic opposition between form and substance, one could regenerate each of the oppositions between the two antagonistic approaches to the treatment of food and the act of eating. In one case, food is claimed as a material reality, a nourishing substance which sustains the body and gives strength (hence the emphasis on heavy, fatty, strong foods, of which the paradigm is pork—fatty and salty—the antithesis of fish—light, lean and bland); in the other, the priority given to form (the shape of the body, for example) and social form, formality, puts the pursuit of strength and substance in the background and identifies true freedom with the elective asceticism of a self-imposed rule. And it could be shown that two antagonistic world views, two worlds, two representations of human excellence are contained in this matrix. Substance—or matter—is what is substantial, not only "filling" but also real, as opposed to all appearances, all the fine words and empty gestures that "butter no parsnips" and are, as the phrase goes, purely symbolic; reality, as against sham, imitation, window-dressing; the little eating-house with its marble-topped tables and paper napkins where you get an honest square meal and aren't "paying for the wallpaper" as in fancy restaurants; being, as against seeming, nature and the natural, simplicity (pot-luck, "take it as it comes", "no standing on ceremony"), as against embarrassment, mincing and posturing, airs and graces, which are always suspected of being a substitute for substance, i.e., for sincerity, for feeling, for what is felt and proved in actions; it is the free-speech and language of the heart which make the true "nice guy", blunt, straightforward, unbending, honest, genuine, "straight down the line" and "straight as a die", as opposed to everything that is pure form, done only for form's sake; it is freedom and the refusal of complications, as opposed to respect for all the forms and formalities spontaneously perceived as instruments of distinction and power. On these moralities, these world views, there is no neutral viewpoint; what for some is shameless and slovenly, for others is straightforward, unpretentious; familiarity is for some the most absolute form of recognition, the abdication of all distance, a trusting openness, a relation of equal to equal; for others, who shun familiarity, it is an unseemly liberty.

The popular realism which inclines working people to reduce practices to the reality of their function, to do what they do, and be what they are ("That's the way I am"), without "kidding themselves" ("That's the way it is"), and the practical materialism which inclines them to censor the expression of feelings or to divert emotion into violence or oaths, are the near-perfect antithesis of the aesthetic disavowal which, by a sort of essential hypocrisy (seen, for example, in the opposition between pornography and eroticism) masks the interest in function by the primacy given to form, so that what people do, they do as if they were not doing it.

The Visible and the Invisible

But food—which the working classes place on the side of being and substance, whereas the bourgeoisie, refusing the distinction between inside and outside or "at home" and "for others", the quotidian and the extraquotidian, introduces into it the categories of form and appearance—is itself related to clothing as inside to outside, the domestic to the public, being to seeming. And the inversion of the places of food and clothing in the contrast between the spending patterns of the working classes, who give priority to being, and the middle classes, where the concern for "seeming" arises, is the sign of a reversal of the whole world view. The working classes make a realistic or, one might say, functionalist use of clothing. Looking for substance and function rather than form, they seek "value for money" and choose what will "last". Ignoring the bourgeois concern to introduce formality and formal dress into the domestic world, the place for freedom—an apron and slippers (for women), bare chest or a vest (for men)—they scarcely mark the distinction between top clothes, visible, intended to be seen, and underclothes, invisible or hidden—unlike the middle classes, who have a degree of anxiety about external appearances, both sartorial and cosmetic, at least outside and at work (to which middle-class women more often have access).

Thus, despite the limits of the data available, one finds in men's clothing (which is much more socially marked, at the level of what can be grasped by statistics on purchases, than women's clothing) the equivalent of the major oppositions found in food consumption. In the first dimension of the space, the division again runs between the office workers and the manual workers and is marked particularly by the opposition between grey or white overalls and blue dungarees or boiler-suits, between town shoes and the more relaxed moccasins, kickers or sneakers (not to mention dressing-gowns, which clerical workers buy 3.5 times more often than manual workers). The increased quantity and quality of all purchases of men's clothing is summed up in the opposition between the suit, the prerogative of the senior executive, and the blue overall, the distinctive mark of the farmer and industrial worker (it is virtually unknown in other groups, except craftsmen); or between the overcoat, always much rarer among men than women, but much more frequent among senior executives than the other classes, and the fur-lined jacket or lumber jacket, mainly worn by agricultural and industrial workers. In between are the junior executives, who now scarcely ever wear working clothes but fairly often buy suits.

Among women, who, in all categories (except farmers and farm labourers), spend more than men (especially in the junior and senior executive, professional and other high-income categories), the number of purchases increases as one moves up the social hierarchy; the difference is greatest for suits and costumes—expensive garments—and smaller for dresses and especially skirts and jackets. The topcoat, which is increasingly frequent among women at higher social levels, is opposed to the "all-purpose" raincoat, in the same way as overcoat and lumber jacket are opposed for men. The use of the smock and the apron, which in the working classes is virtually the housewife's uniform, increases as one moves down the hierarchy (in contrast to the dressing-gown, which is virtually unknown among peasants and industrial workers).

The interest the different classes have in self-presentation, the attention they devote to it, their awareness of the profits it gives and the investment of time, effort, sacrifice and care which they actually put into it are proportionate to the chances of material or symbolic profit they can reasonably expect from it. More precisely, they depend on the existence of a labour market in which physical appearance may be valorized in the performance of the job itself or in professional relations; and on the differential chances of access to this market and the sectors of this market in which beauty and deportment most strongly contribute to occupational value. A first indication of this correspondence between the propensity to cosmetic investments and the chances of profit may be seen in the gap, for all forms of beauty care, between those who work and those who do not (which must also vary according to the nature of the job and the work environment). It can be understood in terms of this logic why working-class women, who are less likely to have a job and much less likely to enter one of the occupations which most strictly demand conformity to the dominant norms of beauty, are less aware than all others of the "market" value of beauty and much less inclined to invest time and effort, sacrifices and money in cultivating their bodies.

It is quite different with the women of the petite bourgeoisie, especially the new petite bourgeoisie, in the occupations involving presentation and representation, which often impose a uniform (*tenue*) intended, among other things, to abolish all traces of heterodox taste, and which always demand what is called *tenue*, in the sense of "dignity of conduct and correctness of manners", implying, according to the dictionary, "a refusal to give way to vulgarity or facility". (In the specialized "charm schools" which train hostesses, the working-class girls who select themselves on the basis of "natural" beauty undergo a radical transformation in their way of walking, sitting, laughing, smiling, talking, dressing, making-up etc.) Women of the petite bourgeoisie who have sufficient interests in the market in which physical properties can function as capital to recognize the dominant image of the body unconditionally without possessing, at least in their own eyes (and no doubt objectively) enough body capital to obtain the highest profits, are, here too, at the site of greatest tension.

The self-assurance given by the certain knowledge of one's own value, especially that of one's body or speech, is in fact very closely linked to the position occupied in social space (and also, of course, to trajectory). Thus, the proportion of women who consider themselves below average in beauty, or who think they look older than they are, falls very rapidly as one moves up the social hierarchy. Similarly, the ratings women give themselves for the different parts of their bodies tend to rise with social position, and this despite the fact that the implicit demands rise too. It is not surprising that petit-bourgeois women—who are almost as dissatisfied with their bodies as working-class women (they are the ones who most often wish they looked different and who are most discontented with various parts of their bodies), while being more aware of the usefulness of beauty and more often recognizing the dominant ideal of physical excellence—devote such great investments, of self-denial and especially of time, to improving their appearance and are such unconditional believers in all forms of cosmetic voluntarism (e.g., plastic surgery).

As for the women of the dominant class, they derive a double assurance from their bodies. Believing, like petit-bourgeois women, in the value of beauty and the value of the effort to be beautiful, and so associating aesthetic value and moral value, they feel superior both in the intrinsic, natural beauty of their bodies and in the art of self-embellishment and everything they call *tenue,* a moral and aesthetic virtue which defines "nature" negatively as sloppiness. Beauty can thus be simultaneously a gift of nature and a conquest of merit, as much opposed to the abdications of vulgarity as to ugliness.

Thus, the experience par excellence of the "alienated body", embarrassment, and the opposite experience, ease, are clearly unequally probable for members of the petite bourgeoisie and the bourgeoisie, who grant the same recognition to the same representation of the legitimate body and legitimate deportment, but are unequally able to achieve it. The chances of experiencing one's own body as a vessel of grace, a continuous miracle, are that much greater when bodily capacity is commensurate with recognition;

and, conversely, the probability of experiencing the body with unease, embarrassment, timidity grows with the disparity between the ideal body and the real body, the dream body and the "looking-glass self" reflected in the reactions of others (the same laws are also true of speech).

Although it is not a petit-bourgeois monopoly, the petit-bourgeois experience of the world starts out from timidity, the embarrassment of someone who is uneasy in his body and his language and who, instead of being "as one body with them," observes them from outside, through other people's eyes, watching, checking, correcting himself, and who, by his desperate attempts to reappropriate an alienated being-for-others, exposes himself to appropriation, giving himself away as much by hyper-correction as by clumsiness. The timidity which, despite itself, realizes the objectified body, which lets itself be trapped in the destiny proposed by collective perception and statement (nicknames etc.), is betrayed by a body that is subject to the representation of others even in its passive, unconscious reactions (one feels oneself blushing). By contrast, ease, a sort of indifference to the objectifying gaze of others which neutralizes its powers, presupposes the self-assurance which comes from the certainty of being able to objectify that objectification, appropriate that appropriation, of being capable of imposing the norms of apperception of one's own body, in short, of commanding all the powers which, even when they reside in the body and apparently borrow its most specific weapons, such as "presence" or charm, are essentially irreducible to it. This is the real meaning of the findings of the experiment by W. D. Dannenmaier and F. J. Thumin, in which the subjects, when asked to assess the height of familiar persons from memory, tended to overestimate most of the height of those who had most authority or prestige in their eyes.[21] It would seem that the logic whereby the "great" are perceived as physically greater than they are applies very generally, and that authority of whatever sort contains a power of seduction which it would be naive to reduce to the effect of self-interested servility. That is why political contestation has always made use of caricature, a distortion of the bodily image intended to break the charm and hold up to ridicule one of the principles of the effect of authority imposition.

Charm and charisma in fact designate the power, which certain people have, to impose their own self-image as the objective and collective image of their body and being; to persuade others, as in love or faith, to abdicate their generic power of objectification and delegate it to the person who should be its object, who thereby becomes an absolute subject, without an exterior (being his own Other), fully justified in existing, legitimated. The charismatic leader manages to be for the group what he is for himself, instead of being for himself, like those dominated in the symbolic struggle, what he is for others. He "makes" the opinion which makes him; he constitutes himself as an absolute by a manipulation of symbolic power which is constitutive of his power since it enables him to produce and impose his own objectification.

THE UNIVERSES OF STYLISTIC POSSIBLES

Thus, the spaces defined by preferences in food, clothing or cosmetics are organized according to the same fundamental structure, that of the social space determined by volume and composition of capital. Fully to construct the space of life-styles within which cultural practices are defined, one would first have to establish, for each class and class fraction, that is, for each of the configurations of capital, the generative formula of the habitus which re-translates the necessities and facilities characteristic of that class of (relatively) homogeneous conditions of existence into a particular life-style. One would then have to determine how the dispositions of the habitus are specified, for each of the major areas of practice, by implementing one of the stylistic possibles offered by each field (the field of sport, or music, or food, decoration, politics, language etc.). By superimposing these homologous spaces one would obtain a rigorous representation of the space of life-styles, making it possible to characterize each of the distinctive features (e.g., wearing a cap or playing the piano) in the two respects in which it is objectively defined, that is, on the one hand by reference to the set of features constituting the area in question (e.g., the system of hairstyles), and on the other hand by reference to the set of features constituting a particular life-style (e.g., the working-class life-style), within which its social significance is determined.

SOURCES

The survey on which the work was based was carried out in 1963, after a preliminary survey by extended interview and ethnographic observation, on a sample of 692 subjects (both sexes) in Paris, Lille, and a small provincial town. To obtain a sample large enough to make it possible to analyse variations in practices and opinions in relation to sufficiently homogeneous social units, a complementary survey was carried out in 1967–68, bringing the total number of subjects to 1,217. Because the survey measured relatively stable dispositions, this time-lag does not seem to have affected the responses (except perhaps for the question on singers, an area of culture where fashions change more rapidly).

The following complementary sources (C.S.) were also used:

I. The 1966 survey on "businessmen and senior executives" was carried out by SOFRES (Société française d'enquêtes par sondages) on behalf of the Centre d'études des supports de publicité (CESP). The sample consisted of 2,257 persons aged 15 and over, each living in a household the head of which was a large industrial or commercial employer, a member of the professions, a senior executive, an engineer, or a secondary or higher-education teacher. The questionnaire included a set of questions on reading habits and the previous few days' reading of daily, weekly and monthly newspapers and magazines, use of radio and TV, standard of living, household equipment, life-style (holidays, sport, consumption), professional life (conferences, travel, business meals), cultural practices and the principal basic data (educational level, income, population of place of residence etc.). I had access to the whole set of distributions by the socio-occupational category of the head of household or individual.

II. The regular survey by INSEE (Institut national de la statistique et des études economiques) on household living conditions and expenditure was based in 1972 on a representative sample of 13,000 households. It consists of a survey by questionnaire dealing with the characteristics of the household (composition, ages, occupation of the head), accommodation and facilities, major expenditure (clothing, fuel etc.), periodic expenditure (rent, service charges etc.), combined with analysis of account books for current expenditure, left with each household for a week, collected and checked by the interviewer. This survey makes it possible to assess the whole range of expenditure (except certain major and infrequent items such as air travel, removal expenses etc.), as well as items of consumption not preceded by purchase (food in the case of farmers, items drawn from their stocks by craftsmen and shopkeepers), which are evaluated at their retail price to allow comparison with the other categories of households. This explains why consumption is considerably higher than income in the case of farmers and small businessmen (categories which are always particularly prone to under-declare their income). For the overall findings, see G. Bigata and B. Bouvier, "Les conditions de vie des ménages en 1972", *Collections de l'INSEE*, ser. M, no. 32 (February 1972). The data presented here come from secondary analysis of tables by narrow categories produced at my request.

The other surveys consulted are simply listed below. These studies, almost always devoted to a particular area of cultural activity, are generally based on relatively limited samples. They mostly use a classification which groups the occupations into five categories: (1) *agriculteurs* (farmers and farm labourers); (2) *ouvriers* (industrial manual workers); (3) industrial and commercial employers; (4) clerical workers and junior executives; (5) senior executives and the "liberal professions".

III. INSEE, "La consommation alimentaire des Français", *Collections de l'INSEE*. (The regular INSEE surveys on eating habits.)

IV. SOFRES, *Les habitudes de table des Français* (Paris, 1972).

V. SOFRES, *Les Français et la gastronomie*, July 1977. (Sample of 1,000.)

Notes

[1] The gaps are more clear-cut and certainly more visible as regards education than income, because information on incomes (based on tax declarations) is much less reliable than information on qualifications. This is especially true of industrial and commercial employers (who, in the CESP survey—C.S. I—provided, along with doctors, the highest rate of non-response to the questions about income), craftsmen, shopkeepers, and farmers.

[2] It follows from this that the relationship between conditions of existence and practices or the meaning of practices is not to be understood in terms either of the logic of mechanism or of the logic of consciousness.

[3] In contrast to the atomistic approach of social psychology, which breaks the unity of practice to establish partial "laws" claiming to account for the products of practice, the opus operatum, the aim is to establish general laws reproducing the laws of production, the modus operandi.

[4] Economic theory, which treats economic agents as interchangeable actors, paradoxically fails to take account of the economic dispositions, and is thereby prevented from really explaining the systems of preferences which define incommensurable and independent subjective use-values.

[5] An ethic, which seeks to impose the principles of an ethos (i.e., the forced choices of a social condition) as a universal norm, is another, more subtle way of succumbing to *amor fati*, of being content with what one is and has. Such is the basis of the felt contradiction between ethics and revolutionary intent.

[6] "Bourgeois" is used here as shorthand for "dominant fractions of the dominant class", and "intellectual" or "artist" functions in the same way for "dominated fractions of the dominant class".

[7] F. Nietzsche, *Der Wille zur Macht* (Stuttgart, Alfred Kröner, 1964), no. 943, p. 630.

[8] Bananas are the only fruit for which manual workers and farm workers have higher annual per capita spending (FF 23.26 and FF 25.20) than all other classes, especially the senior executives, who spend most on apples (FF 31.60 as against FF 21.00 for manual workers), whereas the rich, expensive fruits—grapes, peaches and nuts—are mainly eaten by professionals and industrial and commercial employers (FF 29.04 for grapes, 19.09 for peaches and 17.33 for nuts, as against FF 6.74, 11.78 and 4.90, respectively, for manual workers).

[9] This whole paragraph is based on secondary analysis of the tables from the 1972 INSEE survey on household expenditure on 39 items by socio-occupational category (C.S. II).

[10] A fuller translation of the original text would include: "les *nourritures* à la fois les plus *nourrissantes* et les plus *économiques*" (the double tautology showing the reduction to pure economic function.)" (Translator's note.)

[11] In the French: "le gros et le gras, gros rouge, gros sabots, gros travaux, gros rire, grosses blagues, gros bon sens, plaisanteries grasses"—cheap red wine, clogs (i.e., obviousness), heavy work, belly laughs, crude common sense, crude jokes (translator).

[12] K. Marx, *Capital*, I (Harmondsworth, Penguin, 1976), 482 (translator).

[13] One fine example, taken from Böhm-Bawerk, will demonstrate this essentialism: "We must now consider a *second* phenomenon of human experience—one that is heavily fraught with consequence. That is the fact that we feel less concerned about future sensations of joy and sorrow simply because they do lie in the future, and the lessening of our concern is in proportion to the remoteness of that future. Consequently we accord to goods which are intended to serve future ends a value which falls short of the true intensity of their future marginal utility. *We systematically undervalue our future wants and also the means which serve to satisfy them.*" E. Böhm-Bawerk, *Capital and Interest*, II (South Holland, Ill., 1959), 268, quoted by G. L. Stigler and G. S. Becker, "De gustibus non est disputandum", *American Economic Review*, 67 (March 1977), 76–90.

[14] We may assume that the deep-seated relation to the future (and also to one's own person—which is valued more at higher levels of the social hierarchy) is reflected in the small proportion of manual workers who say that "there is a new life after death" (15 percent, compared with 18 percent of craftsmen and shopkeepers, office workers and middle managers, and 32 percent of senior executives).

[15] It is not superfluous to point out that this art, which has its recognized virtuoso, the "life and soul of the party", can sink into the caricature of jokes or remarks that are defined as stereotyped, stupid or coarse in terms of the criteria of popular taste.

[15] The oppositions are much less clear-cut in the middle classes, although homologous differences are found between primary teachers and office workers on the one hand and shopkeepers on the other.

[16] *La bouffe:* "grub", "nosh"; *grande bouffe:* 'blow-out" (translator).

[17] The preference for foreign restaurants—Italian, Chinese, Japanese and, to a lesser extent, Russian—rises with level in the social hierarchy. The only exceptions are Spanish restaurants, which are associated with a more popular form of tourism, and North African restaurants, which are most favoured by junior executives (C.S. IV).

[18] *Les gros:* the rich; *grosse bouffe:* bulk food (cf. *grossiste:* wholesaler, and English "grocer"). See also note 17 above (translator).

[19] One could similarly contrast the bowl, which is generously filled and held two-handed for unpretentious drinking, and the cup, into which a little is poured, and more later ("Would you care for a little more coffee?"), and which is held between two fingers and sipped from.

[20] Formality is a way of denying the truth of the social world and of social relations. Just as popular "functionalism" is refused as regards food, so too there is a refusal of the realistic vision which leads the working classes to accept social exchanges for what they are (and, for example, to say, without cynicism, of someone who has done a favour or rendered a service, "She knows I'll pay her back"). Suppressing avowal of the calculation which pervades social relations, there is a striving to see presents, received or given, as "pure" testimonies of friendship, respect, affection, and equally "pure" manifestations of generosity and moral worth.

[21] W. D. Dannenmaier and F. J. Thumin, "Authority Status as a Factor in Perceptual Distortion of Size", *Journal of Social Psychology,* 63 (1964), 361–365.

INDEX

319

CPSIA information can be obtained at www.ICGtesting.com
Printed in the USA
LVOW12s1605141014

408499LV00003B/10/P